DEARING AND BEYOND

14–19 Qualifications, Frameworks and Systems

Edited by Ann Hodgson and Ken Spours

KOGAN
PAGE

London • Stirling (USA)

First published in 1997
Reprinted 1997

Apart from any fair dealing for the purposes of research or private study, or criticism or review, as permitted under the Copyright, Designs and Patents Act 1988, this publication may only be reproduced, stored or transmitted, in any form or by any means, with the prior permission in writing of the publishers, or in the case of reprographic reproduction in accordance with the terms of licences issued by the Copyright Licensing Agency. Enquiries concerning reproduction outside those terms should be sent to the publishers at the undermentioned address:

Kogan Page Limited
120 Pentonville Road
London N1 9JN
and
22883 Quicksilver Drive
Stirling, VA 20166, USA

© Ann Hodgson and Ken Spours, 1997

British Library Cataloguing in Publication Data

A CIP record for this book is available from the British Library.

ISBN 0 7494 2160 6

Typeset by Kogan Page
Printed and bound in Great Britain by Clays Ltd, St Ives plc

Contents

Notes on the Contributors

Andy Green is a Reader in Education at London University's Institute of Education and a member of the Post-16 Education Centre. He has written widely on comparative education history and policy and his publications include *Education and State Formation* (Macmillan, 1991); *Education, Youth and Work: World Yearbook of Education 1995* (edited with L Bash) (Kogan Page, 1995), and *Education, Globalization and the Nation State* (Macmillan, 1997). He is currently working on an ESRC-funded project entitled Education and Training for a High Skills Economy.

Ann Hodgson has been a teacher, lecturer, editor and civil servant. Currently she works as a researcher at the Post-16 Education Centre at London University's Institute of Education and as 14–19 Advisor for Tower Hamlets LEA. From 1992 to 1995, Ann was the Research Officer on the Hamlyn Post-16 Unified Curriculum Project and, since November 1995, she has been working on the Value-Added and Attainment Research and Development Project. Ann has co-authored and edited a number of publications related to these two projects.

Tom Leney is a Research Consultant to the Post-16 Education Centre. He has undertaken extensive research into European education systems and his work at the centre includes contributions to the Unified Curriculum Project and the Learning for the Future Project, as well as research for the Engineering Council and a collaborative project with the *Institut National de Recherche Pédagogique* in Paris. He currently works as a National Casework Official for the Association of Teachers and Lecturers, providing a lead on local government reorganization across England and Wales.

Tim Oates is Director of Research at the National Council for Vocational Qualifications. Having worked on a number of national evaluation projects in the field of vocational qualifications, much of his recent work has focused on the development of key skills. Concerned particularly with the analysis of change and policy development, he maintains a strong interest in the relationship between assessment and learning.

David Raffe is Director of the Centre for Educational Sociology within the University of Edinburgh's newly launched Institute for the Study of Education and Society of which he is Co-director. David holds a personal Chair in the Sociology of Education at the University of Edinburgh. His research interests encompass secondary-school and post-compulsory education, training and the labour market. With Michael Young he is Co-director of the Unified Learning Project within the ESRC-funded Learning Society Programme. He has chaired the ESF Network on Transitions in Youth for the last three years and is a member of the Scottish Skills Forum.

Ken Spours is a Lecturer and Research Officer at the Post-16 Education Centre, Institute of Education, University of London. From 1990 to 1994 he was TVEI Inspector and Director in the London Borough of Tower Hamlets. Ken was one of the authors of the IPPR document *A British Baccalaureate* (1990), which originally proposed a unified system for 14–19 qualifications, and he is currently working with Michael Young on the ESRC-funded Unified Learning Project.

Geoff Stanton is a Senior Research Fellow at the School of Post-Compulsory Education and Training, University of Greenwich, and also works as a freelance consultant. For eight years he was Director of the Further Education Unit (FEU), before which he was Head of Department in an FE college and Vice Principal at a tertiary college. He has taught in schools and colleges and in FE Teacher Training. He has been on policy committees at NCVQ, the RSA Examinations Board and City and Guilds. He is a Fellow of the Royal Society of Arts.

Lorna Unwin is a Senior Lecturer in the Division of Education, University of Sheffield, and Director of the Centre for Research in Post-Compulsory Education and Training. She has taught in further and adult education and worked with workplace trainers in industry. Her research interests include the impact of apprenticeship on communities and vocational education and training policy.

Tony Watts OBE is Director of the National Institute for Careers Education and Counselling, which is a network organization sponsored by the Careers Research Advisory Centre in Cambridge (at which he was co-founder). He has written many books and articles, including (with NICEC colleagues) *Rethinking Careers Education and Guidance: Theory, policy and practice* (Routledge, 1996). He has acted as a consultant to a number of international organizations, including the European Commission, OECD and UNESCO. He is editor of the *British Journal of Guidance and Counselling*, and a Visiting Fellow at the University of London's Institute of Education.

Michael Young is Head of the Post-16 Education Centre. He is Co-director of two projects: with David Raffe on the Unified Learning Project, an ESRC-funded project within their Learning Society Programme, and with John Woolhouse on the Learning for the Future Project. He is also the English leader of an eight-country project, funded by the European Union within their Leonardo da Vinci Programme, on post-16 education strategies and improving parity of esteem of vocational education. Michael's special research interests are in qualifications, curriculum and learning in the post-compulsory system and in new relationships between education and work.

Introduction: Dearing and Beyond

This book is published at a time when the English education and training system is at a watershed. The *Dearing Review of Qualifications for 16–19 Year Olds* was a recognition of this fact. After years of gradual and unplanned reform and some advances in both participation and achievement, it is now clear that we have reached a critical point in the English system. Evidence suggests that there is a 'peaking' of rises in full-time post-16 participation, and achievement rates could soon follow this trend. Both are of concern in the light of revised national targets and adverse comparisons with international competitor systems.

Looked at in historical terms, it is possible to see the Dearing Review as a recognition that the triple-track qualifications system, formalized in the 1991 White Paper, is not able to make significant further gains beyond the current position. This is certainly the view expressed in Chapter 1, which provides an historical and conceptual analysis of the period leading up to the Dearing Review and sets the Review itself in this context.

This book attempts to provide four things by its focus on qualifications, frameworks and systems. First, it offers a vision of a unified 14–19 qualifications system which, it argues, will overcome the historical and deep-seated divisions that are reflected in track-based qualifications and are preventing further rises in participation and achievement. Second, it provides a critical review of the current system and in particular the role of the three qualifications tracks. Third, it analyses the Dearing reform agenda, focusing on the potential of a framework approach to build a consensus on a move towards a unified qualifications system. Finally, it identifies barriers to whole system-wide change and proposes strategies for a 'steps and stages' approach to reform of the system. A constant theme throughout the book is the use of international comparison as a means of both analysing the English system and as a way of evaluating strategies for change.

It is argued in several points throughout the book that the fragmented English system needs a strong vision of future reform in order to make the 'step change' that is required at this point in its history. This vision of a future system originated in *A British Baccalaureate*, published by the Institute of Public Policy Research in 1990. Despite the White Paper with its consolidation of a divided 14–19

1

qualifications system, the calls for a unified system have not abated. In fact, ideas about the form that unification should take have come from increasing numbers of those in education and beyond. These debates revolve around the distinctive-ness and purposes of qualifications, the need for flexibility to promote access and combination of study and arguments for a broader and more demanding post-16 curriculum to meet the needs of the 21st century. These visions and interpreta-tions are articulated in Chapters 1 and 13.

Throughout the book it is argued that the Dearing Report, amidst all its ambiguities, provides a possible platform for future change. This argument is laid out in detail in Chapter 2, and other chapters in the book return to Dearing as a starting point in their discussion of 'tools for reform'. Chapter 2 argues that the Dearing Report should be judged not only on its recommendations, but also in the light of its inherent assumptions and what it omits to discuss.

Chapters 3, 4 and 5 review the current qualifications tracks. A-levels, it is argued in Chapter 3, distort the qualifications system and are, in their current form, a major barrier to whole-system change. At the same time, it is recognized that A-levels have educational strengths which could form the basis of an 'ad-vanced level curriculum' of the future. On the other hand, according to Chapter 4, GNVQs suffer from major design weaknesses. This chapter suggests the need not only for a drastic reform of these qualifications, but also a reconceptualization of broad vocational education. Chapter 5 tackles the issue of the work-based route and argues for a recognition of the future importance of this type of learning. The chapter sees potential in the development of modern apprenticeships.

Potential tools for reform of the qualifications system are discussed in Chapters 6–11. The issue of general education and the role of core skills is highlighted in Chapter 6, which argues for a new approach to the core curriculum post-16 and highlights the limitations of the core – or key – skills approach. Chapter 7 recognizes the divided history of modularization in this country and argues that the different reform traditions in academic and vocational qualifications have to be reconciled in order to use this tool as a way of designing a future unified qualifications system. This argument is taken further in Chapter 8, which looks at the development of a common language for describing achievement, as well as the use of the 'unit' as the common building block for a unified system. The unintended outcomes of assessment reform form the core concern of Chapter 9. This chapter, while recognizing the ideological nature of many of the debates on assessment, argues for the development of types of assessment which maximize achievement. Chapter 10 analyses models of student guidance in a changing education and training system and makes a case for the 'systemic model' of guidance as an integral part of a unified curriculum. Chapter 11 turns to the role of institutions in the educational reform process. Using value-added as a case-study, it recognizes that a strength of the English system has been the 'bottom-up' character of process-based reform, but that this on its own is not enough and now needs to be reinforced by whole-system change.

Several chapters in the book make use of international comparison, but Chapter 12 looks in detail at recent reforms in the Scottish post-compulsory education and training system. It argues the case for the use of 'home international' comparisons as a powerful analytical tool in the discussion of reform in geographically adjacent systems. This chapter identifies some important lessons that can be drawn from the Scottish experience and which should inform the debates about unification in England.

The final chapter discusses the challenges of the change process in the context of the English system. It starts from a recognition that radical reform of the 14–19 qualifications system is necessary but will not be easy. There is therefore a need for strong and inclusive visions and debates to build a consensus for reform. The chapter also promotes a staged approach to change which pursues several strands of reform simultaneously.

This book argues throughout that the discussion of system change in England needs to move away from ideological positions and critique and towards a strategic debate about the process of change involved in creating a unified system. This means concentrating on implementation and resourcing issues as well as issues of qualifications design.

The final message of this book is that the process of change will need to be dynamic but gradual, planned and managed. This process will also need to be open and inclusive, so that a broad alliance of forces in education and beyond can be harnessed in the shaping of a future 14–19 qualifications system.

Ann Hodgson and Ken Spours

CHAPTER 1

From the 1991 White Paper to the Dearing Report: A Conceptual and Historical Framework for the 1990s

Ann Hodgson and Ken Spours

Participation, achievement, qualifications and reform

Over the last 15 years, a strong relationship has become apparent between the problems of low levels of participation and achievement for 16–19-year-olds, the nature of the qualifications system and arguments for the reform of the education and training system in England. This chapter will argue that for most of this period, actual changes to the system in this country were largely determined by this relationship rather than by planned local or national reform. It will suggest that throughout the 1980s, the education reform process in England could largely be seen as reactive and piecemeal. However, towards the end of this period, and certainly by the time of the White Paper, *Education and Training for the 21st Century* (DfE/ED/WO, 1991) there were more concerted efforts by national government to shape the system in a more proactive and wholesale way.

Debates about the nature of reform have mirrored this trend. Throughout the latter half of this century there have been a number of debates about the role, purpose and effects of the qualifications system in this country (Broadfoot, 1986; Cathcart and Esland, 1990). However, proposals for reform have usually revolved around changes to one aspect of that structure (eg, 16+ school examinations, Youth Training and work-based training) rather than suggestions for any radical overhaul of the system.

Since the late 1980s and early 1990s, however, proposals for reform of the English education and training system (eg, Finegold *et al.*, 1990; National Commission on Education, 1993, 1995; Royal Society, 1991) have been characterized by a more whole-system approach. The debates about qualification tracks, frameworks and unified qualifications systems on which this chapter, and indeed the book as a whole concentrate, can all be seen as part of this new more proactive and systemic approach to reform.

What this chapter also argues is that while debates about the vision of the English education and training system for the 21st century need to take place at this kind of systemic level, there is also a need for a more pragmatic approach to the implementation of the vision. Proactive developments, particularly at national government level, need to be seen critically; they can easily become little more than the blinkered pursuit of a particular ideology and, as such, can stifle local and institutional innovation. Much of the local and regional reform that characterized the 1980s was, in fact, only able to take place because of the absence of any clear national strategy.

This book, like the Learning for the Future Project (Richardson *et al.*, 1995a), argues that, with the vision of a unified system in mind, there should be a staged approach to reform. We argue that this type of approach requires a re-examination of the piecemeal and local reforms that have been introduced over the last 15 years and the role that they might play in a new context. This re-examination does not see each reform merely as an individual reactive response to a static system, but rather as one of a number of potential tools for change in a gradual move towards a more unified system. Given the English context with its voluntarism, its autonomous institutions and its competing awarding and validating bodies, the potential for factions to develop is rife and consensus, at both a theoretical level and at the level of practical implementation, is hard to achieve.

The need to build a consensus on the vision of the future English education and training system and on the steps towards this vision is therefore of paramount importance. It is this difficult process of disentangling the different strands of reform and the different interests of the key players in the debates about these reforms and then building some kind of consensus between them, that this and subsequent chapters of the book will attempt to address.

From a nationally reactive/locally dynamic system to a nationally proactive/locally reactive system

Throughout the 1980s, the post-16 education and training system in England was characterized as a 'low participation/low achievement system' in comparison with others in Europe and beyond (Finegold *et al.*, 1990; Raffe, 1992). Its main features were low full-time post-16 participation rates (below 50 per cent), accompanied by low levels of work-based training. During this period, the English system also had the highest level of economically active 16–19-year-olds among the OECD countries and high levels of youth unemployment (Spours, 1995b). A large proportion of young people – as many as 30 per cent – were involved in emergency training schemes such as the Youth Training Scheme (YTS) which soon developed a reputation for low quality and low qualifications outcomes. In comparison with its European competitors, the English system was thus identified as producing far fewer qualified young people, particularly in the area of vocational qualifications (Ryan, 1992). By the early 1990s, there were increasing arguments for the need to reform the education and training system in this country to raise levels of participation and achievement (Raffe and Rumberger, 1992). These were strengthened by skill comparisons with emerging Pacific economies such as Taiwan and Singapore (Steedman and Green, 1997 forthcoming).

Throughout the late 1980s and early 1990s, however, the English post-16 system was, in fact, already experiencing significant changes due to steady rises in full-time participation and a weakening of the power of the youth labour market. It was at this time that it moved from being a 'low participation system' to a 'medium participation system' (Spours, 1995a). Between 1987 and 1994, full-time participation at 16 rose from under 50 per cent to about 70 per cent. Attainment at GCSE and at A-level also improved during this period by an average of two per cent annually. While these changes were regarded by some as successes for the system, the system still manifested considerable relative weaknesses in terms of participation and achievement. Compared with other countries, full-time post-16 participation remained low in England (by the early 1990s most European countries had achieved participation rates of between 85 to 90 per cent at 16) and increased participation at 16 was not matched by significant increases in qualifications rates, because it was short-lived and fell away rapidly at 17 and 18 (Raffe, 1992).

It could be argued that this change in the character of the system was not due to the impact of educational reforms at either a local or a national level, but rather to the reactions of young people and their parents to the economic and wider societal changes of the late 1980s and early 1990s. The only real exception to this was the expansion of higher education and the positive effect of the introduction of GCSE on both achievement and, therefore, post-16 participation between 1987 and 1994 (Gray *et al.*, 1993). The new vocational qualifications, which were introduced into the system from 1986 onwards, and particularly General National Vocational Qualifications (GNVQs) were essentially a reactive response to increasing participation rates rather than an incentive to increased participation or achievement. The English system was therefore drifting towards higher levels of participation and achievement in the mid-1990s mainly as a result of the impact of the recession on the youth labour market.

However, as participation rates begin to wane and achievement levels begin to peak in the mid-1990s (Spours, 1995b), it is clear that 'reactive drifting' is no longer an adequate policy option. The stark necessity of encouraging the trend towards a 'high participation/high achievement' education and training system in order to compete with other European and Pacific Rim systems suggests that a greater degree of system shaping is essential. The issue for the late 1990s is not whether the English education and training system needs reform, but what form it should take. Should the system become more education-based, more work-based or simply retain its pluralistic mixed character to reflect differing patterns of demand? What does this mean for the shape of the qualifications structure?

We have argued above that planned reform played little part in shaping the character and structure of the education and training system of the late 1980s. Nevertheless, throughout the 1980s the gradual shifts in participation, led to several attempts at piecemeal reform of the qualifications system. Early in the decade these were largely responses to youth unemployment and included the development of YTS for those in the work-based route and the Certificate of Pre-Vocational Education (CPVE) for those opting to stay on in full-time education. In the late 1980s, however, there was a more active attempt to shape the system and to develop a more coherent approach by building a national qualifications framework, through the setting up of the National Council for Vocational Qualifications (NCVQ). By the early 1990s, with the adoption by the government of National Targets for Education and Training (NTETs) and the introduction of a new funding mechanism for further education (FEFC, 1993), the reform process had moved from being largely reactive to increasing post-16 participation rates, to being actively designed to stimulate participation growth and to raise levels of achievement, albeit at lower unit costs.

Looking at the recent history of the English education and training system through the links between participation, achievement and qualifications highlights three trends. First, there is the fact that the response of national qualifications has been essentially reactive to changes in participation. The second trend is that the strong tradition of local 'bottom-up' reform (eg, records of achievement, unitization/modularization) was able to flourish in this 'drifting reactive' system. The third trend has been a gradual move to a focus on achievement through exhortation (NTETs in a context of international comparisons), a stress on accountability (league tables, OFSTED, FEFC) and national qualifications reform (Dearing, 1996; DfE/ED/WO, 1991). In this sense, over the last 15 years, reform of the English education and training system could be characterized as moving from a 'nationally reactive/locally dynamic phase' to a more 'nationally proactive/locally reactive phase', while at the same time retaining its voluntaristic and market-led nature.

Reform, qualifications and the problem of consensus

Despite recent reforms, the weaknesses of the English system continue to be highlighted by international comparisons (Steedman and Green, 1997 forthcoming). There is a general consensus that reform is required to raise levels of national performance but there is little real agreement as to what this reform should be. The problem for the English system, in contrast to Scotland for instance, is its scale and diversity and the fact that there has been no tradition of strategic reform (Raffe et al., 1996). Consensus for change, linked to this context and history, is going to continue to be difficult to achieve.

However, the issue of qualifications reform has been, and continues to be, central to the debate on system reform. This is because qualifications, or at least public examinations, have, in the English context, always been seen as shaping the curriculum (Hargreaves, 1989; Wolf, 1992a). Studies of international comparisons have also tended to link qualifications rates and economic competitiveness (DTI, 1995; Green and Steedman, 1993; Prais, 1987; Ryan, 1992; Steedman and Green, 1997 forthcoming).

It could be argued that the English system is developing into a 'credentialist' system later than other countries (Young, 1995). In such a system, qualifications act as an articulator between the aspirations of individuals which, generally speaking, have risen over the last decade, the needs of society, in terms of national skills and competition, and schools and colleges that deliver certification.

The specific nature of the debate on reform of the qualifications system appears to revolve round the need to promote further participation at the same time as securing higher educational achievement and ensuring that curriculum design meets the needs of the society of the future. The main strands of this debate centre on the following five key issues.

First, there is the balance between calls for flexibility and differentiation, in order to encourage and sustain participation and achievement (Dearing, 1996) and the demand for a stronger element of general education in initial education and training to raise levels of achievement for all students (Crombie-White *et al.*, 1995; Finegold *et al.*, 1990; National Commission on Education, 1993, 1995; Royal Society, 1991). Second, there is a need to consider the future of the academic track and the form of general education required to stimulate participation, to fulfil skill and social needs and to raise achievement. Third, it is important to understand the consequences of responding to new types of participation by introducing a distinctive vocational curriculum and the implications of this for both student progression and divisions within the system. Fourth, there is the problem of overcoming the long-standing weakness of vocational education in England and of ensuring the development of specialized vocational education and work-based training which can meet the needs of the 21st century. Finally, there is a need to balance increasing demands for modular qualifications and modular delivery of the curriculum with concerns about maintaining national standards and coherence.

At the heart of all these debates is the issue of how to improve and sustain participation, to raise levels of achievement and to develop clear progression routes. The current debates also echo the past. Are there two types of mind – academic and vocational? (MoE, 1959). Should there be a strong distinction between the academic and vocational tracks? The debate around reform focuses relentlessly on the role of qualifications; however, this is in a context where it is impossible to ignore the effects of funding, labour markets and institutional competition.

The combination of voluntarism, academic and vocational division and the search for a national framework were best expressed in the 1991 White Paper

Education and Training for the 21st Century (DfE/ED/WO, 1991). It is therefore this document that we take as the starting point for our discussion of qualifications reform.

The historical development of 14–19 qualifications in England since 1991

The early 1990s and the period surrounding the publication of the White Paper, *Education and Training for the 21st Century* was an important moment both in terms of the direction of government policy and in the debate about qualifications reform.

The White Paper marked a significant development of the national qualifications framework and was designed to set the agenda for government policy on post-16 education and training for the next five years. *Education and Training for the 21st Century* contained a number of themes which signalled a more centralist and system-wide approach to qualifications reform, within a clear market context that stressed the power and autonomy of individual students and individual institutions. These included:

- The formalization of a triple-track national qualifications framework based on an academic track (A-levels), a broad vocational track (GNVQs) and an occupationally specific track (NVQs).
- The establishment of the quasi competence-based GNVQ as a middle track which was intended to provide a progression route to both work and further study.
- Restrictions on assessed course-work in GCSEs and A-levels with the intention that fewer students should participate in the academic track.
- Proposals for overarching advanced and general diplomas.
- The creation of a qualifications framework to link the three tracks though a limited alignment of levels and unit design. This was intended to facilitate some mixing of academic and broad vocational qualifications in individual study programmes.
- Further movement towards an education and training market and the end to local planning of post-16 education with the incorporation of FE colleges.
- Proposals for the wider introduction of youth training credits.

The 1991 White Paper thus represented the development of a divided national qualifications framework based on three tracks with distinctive curricula and assessment regimes. The two dominant features of these proposals were first, the attempts to 'retrench' the academic track by restricting participation in A-levels through assessment policy; and second, the efforts to encourage participation away from the academic track and into the broad vocational track by introducing GNVQs which were intended to be delivered in schools as well as colleges. The White Paper's proposed changes in both the academic and the broad vocational tracks would in fact dominate the qualifications reform agenda for the next five years. The proposals for overarching diplomas, however, quickly disappeared and only surfaced again during the Dearing Review of 1996.

At one level, the White Paper could still be seen as a series of responses to the rapid rises in full-time post-16 participation which had been taking place since 1987. It reflected an anxiety that the surge of participation in A-levels, now about 35 per cent of the age group, would dilute standards. It also responded to concerns that the area in which England compared worst with continental systems was in participation and achievement at intermediate level (our Level 3) vocational qualifications (Ryan, 1992). Finally, through its attempt to build a broad voca- tional track, there was an admission that occupationally based NVQs were not appropriate for most full-time 16–19-year-olds, either in terms of providing breadth of skill or knowledge for progression (Watson and Wolf, 1991). Further- more, NVQs could not be effectively delivered by schools, which was where many of the newly participating students were now studying.

At the same time, however, the White Paper also represented an educational and ideological shift away from a series of curriculum and qualifications devel- opments which were beginning to blur distinctions between academic and vocational curricula. In the second half of the 1980s there had been the develop- ment of GCSEs, the extension of assessed coursework in both GCSE and A-level syllabuses, the emergence of the National Curriculum and the commissioning of the Higginson Report on A-levels (DES, 1988). At 14 and beyond, these developments could be seen as attempts to broaden the academic track and to raise levels of achievement. By the late 1980s, and with the effect of Technical and Vocational Education Initiative (TVEI) Extension on 14–19 curriculum develop- ment, local experiments were beginning to take place focusing on modularization (Moon, 1988; Warwick, 1987) and Y-models, which were designed to combine academic and vocational study (Burgess, 1993). The most well-known of these was the Wessex Modular A-level Project (Rainbow, 1993). At the same time, SEAC and NCVQ were discussing the issue of core skills and their relationship to both academic and vocational courses. In Scotland, modular National Certif- icates were being brought in as part of the Scottish Action Plan (Scottish Educa- tion Department, 1983) and the possibility of a common modular framework was being discussed by practitioners and education academics south of the border (Modular Information Network, 1993, 1994; Spours et al., 1989). It was in this climate of curriculum innovation that the design for a unified qualifications system began to take shape and finally emerged in 1990 in the argument for a British Baccalaureate (Finegold et al., 1990).

The 1991 White Paper sought to bring this process of local and regional curriculum development to an abrupt halt. The rejection of the Higginson Report Advancing A-levels (DES, 1988) signalled a reluctance by government to consider reforming the A-level system. Similarly, by 1989, SEAC's work on core skills was quietly brought to a halt because it was seen as an incremental approach to the same type of reform. The national government policy implications of the 1991 White Paper, however, were altogether more serious because this document clearly demonstrated the government's explicit aim of restricting access to A-levels and developing a clear vocational alternative for those who wished to participate in full-time post-16 study – GNVQs. These moves to formalize the academic/vocational division set the tone of qualifications reform up to the Dearing Review and, as Young argues in Chapter 2 of this book, were also echoed in Dearing's Final Report (Dearing, 1996).

However, there are also proposals within the Dearing Report (eg, the four-level qualifications and certification framework) which can be seen as a move beyond the White Paper and the beginnings of a 'weak framework' stage in qualifications reform (Spours and Young, 1996). Dearing's approach to reform can be seen as a desire to stimulate and sustain participation through a common but differentiated and flexible framework, while at the same time using a 'stand-ards' approach – the retention and even reinforcement of 'tried and tested' A-levels – to raising levels of achievement. The major question is to what extent the inherent tensions between these two policy approaches is affected by the potentially conflicting demands of increasing participation and raising levels of achievement.

Tracks, frameworks and unified systems

The debate about qualifications in the mid-1990s is still essentially a debate about participation, achievement and standards which is being fuelled and influenced by the increasing use of international comparisons.

This debate has crystallized into three basic positions: those who believe in retaining three distinctive qualification 'tracks'[1] (the 'trackers'); those who want to see the development of an overarching qualifications framework (the 'frame-workers'); and those who support the development of unified systems (the 'unifiers') (Spours, 1996). In reality, these groupings are an oversimplification: they overlap with each other and each has its own internal variants. They also tend to look to different countries for evidence of ideas or systems or for examples to emulate.

The first group – the 'trackers' – believes that it is important to preserve (and even to accentuate) the distinction between qualifications tracks in order to accommodate different types of ability and to recognize that academic and vocational learning have different purposes (Dearing, 1996). While this position is supported ostensibly by the Right, it also contains academics who are less concerned by the preservation of elite academic education and more concerned about the quality, status and direction of vocational education (Raffe, 1993; Smithers, 1993, 1994). Analyses of German, Austrian and Swiss systems are often used to support this position. These are systems in which the academic and vocational tracks are separate, but in which the vocational track has high status due to the fact that it contains substantial elements of general education, has its own institutions both in the school and higher education system, and has outcomes which are recognized and supported by employers.

The second group – the 'frameworkers' – consists of those who favour flexible frameworks and see these as providing a mechanism for overarching existing qualifications in order to structure their relationship. The main aims of the flexible framework approach are to use 'unitization' as a means of improving access to the curriculum for adults as well as for 16–19-year-olds, to improve individual student choice, to promote personal pacing of learning, to stimulate curriculum reform by making new combinations of study possible and thus to provide a mechanism for the gradual reform of the qualifications tracks.

Frameworks could be seen as a peculiarly English approach to consensus maintenance due to their openness, ambiguity and voluntary nature. Frameworks provide the means by which existing qualifications can continue, but with greater flexibility (although no compulsion) to mix academic and vocational study. This approach involves creating additional certification, thus producing more qualifications complexity and raising issues of the currency of qualifications.

The main reflections on a framework approach to qualifications were put forward by the Further Education Unit (FEU) in its series of documents on developing a credit framework (FEU, 1992, 1993, 1995) and by the Joint Group of Headteachers' Associations in the Joint Statement (AfC *et al.*, 1994). However, there is considerable ambiguity about how far those who support frameworks are intent on transforming qualifications. Some of the signatories to the Joint Statement in 1994, such as HMC, strongly support the retention of A-levels (HMC, 1995) and others, particularly in further education, have been relatively enthusiastic about the GNVQ approach to learning styles as an alternative route to higher education (Higgins and Megson, 1995). Those who support qualifications frameworks appear to be more interested in introducing flexibility rather than in encouraging breadth. They have supported the idea of core/key skills, although often only as an option. However, they have considerable reservations about introducing breadth through core studies – that is the demand that all students study some sort of core curriculum post-16 – on the grounds that it could discourage some students (Kershaw, 1996) and might both increase failure rates and undermine participation.

A third group – the 'unifiers' – are those who argue for a unified qualifications system. This reform originated with the publication by the Institute of Public Policy Research of *A British Baccalaureate* (Finegold *et al.*, 1990) which was then followed by other organizations – notably the Royal Society (1991), the National Commission on Education (1993, 1995) the Labour Party (1996) and Liberal Democrats (Foster, 1995) – who, while varying in their specific proposals, also argued for a unified qualifications system. During the Dearing Review process these organizations were also joined by several teacher unions such as the NUT, NATFHE and NAHT. The 'unifiers' argue for a core curriculum post-16 and the replacement of existing qualifications by one single qualifications structure, rather than the continuation of a framework overarching different qualifications. They also place great emphasis on modularity and assessment strategies which are based on 'fitness for purpose' and believe that a more unified and mutually enriched academic and vocational curriculum is a necessary preparation for increasing participation rates, as well as meeting the knowledge demands of economies in the next century (Young, 1993). Those arguing for a unified qualifications system have also tended to see the implementation of qualifications reform as requiring national regulation in relation to the youth labour market because of its effects on skill requirements and participation.

This threefold typology, however, has to recognize that the three groups do overlap and share some common concerns. All, for example, agree that there is a need for reform of the English post-14 education and training system in order to increase participation and raise levels of achievement. There is also some interesting convergence. Some of the unifiers share the trackers' interest in focusing on continental approaches to vocational education, with a similar perception that there is a problem about the lack of high-level technical demands in many English vocational qualifications, while unifiers and frameworkers both see the potential of unitization and modularity. In reality, therefore, the alignment of these three discernible groups is complex and could continue to shift with the evolving debate.

Since 1990 the arguments for a unified qualifications system have become stronger, though there is also a considerable degree of overlap here with those who support the development of qualifications frameworks. However, there are also important differences and these tend to revolve around issues of compulsion, coherence, voluntarism and flexibility. The unifiers have argued for the need for breadth and a common core post-16 which implies a degree of compulsion. They also use international comparisons to suggest that those countries which do adopt a more common approach to learning post-16 have higher expectations of their young people (Green and Steedman, 1993). Those in favour of frameworks tend towards greater voluntarism, on the basis that a more pragmatic approach to reform is more realistic in the decentralized and diverse English context and is less likely to antagonise learners (AfC *et al.*, 1994). To some extent, the debate about movement towards a more unified system has built a degree of consensus between the frameworkers and the unifiers because there is a mutual acceptance that the unified system is the long-term aim, but that the qualifications system in England will have to pass through a 'Framework Stage' in order to attain this goal (Labour Party, 1996; Spours and Young, 1995). However, there are currently a number of specific debates emerging, the outcomes of which could influence both the direction and pace of change. The section which follows will analyse some of these debates.

Key qualifications and curriculum debates

The key qualifications and curriculum debates of the mid-1990s can be regarded as aspects of the broader debate on tracks, frameworks and qualifications and the form and content of post-compulsory education and training. They are also dimensions of a debate about how to promote improved participation, achievement and higher standards.

General education, breadth and core skills

The nature of general education 14–19 is central to the overall debate about the purpose of the education and training system in England. As the previous section has argued, it is here that there are still the greatest areas of disagreement both between the trackers, frameworkers and unifiers and also within each of these groups. To accept either that the post-16 education and training system in England should have a general education function, or that general education should be part of every post-16 student's study programme would be something completely new for this country. The acceptance of such a position would also have far-reaching practical implications for the system. It would, for example, affect the future development of A-levels, the broad vocational track and the continuing viability of the distinctively English three-year single-subject honours degrees.

Equally contentious is the argument over what constitutes 'breadth' post-16. Is it breadth of content – that is the idea of studying a wider number of subjects which cover a greater range of knowledge domains – or is it simply the idea of a fuller study programme which includes core knowledge areas such as English and mathematics? There are basically three positions on the question of general education and the case for breadth.

First, many of those who argue for making the tracks 'distinctive' take the view (as does Dearing) that general education post-16 should largely be in the form of academic education for those who want to continue to study school subjects, and for the rest it should be limited to the 'key skills' of communications, numeracy and IT (Dearing, 1996; HMC, 1995). 'General education' in any real sense would thus be restricted to the highest achieving 30 per cent of the age group. It could be claimed that all students were being provided with the opportunity for 'breadth', without any need to disrupt the structure or purpose of existing qualifications.

A second position is to argue for greater breadth of content for all those involved in the academic route – a position taken by the Higginson Report (DES, 1988) which argued for five leaner A-levels. This would lead to a qualification not unlike the International Baccalaureate or the German *Abitur*.

A third position on breadth sees the academic track of the future being transformed into more diverse opportunities for general education, in which there would be more subjects to learn and in which there could be a closer link between general education and vocational education (Finegold *et al.*, 1990; NCE, 1993, 1995; Royal Society, 1991). This approach to general education is most closely associated with the unifiers' arguments for a baccalaureate which embraces both general and vocational education and exhibits some of the features of the Swedish upper secondary curriculum.

The issue of core or key skills – usually equated with those skills assessed by GNVQs – is central to this debate. Those in favour of qualifications tracks suggest the idea of 'core skills' for all. However, as Green's chapter in this book points out, there are disagreements about the content of core skills. Some favour a return to maths and English rather than communications and numeracy (Green, 1995; Smithers, 1994; Wolf, 1992b). There has also been a call by some for further study of a modern foreign language to be seen as one of the core elements of all post-16 programmes (Leney, 1995b). Others, like the Dearing Report (1996) and the National Commission on Education Report (1995), favour a broader definition of core skills and include among these personal and interpersonal skills such as 'improving own learning and performance' and 'working with others'. This is a dimension of the general education and breadth debate on which there is more broad agreement between the 'trackers' and 'unifiers', although the former would take a voluntarist approach to the inclusion of these skills in learning programmes whereas the latter would seek to build them into a baccalaureate-style grouped award. The unifiers have argued strongly that core learning in the foundation subjects of English and mathematics would not be enough and have highlighted the need for more conceptual skills for all (Crombie-White *et al.*, 1995; Young *et al.*, 1993).

Vocational education and specialization

A second key issue in the qualifications debate is the future of vocational education. Vocational qualifications have, for the past decade, been dominated by an NCVQ mission to produce a system founded on competence-based outcomes. This approach has its ardent supporters and its vitriolic detractors. There is little consensus and much polarization. The supporters of NVQs point to their access-based approach to assessment, the promotion of job-ready skills and the emphasis on flexibility (Jessup, 1991). The critics point to a lack of underpinning knowledge in NVQs, their bureaucracy (Hyland, 1994) and the low take-up by employers (Robinson, 1996).

A key issue which will inform this debate is that of 'vocational specialization' and what kinds of specialized vocational knowledge and skills are required for productive life in the future (Young and Spours, 1995). Critics of GNVQs argue that these qualifications are neither broad enough to reflect the demand for general education nor specialized enough to be genuinely vocational (FEU/IOE/Nuffield, 1994). Chapter 4 of this book examines this issue in more depth and suggests that the major challenge is how to create vocational specialist study and experience which is both attractive and educationally and technically demanding.

Assessment, achievement and standards

Since 1991 the debate about assessment in 14–19 qualifications has been dominated by arguments for approaches which stress national consistency and the maintenance of educational standards. This argument has been manifest in the decision to restrict assessed coursework in GCSE and A-levels (DfE/ED/WO, 1991) and to promote more external assessment in GNVQs (Capey, 1996, Dearing, 1996).

At the same time there has been a parallel and often polarized argument which associates particular assessment strategies with certain types of study and forms of learning. 'Rigour and standards' in academic qualifications have been associated with terminal examinations and evidence of synoptic learning (SCAA, 1994), while, in vocational qualifications, they have been connected with tightly defined assessment criteria and portfolios of evidence (NCVQ et al., 1995).

The key debate appears to be over how to balance concerns about national consistency with those of achievement and incentivizing learning. Recently, however, it has been argued that the division between internal and external assessment is no longer a valid debate (Macintosh, 1988) and that a range of assessment tools are available which should be used according to their 'fitness for purpose'. This raises the problem of whether it is possible to create a truly common national assessment framework and, if it is, how it might be applied to different qualifications. Chapters 9 and 13 of this book discuss this issue in more depth.

Modularization and unitization

Modularization[2] has been seen by a wide range of educationalists, both in this country and more widely in Europe, as an important tool for improving learning (MIN, 1993, 1994; Raffe, 1992, 1993; Richardson et al., 1995b). It has also been accused of producing a fragmented approach to learning, not sufficiently stressing the grasp of the whole subject and leading to students being over-assessed (Howieson, 1993; Raffe, 1992). Dearing's cautious approach to modularization was shaped by these anxieties.

At the same time, modular A-level syllabuses are as popular as ever, with over 50 per cent of new syllabuses being modular (Richardson et al., 1995b). Moreover, modular syllabuses are associated with a step-by-step approach to learning which encourages higher levels of achievement through hard and consistent work.

Unitization[3] has also been seen as a tool for promoting greater achievement by breaking assessment down into more manageable chunks and by making the curriculum more transparent and accessible for the learner (FEU, 1993; Young et al., 1994). The argument here is that small units, where learning outcomes and assessment criteria are made explicit, provide the learner with the tools to raise her or his achievement. Unitization has been used by further education colleges and the Open College Network mainly to describe learning which has traditionally fallen outside the spheres of formal qualifications with the intention of ascribing some form of accreditation to it.

Both modularization and unitization have thus been seen as powerful tools to promote achievement and access. However, again the key issues of debate are around quality assurance in terms of assessment, and how to make learning more manageable and explicit while maintaining coherent learning programmes. The debate about the role of modularization and unitization as tools for reform of the qualifications system is highlighted at several points in this book (Chapters 6, 7 and 12).

Processes of student guidance and learning self-management

Over the last decade or so the English system has placed a great deal of emphasis on quality of learning and on the role of individuals in managing their own learning. The development of skills associated with recording of achievement and action planning has been part of the educational agenda of the Employment Department, reflecting a strand of progressive employer thinking which has seen future skills as personal generic skills (CBI, 1989, 1993; IoD, 1992). The promotion of these types of process skills, however, has an ambiguous relationship with the qualifications system. Some have seen it as a substitute for hard-edged vocational learning (Smithers, 1994) and others have seen process-based learning as a means of reforming the curriculum without fundamentally reforming qualifications (Chitty, 1991; Harland, 1991; Spours, 1993).

At the same time, as Watts and Young argue in Chapter 10 of this book, the issues of guidance and learning self-management are becoming more not less important, because of the growing emphasis on lifelong learning (Dearing, 1996; Halsall, 1996). The key issue in the qualifications debate is whether or not these processes can be built into the design of qualifications. Some argue that the curriculum needs to be seen as separate from qualifications (Stanton, 1994) and that it is up to institutions (and possibly funding councils) to promote guidance and self-management. Others argue that a qualifications system of the future should incorporate the processes of management of learning and guidance (Crombie-White *et al.*, 1995; Finegold *et al.*, 1990; National Commission on Education, 1995). A unified qualifications system would tend to see itself as all-inclusive and providing accreditation for a wide range of learning, including a student giving evidence of having reflected on her or his progress (Crombie-White *et al.*, 1995, Spours and Young, 1995).

An important strand to this debate is not only what qualifications should or should not contain, but the relationship between national qualifications and the institutions which deliver them (Hargreaves, 1989; Young and Watson, 1992). Schools, colleges and training organizations mediate between individual learners and national qualifications and, in the final analysis, provide the structure through which learning takes place. Traditionally, schools and colleges have exercised a great deal of autonomy in terms of their choices in the post-16 curriculum, notably in the number of A-levels on offer, the number of taught hours for each course and the amount of guidance being offered. This tradition of voluntarism is being challenged by the demands for qualification reform and by calls for greater efficiency (Audit Commission/OFSTED, 1993; FEFC, 1993). The central relationship between reform of qualifications and the role of institutions is tackled in Chapter 11 of this book.

Strategic implications of the debates on 14–19 qualifications

Fundamentally, the debate about the English 14–19 qualifications system is a debate about whether it evolves in a more unified direction or whether it remains a distinctive track-based system, emphasizing the division between academic and vocational learning and certification. Those who advocate a unified system tend to focus on the link between the economic needs of the future and the design of a qualifications system to meet these needs. (Finegold *et al.*, 1990; National Commission for Education, 1993, 1995; Richardson *et al.*, 1995a).

The major thrust of this argument is that the projected development of 'smart' production methods will require workers who can think creatively, understand how organizations work and can link theory and practice (Young *et al.*, 1993). It is important, therefore, that the education and training system encourages the development of the type of skills and knowledge which will fulfil these requirements. In terms of curricula and qualifications, this could be interpreted as meaning that academic learning needs to be more applied and vocational learning needs greater theoretical content to be able to develop both conceptual and technical capability in students (Prospect Centre, 1992; Reich, 1991). Since, it is argued, attempts to establish 'parity of esteem' between academic and vocational qualifications in the English historical and social context have moved little beyond rhetoric, the only realistic course for reform of English 14–19 qualifications is to bring academic and vocational learning closer together.

The development of unifying strategies is also part of a wider international trend, though the strategies for promoting parity of esteem for vocational qualifications differ according to the type of education and training system. Unified and integrated qualifications systems are being developed in Norway, Sweden, Finland and Scotland, based either on modularity, on high degrees of general education in all programmes or on delivery in comprehensive post-16 institutions. At the same time, countries with traditionally strong work-based systems, such as Germany and Austria, are attempting to modernize and enhance vocational education by the introduction of more general education into their vocational programmes and by creating new vocational qualifications which extend progression into higher education (Lasonen, 1996).

What a study of the current direction of European education and training systems shows, therefore, is that even the most robust and well-regarded two-track systems are in a process of change. In comparative terms, the English system is in a state of flux and can be seen as approaching a watershed. It is still very much a divided system, but new linkages between the tracks are considered in the Dearing proposals.

Any strategic approach to system reform will have to address the issues of complexity and coherence. One of the reasons for the problems of incoherence in English qualifications arrangements has been the tendency of the reform process to lead to additions to the system, rather than to produce rationalization. This has been the dominant history of qualifications reform since the early 1980s and the Dearing proposals for new overarching certification can be seen as part of this tradition. At one level, a qualifications system based on tracks has a superficial simplicity – everyone knows where they are – but in reality it is infinitely more complex. First, students increasingly do not want to confine themselves to one track but would like the right to move between tracks (Hodgson, 1994). Second, the nature of the current academic track limits its ability to increase substantially in size. This effectively consigns the majority of the post-16 cohort to a vocational form of education. Third, over 60 per cent of qualifications, albeit mostly vocational ones, still lie outside the tracks defined as A-levels, GNVQs and NVQs (FEFC, 1996).

A divided system, in its attempt to absorb increasing numbers of students, is producing more division, proliferation and potential confusion. A unified system, based on a single modular structure, promises greater simplicity of design since it could include all types of learning which could be unitized to fit into a single framework. At the same time, however, a unified modular system would produce more complex choices for individual students and would demand a critical new role for guidance (see Chapters 8 and 10).

The development of unified qualifications systems is at a very early stage right across Europe. There are no tried and tested models. Even in Sweden and Finland the current developments are the result of reforms introduced in the late 1980s and early 1990s and these are still evolving. Scotland's experiment in the form of *Higher Still* will not start until 1998 and, in any case, still does not embrace the full range of work-based qualifications. So the movement towards more unified systems poses many challenges and problems, particularly in the English context.

One of the most important of these is the fact that qualifications reform is not only about content and design, but also about how these relate to the context of change. How these issues are tackled may prove as influential as the content of the reform itself in determining successful outcomes (Raffe, 1984). The English system is deeply divided and fragmented and strong arguments have been made that successful reform can only be achieved in steps and stages (Spours and Young, 1995). The Learning for the Future Project argued that the qualifications system could be reformed by moving to a unified system through first developing a genuine national framework that included all existing qualifications. A critical issue for such a strategy is how far the Dearing proposals signify a movement in this direction and how this can be built upon. This is something to which each of the chapters in this book returns.

Consideration of the reform process must take into account the sheer complexity of the English context and its traditions of voluntarism. These features have in some ways been extended by recent Conservative education policy, which has combined greater central control (through funding and qualifications) with greater freedom for institutions. Is it the case that a unified system will have go with the grain of major features of the English system? Many of these features can appear negative; they include electivism in subject choice, the dominant role of universities in determining the nature of general education, the vested interest of competing awarding and validating bodies, competence-based vocational education and a weak employer demand for qualified workers. Or can we try to go with the positive aspects of the system and in particular its traditions of local innovation? A clear national strategy will have to be balanced with a strong response from below. This points to a long reform process (ten years or more) which tries to combine a vision of change with consultation and a realistic timescale for reform. The key question for teachers and lecturers is whether they are ready to be directly involved in this long-haul approach to change (Higham *et al.*, 1996). It is also important that amidst the current policy flux and confusions, teachers and lecturers feel that a transformed post-14 qualifications system is ultimately attainable.

This book aims to provide three things to support the process of change: first, a clear picture of the current position in relation to 14–19 qualifications and their context; second, a vision of the kind of unified 14–19 qualifications system needed to meet the challenges of the 21st century; finally, an analysis of both the tools for reform and the processes of change which might help to translate vision into reality.

Notes

1. The terms 'tracks' and 'pathways' are often used synonymously. Dearing, for example, uses the term 'pathways' when in fact he is referring to what others describe as 'tracks'. The degree of difference between various qualifications defines whether they constitute a track or not. A track can be defined by four dimensions of distinctiveness: purposes, content, assessment and structure. For instance, both A-levels and GNVQs could be described as tracks, because they are meant to serve different purposes and have very little overlap of content and assessment (Coates and Hamilton, 1996).
2. The term 'modularization' is used here to describe a way of breaking down whole qualifications into smaller units of learning, which may be separately assessed but which are also governed by some form of overall assessment. This term as defined here is most often used, therefore, to describe changes to linear A-level syllabuses.
3. Unitization is the breaking down of the curriculum into 'units'. In the definition of the FEU, 'A unit is a coherent set of learning outcomes' (FEU, 1995, p.6).

References

Association for Colleges, The Girls' School Association, The Headmasters' Conference, The Secondary Heads Association, The Sixth Form Colleges' Association and The Society for Headmasters and Headmistresses In Independent Schools (1994) *Post-Compulsory Education and Training: A Joint Statement*, London: AfC.

Audit Commission/OFSTED (1993) *Unfinished Business: Full-time Education Courses for 16–19 Year Olds*, London: HMSO.

Broadfoot, P (1986) 'Alternatives to Public Examinations' in Nuttall, D (ed.) *Assessing Educational Achievement*, London: Falmer Press.

Burgess, M (1993) 'Linking BTEC and A/AS Levels', in Richardson, W, Woolhouse, J and Finegold, D (eds) *The Reform of Post-16 Education and Training in England and Wales*, Harlow: Longman.

Capey, J (1996) *Review of GNVQ Assessment*, London: National Council for Vocational Qualifications.

Cathcart, H E and Esland, G M (1990) 'The Compliant Creative Worker: The Ideological Reconstruction of the School Leaver', in Esland, G (ed.) *Education, Training and Employment. Vol. 2: The Educational Response*, Buckingham: Open University Press.

Chitty, C (ed.) (1991) *Post-16 Education: Studies in Access and Achievement*, London: Kogan Page.

Coates, P and Hamilton, J (1996) '16–19 Coherence Project', in Dearing, R, *Review of Qualifications for 16–19 Year Olds*, London: SCAA.

Confederation of British Industry (1989) *Towards a Skills Revolution*, London: CBI.

Confederation of British Industry (1993) *Routes for Success. Careership: A Strategy for All 16–19 Year Old Learners*, London: CBI.

Crombie-White, R, Pring, R and Brockington, D (1995) *14–19 Education and Training: Implementing a Unified System of Learning*, London: Royal Society of Arts.

Dearing, Sir Ron (1996) *Review of Qualifications for 16–19 Year Olds*, London: SCAA.

Department of Education and Science (1988) *Advancing A-levels: Report of the Committee chaired by Professor Higginson*, London: HMSO.

Department of Trade and Industry (1995) *Competitiveness: Helping Business to Win*, London: HMSO.

Department for Education/Employment Department/Welsh Office (1991) *Education and Training for the 21st Century*, London: HMSO.

Finegold, D, Keep, E, Miliband, D, Raffe, D, Spours, K and Young, M (1990) *A British Baccalaureate: Overcoming Divisions Between Education and Training*, London: Institute for Public Policy Research.

Foster, D (1995) 'Heat and Light', *Education*, 10 March.

Further Education Funding Council (1993) *Funding Learning*, Coventry: FEFC.

Further Education Funding Council (1996) 'Student Numbers at Colleges in the Further Education Sector in England in 1994–5', Press Release 23 January, Coventry: FEFC.

Further Education Unit (1992) *A Basis for Credit?* London: FEU.

Further Education Unit (1993) *Beyond a Basis for Credit*, London: FEU.

Further Education Unit (1995) *A Framework for Credit: A Common Framework for Post-14 Education and Training for the 21st Century*, London: FEU.

Further Education Unit, Institute of Education and Nuffield Foundation (1994) *GNVQs 1993–1994: A National Survey Report*, an Interim Report of a Joint Project, The Evaluation of GNVQs: Enrolment and Delivery Patterns and Their Policy Implications, London: FEU.

Gray, J, Jesson, D and Tranmer, M (1993) *Boosting Post-16 participation in Full-time Education: A Study of Some Key Factors in England and Wales*, Youth Cohort Study No 20, Sheffield: Employment Department.

Green, A (1995) 'Core Skills and Progression in Post-Compulsory Education and Training in England and France', *Comparative Education*, **31**, 1.

Green, A and Steedman, H (1993) *Education Provision, Education Attainment and the Needs of Industry: A review of the Research for Germany, France, Japan, the USA and Britain*, National Institute of Economic Research, Report No 5, London: NIESR.

Halsall, R (1996) 'Core Skills – The Continuing Debate', in Halsall, R and Cockett, M (eds) *Education and Training 14–19: Chaos or Coherence?*, Manchester Metropolitan University Series, London: David Fulton.

Hargreaves, A (1989) *Curriculum and Assessment Reform*, Buckingham: Open University Press.

Harland, J (1991) 'Upper Secondary Education in England and Wales. An Overview of Curriculum Pathways', in Chitty, C (ed.) *Post-16 Education: Studies on Access and Achievement*, London: Kogan Page.

Headmasters' Conference, The (1995) *Education 14–19*, Leicester: HMC.

Higgins, T and Megson, C (1995) 'GNVQs are good for you: it's official', *Education*, 24 November.

Higham, J, Sharp, P and Yeomann, D (1996) *The Emerging 16–19 Curriculum Policy and Provision*, London: David Fulton.

Hodgson, A (1994) *What's in it for Me? A Study of Student Aspirations and Achievement 1992–1994*, London: Tower Hamlets TVEI.

Howieson, C (1993) 'Parity of Academic and Vocational Awards: The Experience of Modularisation in Scotland', in Wolf, A (ed.) *Parity of Esteem: Can Vocational Awards Ever Achieve High Status? International Centre for Research on Assessment*, Institute of Education, University of London.

Hyland, T (1994) *Competence, Education and NVQs: Dissenting Perspectives*, London: Cassell.

Institute of Directors (1992) *Performance and Potential: Education and Training for a Market Economy*, London: IoD.

Jessup, G (1991) *Outcomes – NVQs and the Emerging Model of Education and Training*, London: Falmer Press.

Kershaw, N (1996) 'Stirred but not shaken', *TES*, 10 May.

Labour Party (1996) *Aiming Higher: Labour's Proposals for the Reform of the 14–19 Curriculum*, London: Labour Party.

Lasonen, J (1996) *Reforming Upper Secondary Education in Europe: Surveys of Strategies for Post-16 Education to Improve the Parity of Esteem for Initial Vocational Education in Eight European Educational Systems*, Finland: University of Jyväskylä Press.

Leney, T (1995a) 'Lessons from the Scots: Background and Prospects for the Reform of Post-Compulsory Education in Scotland' in Young, M, Hodgson, A and Leney, T (eds) *Unifying the Post-Compulsory Curriculum: Lessons from France and Scotland*, Unified 16+ Curriculum Series Number 9, Post-16 Education Centre, Institute of Education, University of London.

Leney, T (1995b) 'Lessons from the French: Post-Compulsory Education in France', in Young, M, Hodgson, A and Leney, T (eds) *Unifying the Post-Compulsory Curriculum: Lessons from France and Scotland*, Unified 16+ Curriculum Series Number 9, Post-16 Education Centre, Institute of Education, University of London.

Macintosh, H (1988) 'Modular Units and Credit Systems', in Murphy, P and Torrance, E (eds) *The Changing Face of Educational Assessment*, Buckingham: Open University Press.

Ministry of Education (1959) *15 to 18: Report of the Central Advisory Council for Education – England (Vol. 1)*, London: HMSO.

Modular Information Network (1993) *The Gloscat Project*, Case Study No 2, April, Addlestone: MIN.

Modular Information Network (1994) *The Somerset Modular Scheme 1983–1993*, Case Study No 8, February, Addlestone: MIN.

Moon, B (ed.) (1988) *Modular Curriculum*, London: Paul Chapman.

National Commission on Education (1993) *Learning to Succeed: A Radical Look at Education Today and a Strategy for the Future, Report of the Paul Hamlyn Foundation National Commission on Education*, Oxford: Heinemann.

National Commission on Education (1995) *Learning to Succeed: The Way Ahead. Report of the Paul Hamlyn Foundation National Commission on Education*, London: National Commission on Education.

NCVQ (1987) *The National Qualification Framework*, London: NCVQ.

NCVQ, BTEC, CGLI and RSA Examinations Board (1995) *GNVQ Quality Framework*, London: NCVQ.

Prais, S J (1987) 'Educating for Productivity: Comparisons of Japanese and English Schooling and Vocational Preparation' *National Institute Economic Review*, February.

Prospect Centre, The (1992) *Growing an Innovative Workforce. Forward Looking Education and Training for Forward Looking Business*, London: The Prospect Centre.

Raffe, D (1984) 'The Content and Context of Educational Reform' in Raffe, D, *Fourteen to Eighteen*, Aberdeen: Aberdeen University Press.

Raffe, D (1992) *Participation of 16–18 Year Olds in Education and Training*, NCE Briefing Paper No 3, National Commission on Education.

Raffe, D (1993) 'Tracks and Pathways: Differentiation in Education and Training Systems and Their Relation to the Labour Market', paper presented to the First Conference of the European Research Network on Transitions in Youth, Barcelona.

Raffe, D and Rumberger, R (1992) 'Education and Training for 16–18 Year Olds' in McFarland, L and Richardson, W (eds) *Something Borrowed, Something Blue? A Study of the Thatcher Government's Appropriation of American Education and Training Policy: Part I, Volume 2 Oxford Studies in Comparative Education*, Yatton: Triangle Press.

Raffe, D, Howieson, C, Spours, K and Young, M (1996) 'Unifying Academic and Vocational Learning: English and Scottish Approaches', paper presented to the British Association Annual Festival, University of Birmingham, 11 September.

Rainbow, B (1993) 'Post-Compulsory Education: A National Certificate and Diploma Framework', in FEU (ed.), *Discussing Credit*, London: FEU.

Reich, R (1991) *The Work of Nations*, Hemel Hempstead: Simon Schuster.

Richardson, W, Spours, K, Woolhouse, J and Young, M (1995a) *Learning for the Future*, Interim Report, Post-16 Education Centre, Institute of Education, University of London, Centre for Education and Industry, University of Warwick.

Richardson, W, Spours, K, Woolhouse, J and Young, M (1995b) *Current Developments in Modularity and Credit*, Learning for The Future Working Paper 5, Post-16 Education Centre, Institute of Education, University of London and Centre for Education and Industry, University of Warwick.

Robinson, P (1996) *Rhetoric and Reality: Britain's New Vocational Qualifications* Centre for Economic Performance, London: London School of Economics.

Royal Society (1991) *Beyond GCSE: A Report by a Working Group of the Royal Society's Education Committee*, London: The Royal Society.

Ryan, P (1992) (ed.) *International Comparisons of Vocational Education and Training for Intermediate Skills*, London: Falmer Press.

Schools Curriculum and Assessment Authority (1994) *GCE A and AS Code of Practice*, London: SCAA.

Scottish Education Department (1983) *16–18s in Scotland: An Action Plan*, Edinburgh: SED.

Scottish Office (1994) *Higher Still: Opportunity for All*, Edinburgh: HMSO.

Smithers, A (1993) 'All Our Futures: Britain's Educational Revolution', Dispatches, Channel 4 Television.

Smithers, A (1994) 'Interview' *Furthering Education*, 5.

Spours, K (1993) 'The Reform of Qualifications Within a Divided System' in Richardson, R, Woolhouse, J and Finegold, D (eds) *The Reform of Post-16 Education and Training in England and Wales*, Harlow: Longman.

Spours, K (1995a) *Issues of Post-16 Participation, Attainment and Progression*, Working Paper No 17, Post-16 Education Centre, London University Institute of Education.

Spours, K (1995b) *Post-Compulsory Education and Training: Statistical Trends, Learning for the Future Project*, Working Paper No 7, Post-16 Education Centre, London University Institute of Education, Centre for Education and Industry, University of Warwick.

Spours, K (1995c) *The Strengths and Weaknesses of GNVQs: Principles of Design*, Learning for the Future Working Paper 3, Post-16 Education Centre, Institute of Education, University of London and Centre for Education and Industry, University of Warwick.

Spours, K (1996) 'Trackers, Frameworkers and Unifiers: Has Dearing Produced Something for Everyone?', *Furthering Education*, June.

Spours, K and Young, M (1995) *Post-Compulsory Curriculum and Qualifications: Options for Change*, Learning for the Future Working Paper 6, Post-16 Institute of Education, University of London, Centre for Education and Industry, University of Warwick.

Spours, K and Young, M (1996) 'Dearing and Beyond: Steps and Stages to a Unified System', *British Journal of Education and Work*, December.

Spours, K, Mack, D, Jones, J, Sauve, E and Holland, J (1989) *Modularisation and Progression: Issues on the 14–19 Curriculum*, Working Paper No 6, Post-16 Education Centre, London University Institute of Education.

Stanton, G (1994) 'Post-16 Curriculum and Qualifications: Confusion and Incoherence or Diversity and Choice?', in National Commission on Education, *Insight into Education and Training*, London: Heinemann.

Steedman, H and Green, A (1997 forthcoming) *International Comparison of Skill Supply and Demand Centre for Economic Performance*, London School of Economics.

Warwick, D (1987) *The Modular Curriculum*, Oxford: Blackwell.

Watson, J and Wolf, A (1991) 'Return to sender', *TES*, 6 September.

Wolf, A (1992a) *An Assessment-Driven System: Education and Training in England and Wales*, Institute of Education, University of London.

Wolf, A (1992b) *Mathematics for Vocational Students in France and England: Contrasting Provision and Consequences*, NIESR Discussion Paper No 23, London: National Institute of Economic and Social Research.

Wolf, A (1995) 'Awards that pay lip service to flexibility', *TES*, 3 February.

Young, M (1993) 'A Curriculum for the 21st Century? Towards a New Basis for Overcoming Academic/Vocational Divisions', *British Journal of Educational Studies*, **40**, 3.

Young, M (1995) 'Post-Compulsory Education for a Learning Society', *Australian and New Zealand Journal for Vocational Education and Training*, **3**, 1.

Young, M and Spours, K (1995) 'The New Vocationalism? Reflections on the Finnish Polytechnics', in Heikkinen, A (ed.) *Vocational Education and Culture: European Prospects from Theory and Practice*, Finland: University of Tempereen Press.

Young, M and Watson, J (1992) *Beyond the White Paper: The Case for a Unified System at 16+*, December 1991 Conference Report, Post-16 Education Centre, Institute of Education, University of London.

Young, M, Hayton, A, Hodgson, A and Morris, A (1993) *Towards Connectivity: An Interim Approach to Unifying the Post-16 Curriculum*, Unified 16+ Curriculum Series Number 3, Post-16 Education Centre, Institute of Education, University of London.

Young, M, Wilson, P, Oates, T and Hodgson, A (1994) *Building a Credit Framework – Opportunities and Problems*, papers and comments from Hamlyn Seminar 2 held on 29 November at the Institute of Education, University of London, Unified 16+ Curriculum Series Number 4, Post-16 Education Centre, Institute of Education, University of London.

CHAPTER 2

The Dearing Review of 16–19 Qualifications: A Step Towards a Unified System?

Michael Young

Introduction

The publication of the final report of Sir Ron Dearing's Review represents another stage in the evolution of 16–19 qualifications in England and Wales with its proposals for a National Framework with four levels and a new baccalaureate-type Diploma. The recommendations of the Review are in many respects ambiguous, perhaps deliberately so, as it is an attempt to satisfy many different educational and political constituencies. Furthermore, the government has said that the Report is 'an agenda and not a blueprint' and is in the process of deciding which of the recommendations will be taken forward or whether any additional funding will be made available for them to be implemented.

From the point of view of this book, the key question is whether or not the Dearing recommendations, if implemented, represent a step towards a unified system of 16–19 qualifications. At first glance the answer appears straightforward. The Report's strong support for making the three qualifications tracks more distinctive would suggest that one of its primary aims was to reverse such convergence between the tracks as there had been in the last decade. In terms of changing the relationships between the three tracks, therefore, it represents a step back towards sharper divisions, not a step forward to unification. On the other hand, the Report also makes a number of recommendations, such as the merging of NCVQ and SCAA into a single regulatory body, proposals for an Advanced Diploma based on four knowledge domains, and the breaking up of GNVQs into smaller six-unit or even three-unit blocks, all of which establish conditions for a more unified system. The fact that the Report makes recommendations with both unifying and divisive implications suggests that any assessment of whether it represents a stage in the move towards a more unified system will be complex.

In relation to the origins of the Report, the chapter considers three sets of issues. The starting point is the terms of reference given to Dearing by the government. However, terms of reference for a review of qualifications cannot be seen in isolation. They, and the decision to launch the Review, need to be seen as a response to specific developments in the English education and training system. In particular, the terms of reference need to be seen in the context of changes in the system that have taken place since the 1991 White Paper, *Education and Training for the 21st Century* (DfE/ED/WO, 1991), and the extent to which these changes have reflected government policy or have represented a challenge to it.

It was not, however, only government to which Sir Ron listened. Indeed, it is difficult to think of a report on which there was wider consultation with those involved professionally. What follows is a consideration of the possible influence of different professional and employer interests in shaping the Report. Finally, in relation to factors shaping the Report, I will suggest that it is not only the issues explicitly referred to in its terms of reference, nor the views expressed in the consultation that need to be considered; the Report's recommendations will also have been shaped by its framework of assumptions – those issues that it takes for granted. Two kinds of issues are considered. First, those that appear to have been explicitly excluded from discussion, but are the subject of wider debates, such as the role of coursework and teacher assessment. There are also more fundamental assumptions in the Report about the role and purpose of qualifications and how human abilities are distributed across the population. Both kinds of issues, I will argue, have shaped the Report's recommendations.

The final section of the chapter involves a shift in perspective from a focus on factors influencing the content of the Report, to its possible consequences. The Report is examined in the light of three ways of conceptualizing the process of qualifications change. In the concluding section of the chapter, there is a brief analysis of strategies for building on the Dearing recommendations in the direction of a unified system.

The Dearing Report: consolidation or reform?

The Report makes 198 proposals in all. However, its central organizing theme is undoubtedly that a more coherent national framework of qualifications is needed. The main elements that the Report[1] suggests such a framework should include are:

- three distinct pathways – academic, general vocational and work-based vocational;
- National Certificates at each level and a National Diploma at Level 3;
- four levels to provide for the equivalence of academic and vocational qualifications, including a new Entry Level;
- larger A-level subject 'cores' and more consistency of standards between subjects based on regular five-yearly reviews;

- new proposals for an S-level to provide a challenge for 'high flyers';
- a new lateral AS-level to be taken at the end of one year of study and to be equivalent to half an A-level;
- reorganizing Advanced GNVQs into six-unit and, possibly, three-unit groupings;
- a more explicit emphasis on core skills to be certificated within the overarching National Certificates and the new National Diploma;
- bringing together SCAA and NCVQ into a single body to oversee the newly constructed framework;
- encouraging the merger of the existing academic and vocational examining and validating bodies;
- a rationalization of subjects and fields between the three qualifications tracks, so that the distinctive characteristics of each is clearer;
- a re-launch of Youth Training within a new National Traineeship framework, linking it to Modern Apprenticeships and allowing progression between the two (Dearing, 1996).

In summary then, the Report is concerned to balance proposals for strengthening existing qualifications, especially A-levels, with proposals which develop frameworks within which students can combine elements from more than one qualification. Taken overall, the proposals cannot be described straightforwardly as a 'framework model' since existing qualifications can be awarded independently and thus the tracks are allowed to continue. On the other hand, the proposal for an Advanced Diploma goes beyond other framework models, such as that proposed by the Association for Colleges and others (AfC *et al.*, 1994) and provides an indication of what a Diploma within a unified system might look like.

The key feature in the terms of reference for the Review is consolidation of the proposals of the 1991 White Paper, which established the triple-track qualifications system based on A-levels, GNVQs and NVQs. The importance of consolidation as a theme was underlined by the Secretary of State's requirement that the Review should have particular regard to maintaining the rigour of A-levels and building on the current development of GNVQs and NVQs (Dearing, 1996). However, the terms of reference also required the Review to have regard to increasing participation and achievement and minimizing wastage and to consider proposals for greater coherence and breadth of study post-16 without compromising standards.

Even within the official terms of reference, therefore, the contradiction between consolidation and reform is apparent. Although explicit in the terms of reference, the origins of this contradiction are wider. Three examples will illustrate this point. One of the stated purposes of the Review was to support the achievement of the revised National Targets, notably, that 60 per cent of 21-year-olds should obtain an advanced level qualification by the year 2000. This represents a rise of 42 per cent from the current position in less than five years. This aim to increase achievement has to be set against the requirement in the terms of reference to 'strengthen' A-levels when they are still, numerically, the main Level 3 qualification for 16–19-year-olds and despite the fact they currently have a 30 per cent non-success rate (Spours, 1995).

A second example is the tension between the requirement that the Review should look at the scope for more 'breadth' at the same time as maintaining the rigour of A-levels which, at least since Crowther (MoE, 1959), has been associated with studying a few subjects in depth.

A third example has its origins in the changing economic context and is linked to the government's recognition, in the recent competitiveness White Paper (DTI, 1995), of the need to improve the qualifications of the whole population. This requirement is expressed in the Report's terms of reference as seeking to strengthen the qualifications framework and to make it more coherent. In the Report, coherence is expressed in at least two ways. First, it is found in the strong emphasis on a national system, which locates all qualifications on one of four levels. It is also expressed in the welcome given to the newly-merged DfEE, the proposal for merging SCAA and NCVQ and the encouragement given to the voluntary merger of academic and vocational examining and validating bodies. The contradiction appears when these requirements for greater coherence are set against arguments for retaining the distinctiveness of A-levels. In the past, this distinctiveness was expressed in the very small numbers who got A-levels: about 3 per cent when they were launched in 1951. Also, with the exception of Oxbridge entrance exams, A-levels were the only entry route to university and therefore not comparable to any other qualifications. However, the larger the number of students achieving A-levels, and the more they become part of a national system of qualifications, the less A-levels can claim distinctiveness. The argument for distinctiveness of the qualifications tracks in the Report, therefore, can be seen in part as an attempt to counter the developments that are reducing the 'special' character of A-levels and their association with students of high ability.

It is apparent from the contradictions I have described, that Sir Ron was given a tightrope on which to walk in undertaking his Review. It follows that in trying to assess the final recommendations of the Report, the factors beyond the Review's terms of reference may be as important as the terms themselves. I first turn, therefore, to the possible impact of recent policy developments since the 1991 White Paper (DfE/ED/WO, 1991), which was the last major government pronouncement on 16–19 qualifications prior to the Dearing Report itself.

The Dearing Report in context

The 1991 White Paper appeared at a time when a powerful movement for a unified system was beginning to emerge. A-levels were being broadened both in content and assessment (see Chapter 3). The unifying potential of modularization was also being explored and there were signs of convergence between the academic and the broad vocational routes of the time with the emergence of

Y-models[2] involving modular A-levels and BTEC National Diplomas (Burgess, 1993). At the same time, a series of reports were published (Finegold *et al.*, 1990; Royal Society, 1991) which, for the first time, argued for a unified system and the abolition of A-levels.

With its firm plans for a triple-track system of qualifications and a reduction in the maximum coursework assessment in GCSEs and A-levels to 20 per cent, the White Paper can be seen as a quite explicit attempt both to put a block on these 'unifying' developments and to prevent the continued expansion and diversification of the academic track. Its proposals were designed to direct any further post-16 expansion in participation into GNVQs – the new broad vocational route that had been designed to be clearly distinct from A-levels (see Chapter 4). However, despite the restrictions on coursework assessment, A-level pass rates continued to increase (Spours, 1995) and a growing number of new applied A-levels came on stream. By 1996, these had reached 12 per cent of all entries (Pyke, 1996). The demand for modular A-level syllabuses continued to grow (Richardson *et al.*, 1995a) but, as the Dearing Report itself records, fears were expressed that these syllabuses would gradually replace the traditional linear A-levels. Furthermore, the implementation of GNVQs was turning out to be far from straightforward. GNVQs were widely criticized by teachers and academics and there was evidence that student completion rates and progression possibilities were inferior to those in the qualifications that they had replaced (Robinson, 1996; Spours, 1995). The decision to launch a Review of 16–19 qualifications in 1995, and the underlying meaning of consolidation in its terms of reference, can be seen, therefore, as a recognition that all had not worked out as the government had hoped in relation to the agenda mapped out by the 1991 White Paper. The government's decision to initiate the Capey and Beaumont Reviews of GNVQs and NVQs/SVQs is also an indication that it felt obliged to respond to the growing criticisms of these qualifications from the inspectorates – OFSTED (1994) and the Further Education Funding Council Inspectorate (1994).

Professional and other influences on the Dearing Report

As pointed out earlier, Sir Ron consulted widely in preparing his Report, both among professional groups and employers, and in the process received written submissions from many organizations. Not all these submissions were made public. However, a preliminary analysis of the submissions available suggests that there is a substantial professional consensus supporting a more unified approach to the qualifications system than that which is found in the Report itself (Leney and Spours, 1996).

The policies which appeared to have widespread professional support can be divided into two kinds, according to whether or not they were included in Dearing's recommendations. There was near unanimity on the need for the pre-conditions for a more unified system. For example, there was support for a single qualifications framework, the integration of SCAA and NCVQ and of the academic and vocational examining and validating bodies. There were also a number of ways in which respondents went considerably further than Dearing. These included widespread support for unitization of qualifications within a National Qualifications Framework to accommodate breadth as well as depth, a national system of credit accumulation and transfer and a flexible approach to a post-compulsory core that went beyond core skills.

On the other hand, the same research also suggests that there is no professional consensus on moving directly to a unified system and certainly not to one with a significant element of general education, on continental European lines, as a requirement for all students. There were explicit reservations, for example, about too large a core and a wariness about going back to very high levels of course-work assessment. Many of the proposals associated with baccalaureate-type models for a unified system[3] were seen as making too heavy a demand on teacher work-loads, especially if they were not linked to new funding. There are valuable lessons, therefore, to be drawn from the analysis of the submissions to Dearing.

Sir Ron gives considerable importance to the views of employers; they are the first group to whose views he refers. Three features of their views, as summarized in the Report, are worth mentioning. First, employers' concerns tend to be general rather than specific and do not reflect deeply-held views about particular qualifications. Second, they make a strong plea for simplicity and clarity as features of any new qualifications framework. Third, they see improving core skills as a major priority. The most striking omission in the Report's response to employers' views is the absence of any attempt to include the assessment of a broader spread of core skills, such as interpersonal skills, management of learning and problem solving, within the qualification system. This is a view of a core skills agenda promoted by the CBI (1989, 1993). While the employers' views on core skills are warmly endorsed in the Report, formal assessment in the new Certificates and Diploma is limited to what the Report refers to as the three 'key skills' currently associated with GNVQs.

Any broader assessment of the influence of professional and employer perspectives is inevitably speculative without further research. But the stronger concept of a framework, endorsed by many involved in education, and the plea for a wider range of core skills from employers, appear to have come up against the requirement, expressed in the Review's terms of reference, that A-levels should not be changed.

The framework of assumptions of the Dearing Report

Any report on educational policy engages in issues of public educational debate, both in terms of what it does discuss and what it fails to consider. The Dearing Report is no exception. The most obvious examples of the former are its support for core skills in their current form, its rejection of the need to consider the redesign of GNVQs and its detailed discussion of the advantages and disadvantages of modular and linear A-levels. The most striking example of a widely-debated issue that is hardly discussed in the Report is the role of coursework assessment in GCSE and A-levels. However, there are also assumptions at a deeper level which are likely to have had a significant influence on the Report's final recommendations.

The kind of assumptions to which I am referring become explicit when the view of 16–19 education expressed in the Report is contrasted with views of post-compulsory education in other comparable European countries. The Report sees 16–19 education in England as 'pluralist', 'divided' and as substantially 'permissive' or 'voluntarist'. The concept of pluralism in the Report is reflected in Dearing's enthusiasm for different types of qualifications for different levels of ability. Related to this is the notion of a divided curriculum based on the argument for the distinctiveness of academic and vocational programmes. All of this was intended to take place in a voluntary system where there should be no formal or additional requirements placed on 16–19 students or institutions beyond the demands of the qualifications they had chosen. These are not only features of the administration of qualifications; they represent values associated with diversity, with a view that students can be distinguished, in terms of whether they are 'academic' or 'vocational', and with the idea of freedom of choice. It is these values, though they are not explicitly referred to, that are largely endorsed by the Report and that inevitably shape its recommendations.

However, it is again useful to notice a tension between the requirements of the Report to be 'conservative', in the sense of protecting traditional values, and, at the same time, its need to be 'reformist' to respond to the pressures on the system as a whole to be more flexible, efficient and attainment-oriented. This tension can be exemplified by three examples. The first concerns the Report's discussion of A-level standards. Despite the lack of evidence, the Report takes very seriously the view that higher A-level pass rates may mean lower standards rather than being the result of more focused teaching and harder work by students. There are, therefore, a number of proposals for making A-levels 'stronger', including bringing all subjects up to the level of difficulty of maths and physics. One consequence of this is likely to be that slower-learning students will be forced towards the broad vocational track. In other words, the assumption, which goes back a long way in English educational history, is that general or academic education is only for the elite. In a similar vein, though again recognizing the lack of evidence, the Report supports the view that modular syllabuses, in that they tend to lead to higher pass rates without emphasizing the need to master and memorize bodies of knowledge at the end of a course, also lead to a lowering of standards. Its recommendation that all A-level syllabuses should converge towards a part modular/part linear model can be seen as a compromise. It is an attempt to bridge the divide between the 'conservative' view that traditional linear A-levels should be retained and the 'reformist' view that modular syllabuses are more efficient instruments of learning. The psychological assumption underpinning the linear approach to syllabuses is that the pool of students with high ability is limited and tests, such as three-hour unseen written examinations, need to be devised to select out this

31

'pool'. In contrast, the modular approach sees the same 'pool of ability' as significantly shaped by how it is tested, by the skills of the teachers and by the motivations and study skills of students. It is this reformist assumption that the pool of ability in the population is not fixed that, to some extent, underpins the idea of progressively rising National Targets. The Report, like government policy, cannot resolve this contradiction. It reflects conflicting assumptions which go far beyond the issue of modular syllabuses. In South-East Asian and many European countries, it is an issue that is largely resolved in favour of the reformist view and the acceptance that there are powerful economic reasons against assuming that there is some 'natural' limit to the human resources of a country (Green, 1993).

In its discussion of the issue of breadth, the Report goes back to the Crowther Report (MoE, 1959) and its defence of the peculiarly English view that students learn to 'think' best by having to specialize in two or three subjects at advanced level. This assumption, which the Report recognizes may no longer be appropriate nearly 40 years later, lies at the heart of the case for retaining A-levels in their present form and, therefore, is not directly challenged. Instead, a new National Diploma in addition to A-levels is proposed as a compromise. The Diploma would offer breadth by accrediting study in four domains as well as core skills. We have, therefore, if we exclude the International Baccalaureate, the basis for a baccalaureate-type award emerging for the first time in England. It is possible that at some point a government might think breadth of study too important a criterion for the 16–19 curriculum to be left to the vagaries of individual and institutional choice. One alternative would be that a Diploma, like two A-levels today, could become the minimum requirement for university entry for 18/19-year-olds.

This section has considered how Sir Ron Dearing's recommendations are shaped as much by his assumptions as by his overt aims. For example, he is sceptical of the role of state intervention and prefers to leave things to voluntary initiative and the market. These views are not argued but assumed. Similarly, he places a high value on diversity. This means that differences such as academic/vocational divisions become examples of diversity and thus opportunities for choice, whereas they might be seen as inequalities and so barriers to choice.

The Report is full of compromises, some leaning towards the past and some giving pointers to the future. For example, in the discussion of A-level standards, Dearing is clearly trying to find a balance between the need to increase the number of people who are qualified and the anxiety that we have already tapped the 'pool of ability'. Here he leans towards the pool of ability argument and the recommendation is to limit the scope for modularization. Another example, but pointing to the future, is his response to the many people in the consultation who wanted A-levels broadened. Here he satisfies those who want no change by making his proposal for the Advanced Diploma voluntary. However, the Diploma could at a later point become the model for a single qualification at 18+. In a complex balancing of different interests, Sir Ron is creating a basis for reforms which could go well beyond his terms of reference.

The Dearing Report and the process of qualification change

Assessing a report such as Dearing's requires not only that it is seen as a product of its terms of reference, its assumptions and the context in which it was launched; it also needs to be seen as part of a process of educational change and as one of the factors that might influence that change. This section considers the Dearing Report from the perspective of three approaches to qualifications change, which I shall refer to as 'evolutionary', 'multi-dimensional' and 'contextual'.

The evolutionary approach

The evolutionary approach is another way of addressing the 'steps and stages' model of change developed in the Learning for the Future Project (Richardson *et al.*, 1995b). The concept of steps and stages was an attempt to overcome the weaknesses of seeing change in terms of a simple shift from a divided to a unified system, implicit in the IPPR Report, *A British Baccalaureate* (Finegold *et al.*, 1990). It also arose from a recognition that during the early 1990s a number of proposals for the qualifications system had been developed that could not easily be classified as either tracked or unified models. The most significant of these proposals, from the point of view of influencing the Dearing Report, was the idea of a 'common framework' launched by the Associations of Heads' Group (AfC *et al.*, 1994). The Joint Statement by this group proposed that all qualifications should be brought within a single framework under one popular title.

The Joint Statement went on to support unitization of assessment as a way of enabling students to build their own programmes of study. The framework proposed in the Joint Statement is permissive rather than prescriptive, and envisages that existing qualifications will continue to be used. In that sense it is distinguishable from proposals for a unified system such as that being developed in Scotland, where both previous qualifications (Highers and National Certificates) will be modularized within a 'unified framework' (see Chapter 12). On the other hand, the Joint Statement proposal is clearly a step towards a more unified system. It envisages a shift from a system of entirely separate qualifications to one in which all qualifications are part of a common framework.

In contrast to the Joint Statement, the Dearing proposals are a 'framework' in only the weakest sense. This is for two reasons. First, Dearing's National Framework only refers to levels and neither GNVQs, NVQs nor A-levels will have to be changed to be part of the framework. Second, the frameworks for the proposed new National Certificates and Advanced Diploma are additional to existing qualifications. They are not, as the Joint Statement recommended, a proposal for bringing existing qualifications within a single framework under one popular title. Despite these limitations, a National Framework of levels is a minimum basic condition for a unified system and is not something we have had in the past in the UK. For this reason, it is useful to describe the Dearing proposals as representing a 'weak framework/strong track' approach (Spours and Young, 1996).

From the point of view of the future development of a unified system, the evolutionary approach suggests two related strategies that could build on a weak framework/strong track approach like Dearing's. They are improving the qualifications tracks and strengthening the framework. However, each strategy highlights the importance of linking the earlier analysis of the origins of the Report to seeing it as a basis for future reform. Within the requirement on Dearing to consolidate existing qualifications, it is difficult to see any practical strategy for significantly improving qualifications. The strategy of strengthening the framework suggests more possibilities, not least because the concept of framework remains ambiguous and open to interpretation.

The multi-dimensional approach

This approach to qualification change (Raffe *et al.*, 1996) begins by identifying two limitations of the 'evolutionary' approach. First, the idea of a Framework Stage may not be applicable to all examples of qualification change. The concept of framework is better seen as describing a unique feature of English educational history and its various attempts to bring qualifications together without changing them (Spours, 1993). Second, a 'multi-dimensional' approach recognizes that qualifications systems consist of a number of different dimensions and that therefore a unilinear change, through a series of steps and stages, is only one possibility. Qualification systems can be unified in some dimensions and not in others. For example, the bodies that regulate qualifications might be unified, but certification could still remain divided.

The multi-dimensional approach views the process of qualifications change in terms of a series of inter-related dimensions. Five dimensions can initially be distinguished – government, regulation, validation, certification and assessment – which are hierarchically related to each other, though each has some autonomy from the level above.[4] A multi-dimensional approach to the process of unification presents a somewhat different picture of the Dearing Report to that outlined earlier. The Dearing Report's welcome for the establishment of a single government department for education and training, the DfEE, with a single Director of Qualifications, and its argument for a single regulatory agency to replace SCAA and NCVQ, represent a step towards a unified system. The Report also encourages mergers between the academic and vocational examining and validating bodies, such as that already completed between BTEC and ULEAC. This means that the organizational basis of a unified validation and certification system is being put into place. It is perfectly possible, of course, as now, for a unified examinations board to operate separate validation and certification systems. However, as more and more students become candidates for qualifications, the economic logic is likely to be for more common systems. Furthermore, the benefits to schools and colleges of dealing with a single unified examining board are likely to accelerate other mergers.

On the remaining dimensions of the qualifications system – certification and assessment – the Dearing recommendations maintain a divided system. The current government is likely to use the more unified administrative and regulative processes to maintain the separate qualifications tracks and to limit the development of common approaches to assessment. However, policies directed to unifying qualifications would be facilitated by the more integrated form of organization that will be a result of the Dearing proposals.

The contextual approach

The limitation of the two approaches to qualifications change considered so far in this chapter is that they do not locate the process of qualifications change in its social and economic context. The evolutionary approach points to the need both for strengthening Dearing's national framework and for reform rather than consolidation of the individual qualification tracks, if the Report is to be a step towards a unified system. On the other hand, the multi-dimensional approach sees some of the Dearing proposals as establishing necessary conditions for any future unification strategy that might be undertaken by a new government.[5] A third approach to qualifications change, which it is only possible to consider briefly here, is what I shall call a 'contextual' approach. It would make explicit the links between qualifications change, different political forces and wider social and economic changes.

One way of conceptualizing a contextual approach to qualifications change is through the idea of the 'learning society' as a model of the society of the future (Young, 1995). The idea of a learning society is both a socio-economic and an educational concept. As a socio-economic concept, it is the corollary of the idea of intelligent production and services when the intellectual capacities of all the employees in an organization are developed as a resource for improving the quality of the service or product of a company and the quality of life of a country. As an educational concept, the idea of a learning society represents a profound shift in educational values and a transformation of our ideas about the purposes of qualifications. This shift in focus would be from learning in the preparatory years of post-compulsory education (16–25 years) to learning throughout life. It also signifies a shift from learning in school, colleges and universities to learning in every context where people live and work.

The idea of a learning society, therefore, has profound implications for our view of qualifications that are hardly hinted at in the Dearing Report. Instead of qualifications being primarily a means of selection, either for a place in higher education or a job, they become a means of incentivizing learning. One way of expressing this change would be in a shift from a focus on 'qualifications as outcomes' to focusing on 'qualifying as a process'. Despite a recognition that employers have showed almost total support for lifelong learning, nowhere in the Report is there a recognition that qualifications might need to be redesigned for this to become a reality.

Conclusions: a step towards a unified system?

The three different approaches to qualifications change discussed in the previous section lead to somewhat different assessments of the Dearing Report as a step towards a unified system. The evolutionary approach directs our attention to the changing balance between frameworks and tracks. The Dearing recommendations appear as a partial version of a 'weak framework/strong track' approach, with some pointers to what a unified system might be like. The multi-dimensional approach points to how a number of the Dearing recommendations provide conditions on which a more unified system could be built. On the other hand, it is clear that in the Dearing Report conditions such as the merger of SCAA and NCVQ are associated with quite regressive proposals at the level of curriculum. The contextual approach brings out the greatest weaknesses in the Dearing Report in demonstrating its failure to question the role and purpose of qualifications, or how the qualifications system might have to change in the learning society of the future. It is not only a question of whether the qualifications system is becoming more unified, but of how to design qualifications to encourage learning relationships throughout life as well as within schools and colleges.

This chapter began by asking whether and in what ways the recommendations of the Dearing Report might be seen as a step towards a unified system. It has been argued that a number of its recommendations can be seen as steps forward. The three models of qualifications change can give us some guidelines for building on the Dearing proposals. Each model focuses on distinct aspects of qualifications change – strengthening the framework, extending the process of unification to new dimensions and, more fundamentally, reconstructing the purposes of a qualification. The chapter concludes by considering these strategies as ways of taking the Dearing recommendations forward at a national and institutional level.

Strengthening the framework

It has been my argument here that in trying to fulfil the contradictory demands of consolidation and reform, Dearing has had to move beyond his brief and make proposals that, if implemented, could take us some steps beyond the rigidly track-based system that we have now. The Advanced Diploma, and to a lesser extent the Certificates, represent a shift away from a system based on tracks. The idea of knowledge domains including theoretical and applied knowledge and cross-domain core skills has many of the features of proposals for a unified system.

There are two kinds of ways ahead within the evolutionary model, one strategic, which would concern a new government, and one tactical, for institutions and other agencies. These two levels are obviously inter-dependent. Strategically, a new government could devise ways of extending the scope of the Dearing framework by introducing new framework criteria. This could involve more common approaches to assessment across different qualifications, establishing the three-unit block as the basic component of the system, extending modularization and developing the concept of core or key skills to take into account a wider range of more intellectual skills in areas such as research, analytical and foreign language skills. The framework criteria could also include making the Diploma mandatory. These developments might be seen as improving the existing qualifications, as well as providing the basic components of a more unified qualifications system (see Chapter 13). Tactically, it will be important for institutions, in consortia and in collaboration with universities, to explore the implications for their timetables, both of delivering the Diploma and of introducing new ways of balancing the internal assessment of students with the external accreditation of institutions.

Extending the dimensions

The second model argued that qualifications change is a multi-dimensional process. In relation to Dearing, it was noted that certain unifying conditions were being laid down; a single government department, a single regulating body and unified examining and validating bodies (EVBs). At the same time, on issues of curriculum the Report was, notably in the area of assessment, regressive. The strategic possibilities are for a new government to build on the organizational changes proposed in the Dearing Report and to ask the new merged qualifications authority, in collaboration with the newly merged EVBs, to explore common assessment systems for academic and vocational qualifications. They could also be asked to look at ways of bridging the full-time course/traineeship division. Tactically, the focus on organizational conditions will allow the EVBs to explore new kinds of relationships with schools and colleges when they are awarding both academic and vocational certificates in the same institution.

Redefining qualifications for a learning society

The contextual approach challenges the 'conservative' assumptions that the Dearing Report makes about qualifications. It argues that his essentially credentialist view of qualifications, as primarily involved in sorting people for jobs, is increasingly out of date in a society where the priorities must be to motivate people to continue learning, even when they have left school or college. If, as we argued in the previous section, the new role of qualifications is to incentivize learning, then the National Framework cannot end at Level 3. The four levels in Dearing's proposals have to be linked to further levels associated with higher education and to ways of encouraging people to progress both vertically and horizontally as occupational opportunities change. Credit accumulation and transfer, on the basis of unitization of the curriculum, will take on much more significance in a qualifications framework oriented to lifelong learning. Current qualifications are based on the relative stability of bodies of knowledge, in the case of academic qualifications, and of occupational categories in relation to vocational qualifications.

As relationships between bodies of knowledge (Gibbons *et al.*, 1994) and between occupations (Reich, 1991) become more fluid, the balance between qualifications and frameworks will shift towards 'strong framework/weak qualification' models. In such models, learners will increasingly rely on updating their record of achievement within an all-through national framework, rather than trying to get new qualifications.

In summary, the argument of this chapter is that the Dearing Report's recommendations are best seen as a weak variant of a framework approach which also establishes some of the conditions for moving towards a unified system in the future. With the pace of economic change forcing more and more people to see learning and becoming qualified as a lifelong and not a once-and-for-all process, Dearing's view of qualifications seems disappointingly conservative. Nevertheless, the extent to which his proposals are an agenda rather than a blueprint leaves an openness which provides a basis for future reform.

Notes

1. Many of the Report's recommendations which are of considerable importance are not discussed here for reasons of space. Examples are re-launching the NRA and extending the external testing in GNVQs and NVQs.
2. Y-models are where the first year of a post-16 programme is common to all students on advanced level courses. At the beginning of the second year they have the opportunity to opt for an academic or vocational qualification.
3. As in the proposals by the IPPR (Finegold *et al.*, 1990) and the Royal Society (Royal Society, 1991).
4. An important research question is the extent to which the autonomy of examining and validating bodies will be reduced or extended by proposals such as those in the Dearing Report for merging NCVQ and SCAA. This question and the issue of qualification change more generally is being explored from the perspective of Anglo-Scottish comparisons in the ESRC-funded Unified Learning Project, which is co-directed by David Raffe, Centre for Educational Sociology, University of Edinburgh and Michael Young, Post-16 Education Centre, Institute of Education, University of London.
5. A Labour government elected in 1997 could, if it adopted a policy along the lines of the Party's discussion document, *Aiming Higher* (Labour Party, 1996), build on the Dearing reforms in the direction of a unified system.

References

Association for Colleges, The Girls' School Association, The Headmasters' Conference, The Secondary Heads Association, The Sixth Form Colleges' Association and The Society for Headmasters and Headmistresses in Independent Schools (1994) *Post-Compulsory Education and Training: A Joint Statement*, London: AfC.

Burgess, M (1993) 'Linking BTEC and A/AS Levels' in Richardson, W, Woolhouse, J and Finegold, D (eds) *The Reform of Post-16 Education and Training in England and Wales*, Harlow: Longman.

Confederation of British Industry (1989) *Towards a Skills Revolution*, London: CBI.

Confederation of British Industry (1993) *Routes for Success. Careership: A Strategy for All 16–19 Year Old Learners*, London: CBI.

Dearing, Sir Ron (1996) *Review of Qualifications for 16–19 Year Olds*, London: SCAA.

Department for Education/Employment Department/Welsh Office (1991) *Education and Training for the 21st Century*, London: HMSO.

Department of Trade and Industry (1995) *Competitiveness: Forging Ahead*, London: HMSO.

Finegold, D, Keep, E, Miliband, D, Raffe, D, Spours, K and Young, M (1990) *A British Baccalaureate: Overcoming Divisions Between Education and Training*, London: Institute for Public Policy Research.

Further Education Funding Council (1994) *General National Vocational Qualifications in the Further Education Sector in England*, National Survey Report, Coventry: FEFC.

Gibbons, M, Limoge, C, Nowotny, H, Swartzman, S and Scott, P (1994) *The New Production of Knowledge*, London: Sage.

Green, A (1993) *Educational Achievement in Britain, France, Germany and Japan: A comparative analysis*, Working Paper No. 14, London: Post-16 Education Centre, Institute of Education, University of London.

Labour Party (1996) *Aiming Higher: Labour's Proposals for the Reform of the 14–19 Curriculum*, London: Labour Party.

Leney, T and Spours, K (1996) 'A Comparative Analysis of the Submissions and Responses of the Educational Professional Associations to the Dearing Review', mimeo, London: Post-16 Education Centre, Institute of Education, University of London.

Ministry of Education (1959) *15 to 18: Report of the Central Advisory Council for Education – England, (Vol. 1) – The Crowther Report*, London: HMSO.

OFSTED (1994) *GNVQs in schools 1993/4: Quality and Standards of General National Vocational Qualifications*, London: HMSO.

Pyke, N (1996) 'Modules Could Boost Exam Passes', *TES*, 9 August.

Raffe, D, Howieson. C, Spours, K, and Young, M (1996) 'Unifying Academic and Vocational Learning: English and Scottish Approaches', paper presented to the British Association Annual Festival, University of Birmingham, 11 September.

Reich, R (1991) *The Work of Nations*, London: Simon and Schuster.

Richardson, W, Spours, K, Woolhouse, J and Young, M (1995a) *Current Developments in Modularity and Credit*, Learning for The Future Working Paper 5, Post-16 Education Centre, Institute of Education, University of London and Centre for Education and Industry, University of Warwick.

Richardson, W, Spours, K, Woolhouse, J and Young, M (1995b) *Learning for The Future Interim Report*, Post-16 Education Centre, Institute of Education, University of London, Centre for Education and Industry, University of Warwick.

Robinson, P (1996) *Rhetoric and Reality: Britain's New Vocational Qualifications*, Centre for Economic Performance, London School of Economics.

Royal Society (1991) *Beyond GCSE: A Report by a Working Group of the Royal Society's Education Committee*, London: The Royal Society.

Spours, K. (1993) 'The Reform of Qualifications in a Divided System' in Richardson, W, Woolhouse, J and Finegold, D (eds) *The Reform of Post-16 Education and Training in England and Wales*, Harlow: Longman.

Spours, K (1995) *Post-Compulsory Education and Training: Statistical Trends*, Learning for the Future Working Paper No 7, London: Post-16 Education Centre, Institute of Education, University of London.

Spours, K and Young, M (1996) 'Dearing and Beyond: Steps and Stages to a Unified System', *British Journal of Education and Work*, December.

Young, M (1995) 'Post-Compulsory Education for a Learning Society' *Australian and New Zealand Journal for Vocational Education Research*, **3**, 1.

CHAPTER 3

From A-levels to an Advanced Level Curriculum of the Future

Michael Young and Tom Leney

Introduction

The publication of Sir Ron Dearing's Report on 16–19 qualifications represents yet another chapter in the history of attempts to reform A-levels. This time we have a new twist: Dearing proposes a broad-based Advanced Diploma based on A-levels, but leaves A-levels themselves unchanged. The proposal is a welcome recognition that a broader curriculum can enhance a student's specialist studies. However, as this chapter will argue, by leaving A-levels themselves unchanged, this proposal can only be a very small step towards an advanced level curriculum of the future.

For all the undoubted strengths of A-levels, we can no longer afford an advanced level general education curriculum that reaches only one in three of each cohort. The economy is changing and the jobs of the future will either be casual and part-time or they will require an advanced level qualification or above. When A-levels were launched in 1951, only three in 100 of the cohort gained this qualification. Of the remainder, 10 to 15 per cent left school before 18 and went into office or other service jobs, another 10 to 15 per cent were taken on for either technician or craft apprenticeships at 16, and the remainder got unskilled jobs and left school with no qualifications at all. The peculiarities of A-levels, which make them so different from similar examinations in other countries, did not matter so much in the 1950s. The fact that they were designed to enable universities to select candidates for single-subject honours degrees was less of a problem, not least because many more degrees were in single subjects at that time. Thirty per cent of those who took A-levels failed, but they could still get office jobs, or become nurses or teachers with their O-levels. Vocational courses for apprentices were part-time and operated completely independently of the academic exam system.[1]

In considering the impact of A-levels, we are no longer discussing the education of one in four or five in each cohort, but the seven out of ten who stay on in full-time education. All their futures are determined by A-levels in one way or another. The number of students remaining in full-time post-compulsory education declines steadily at 17 and 18, and includes some of those on A-level courses. Nearly 30 per cent of those who start A-level courses end up with no additional qualification at the age of 18 (Spours, 1995). However, unlike in the 1950s, there are far fewer office jobs and fewer nursing and no teacher training opportunities for those without A-levels; and, of course, far fewer apprenticeships. Among those who achieve good grades, A-levels produce narrow specialists (for example chemists who know no business economics and students of business studies who know no chemistry), who often have to make choices between subjects, all of which they may want to continue. Others try for a balanced curriculum, but end up with bizarre collections of subjects like Spanish, economics and biology. Lower achievers take A-levels and risk failure at 18 or have to opt for GNVQs which are equally, if differently, over-specialized for 16-year-olds. In contrast, therefore, to the debates about A-levels in the 1970s and 1980s, the issue is no longer just the future of A-levels; it is the future of 16–19 education as a whole, shaped powerfully by what happens to A-levels.

It is not only the economy that has changed, nor just the level of participation in full-time post-16 education. The political context is changing as well. It is likely that in the General Election in May 1997, there will be a choice between the present government, wedded to unchanged A-levels as the 'gold standard', and two opposition parties who, somewhat tentatively in the case of the Labour Party, accept the idea that A-levels need to be changed. It will no longer be good enough to criticize A-levels because they are elitist and too narrow; we will need a practical reform strategy and a clear idea of the new curriculum for which we are aiming. This means being clear about the different functions fulfilled by A-levels and about how they are part of a complex system in which schools, colleges, universities and examination boards are inextricably locked together.

The Dearing Report argues that A-levels have reached the limits of the proportion of the cohort who can benefit by them. If this refers to A-levels in their present form, most people would agree. In fact, it is doubtful whether many of those currently achieving only one or two A-levels benefit much from them. The Dearing Report goes on to assume that those who fail or do poorly at A-levels would be better off doing a GNVQ. However, this assumes that such students want to do a vocational course rather than to continue with their general education. Limiting student options to either studying one or two A-levels or a GNVQ is only necessary if A-levels are the only way in which general education can be continued after 16. This chapter will argue that A-levels are no longer an adequate form of general education when we want this to be available to most of the young people who stay on in full-time education after 16. A new kind of advanced level curriculum and a strategy for achieving it are needed. These are the issues discussed in this chapter. First, however, we need to be clear exactly what we mean by the A-level curriculum which, it is claimed, needs reform, about the functions it serves and why it is so resistant to change.

What is the A-level curriculum and what purposes does it serve?

A-levels are single-subject examinations and the examining boards examine subjects, not the curriculum. For them there is no such thing as the A-level curriculum. The A-level curriculum refers to the programme of study that a school or college can offer and that a student can choose, based on A-level subject examinations. It is the responsibility of individual schools and colleges. Despite all the government interventions of the last decade, this has not changed. With the removal of most of the powers of local education authorities, the schools have a greater responsibility for the 16–19 curriculum than ever before. Schools and colleges have, in the past, welcomed this autonomy, with the proviso that they see that much of the power is in the hands of university admissions tutors. However, with the range of post-16 full-time 'choices' continuing to increase – no longer just GNVQs or A-levels, but Dearing's new Certificates and Advanced Diploma as well – schools, in particular, are beginning to say there are too many choices without enough information to assess their implications (Spours, 1996).

Schools' and colleges' autonomy over decisions related to the post-16 curriculum they offer also masks an inequality that has become more marked in the last decade. Though a student's A-level grades are treated as the same, regardless of where she or he has studied, this is far from true for her/his A-level curriculum. A student's A-level curriculum, in other words the whole educational experience of a student taking A-levels, that public schools can offer is much more extensive than that offered at any state school or college. It is little wonder that these schools have much better results – 80 per cent of students in the independent sector now get three A-levels (Walden, 1996).

One way of understanding what a curriculum based on A-levels is like is to contrast it with other European examinations taken at the same age:

A-level curriculum	*Continental curriculum*[2]
1. a small number (four or less) of subjects studied in depth	1. five or more subjects studied in less depth
2. elective/free choice of subjects by students	2. student choice constrained by required core subjects
3. no overall curriculum which candidates have to study	3. overall criteria of what constitutes a curriculum
4. emphasis on end of course external exams	4. various; some have no exams, some use teacher assessment and some rely on A-level type exams

5. no relationships between subjects	5. some require a theory of knowledge course
6. schools/colleges responsible for the whole curriculum	6. examination requirements and national regulations define the whole curriculum
7. no right to HE entry; admission dependent on grades	7. legal right to enter university in most countries if the exam is passed[3]
8. reliability of results dependent on the independence of exam boards	8. reliability dependent on state exams or trust in teachers (eg, Sweden and Germany)
9. a mixture of linear and modular syllabuses.	9. syllabuses not modular.

Over the years, some of these features of the A-level system have been subject to modification. However, despite incremental changes, A-levels have remained, throughout their 45-year history, a highly selective, narrow and elective curriculum. Three inter-linked features of A-levels have had a particular role in making them so resistant to change: the absence of a national body with overall responsibility for the 16–19 curriculum; the autonomy of the schools and colleges over what they offer; and the 'free choice' that students have in deciding their subjects. Even a government committed to changing the A-level system might find it difficult to know where to begin. Another feature of the A-level system that makes it resistant to change is the inter-locking arrangement linking the examination boards, the university teachers who usually chair the subject-examining panels and the sixth form and college teachers who carry out the marking. It is this system which underpins the public confidence in A-levels. Furthermore, it is a system A-level teachers know and it is, at least for them, relatively predictable.

Any change, however educationally sound, is likely to be seen as threatening both by higher education admissions tutors, who are under pressure to recruit the 'best students', and teachers, who are expected to increase the number of their students accepted for university. It is interesting to note that while the English system maximizes the autonomy of the schools and university admissions tutors, it places much less trust in individual teachers than other countries. It is almost as if there is a fear that if the mass of teachers were given more responsibility for examining, as is the case in Sweden and Germany, they would generously grade their own students and undermine A-levels' selective role.

Having briefly identified the main features of the A-level curriculum, we now want to turn to the wider functions of A-levels and will distinguish between their 'ideological' and their 'educational' functions. Much past and current debate has focused on the political and ideological functions of A-levels; for example, they have been criticized as being elitist and giving unfair advantages to public school pupils. It is of course true that A-levels are elitist; but as the main route to university, selection is bound to be one role of any advanced level curriculum. The key questions are, how elitist are A-levels and what other functions do they have?

Whereas, until the 1980s, fewer students passed the Baccalaureate in France than English students passed A-levels, twice as many students now achieve one of the new three-track French Baccalaureates (Watson, 1991). In other words, by remaining exclusive and, as a consequence, devaluing other qualifications, A-levels are part of the reason why levels of post-16 attainment in England are so low. The powerful role of A-levels in selection limits the extent to which they can provide general education to a wider section of the cohort. However, A-levels are not only a gateway to university; like any advanced level curriculum, they also have an educational role. If the educational role of A-levels is forgotten, not only does this deny the real learning that A-level students achieve, but the only option for the critic is to say that more people should be allowed to get them. Inevitably, this leads to the charge of 'lowering standards'.

The educational function of A-levels, as any form of advanced study, is to provide a way of giving students access to specialized knowledge and the concepts and skills that go with it. However, as can be seen from the table on page 42, A-levels and qualifications in other European systems represent very different views of specialist knowledge. The typical European equivalent to A-levels sets out to offer students a broad-based education in the main fields of knowledge, while at the same time allowing them some opportunity to specialize. In the A-level curriculum, there is no attempt to provide a broad-based education; the curriculum consists of a small group of subjects only. Within limits, determined by what a student hopes to do on leaving school, it does not matter which subjects she or he chooses. The A-level curriculum is not designed to develop any particular capacities; the assumption is that any subject sanctioned by the universities must be 'training for the mind'. However, there is no research on what kind of mind training is achieved by subject-based study, or on the different ways in which breadth and specialization can be linked. The result is that the policies of political parties have remained little more than critiques of A-levels or a general endorsement that A-levels should be broader. During the period since 1979, throughout which the 'gold standard' view of A-levels has prevailed, this lack of breadth has been of little practical concern. However, to have a new government committed to the reform of A-levels, but with no clear idea of what to put in their place, could have very serious consequences. Without a clear policy, the new government could be vulnerable to a media campaign in defence of A-levels. If, on the other hand, it did try to introduce reforms that were not thought through, it could find that the merged SCAA/NCVQ got bogged down in differences and technical details as the Schools' Council did in the 1960s and 1970s, and managed ultimately to please no one.

The first task of any strategy for reforming A-levels is therefore to develop alternative models of how breadth and specialization might be linked, as a basis for a reformed qualification. The previous attempts to reform A-levels in the 1960s and 1970s singularly failed to do this. They took for granted that anything less specialized than A-levels was an improvement, without asking why or what might be involved. There are, however, valuable lessons to be learned from these earlier attempts at reform. The next section, following a brief history of previous reform attempts, suggests what these lessons might be.

Lessons from the history of attempts to reform A-levels

In considering the history of A-level reform, we want to begin by making two further distinctions. The first is concerned with the dynamics of change and distinguishes between incremental changes to individual A-levels and structural changes to the A-level system. The second distinction is between different historical periods in which there have been attempts to reform A-levels; the different periods identify the changing context of A-level reform. Examples of incremental changes are changes in content of subject syllabuses, the introduction of new subjects, the development of new subject cores and new forms of assessment, including the shift from linear to modular syllabuses. Each of these types of incremental change has been introduced, at least initially, with little or no political or professional opposition.

Structural changes are those that involve the relationship between subjects, the number and size of subjects relative to a student's whole curriculum, and changes which appear to shift the balance between what are seen as standard and non-standard approaches to syllabuses and assessment. For A-levels, a standard syllabus is linear, it is associated with the subjects of the traditional grammar and public school sixth forms,[4] and its assessment is based on an end of course written examination.

Incremental and structural changes are not entirely independent of each other. A good example of this link was the development in the early 1980s of modular syllabuses and assessment schemes with over 50 per cent coursework assessed by teachers. Initially, these changes were hardly noticed. However, the political climate of the late 1980s and early 1990s changed and the proportion of modular syllabuses continued to grow. In this new context, they were perceived as a threat to the A-level system, that is, to the dominance of linear syllabuses. As a result, many of the modular syllabuses were withdrawn. It seems likely that incremental changes are absorbed into the A-level system so long as they are not seen as affecting its key selective function.

Three phases of attempted reform of A-levels can be distinguished. The first, between 1951 and 1979, was a period of expansion of A-level entries and a long and drawn-out series of unsuccessful attempts to reform A-levels by the Schools' Council. During this period, debates were largely restricted to the professional education community. The period 1979–1991 was one of continued expansion of A-levels and many incremental changes. Only towards the end of this period did the future of A-levels, become a political issue, partly through opposition by the Right to the incremental changes and partly because the Left began to articulate a view of transforming A-levels into a unified curriculum (Finegold *et al.*, 1990). The final period between 1991 and 1996 began with the 1991 White Paper (DfE/ED/WO, 1991) and culminated in the Dearing Report (Dearing, 1996). In this period both professional and political conflicts over A-levels have been more overt and the debate about A-levels has become part of the wider debate about the future of 16–19 education as a whole.

Phase 1: Proposals without reform (1951–1979)

The first chance to evaluate A-levels came in 1959 with the Crowther Report on the Education of 15–18-year-olds (MoE, 1959). However, the opportunity was missed. The view of the Crowther Committee was that able pupils were 'subject minded' and therefore A-levels were the ideal curriculum. Having underwritten A-levels, all Crowther could do was to hope that schools would not allow A-levels to encroach on more than two-thirds of a student's timetable.

Mathieson (1992) traces the sequence of unsuccessful attempts to tackle the question of over-specialization in A-levels that followed Crowther. The issue was first taken up by the Schools' Council in 1966 with a plan to introduce 'major' and 'minor' subjects. Both schools and universities rejected the proposal, doubting that minority subjects would be taken seriously. In the late 1960s, the Dainton Report on the shortage of scientists (DES, 1968) recommended that broadening the sixth form curriculum was the best way to increase the number of students studying science post 16; little notice was taken of it. The Schools' Council tried again in 1973 with N (Normal) and F (Further) levels, both to be studied over two years. Reactions were again negative from both schools and universities. The fact that lower achievers might be able to cope with N levels meant that they would inevitably be devalued as a mechanism for broadening the curriculum of high achievers. In 1979, the new Conservative government announced that A-levels 'were here to stay', with hardly a murmur of dissent.

There are two lessons from this period. The first is that schools and universities are much more tightly bound to the A-level system than has often been recognized. The second lesson is that, unless it can be shown that breadth enhances specialist study, it will always be seen as being at the price of depth, and therefore associated with lower standards.

Phase 2: Incremental changes within a track-based system (1979–1991)

The 1980s were a period of sharp increase in the numbers taking A-levels and of diversification of subjects offered. Four types of incremental change can be identified in this period; the introduction of new subjects, the idea of half subjects (the AS examinations), modular syllabuses and coursework assessment. These will now be discussed briefly.

New subjects

Proposals for changing subject syllabuses or introducing new A-level subjects represent the least radical form of change to A-levels, since they leave the A-level system unchanged. It is not surprising that in the 1980s, when TVEI funding was available to support 14–19 innovations, many new A-level syllabuses were introduced. Considerable attention was initially given to an A-level in general studies as a way of broadening the A-level curriculum (Smithers, 1994). However, although candidate numbers expanded fast, most universities would not accept general studies as a subject for admissions purposes.[5]

The diversifying of A-level subjects in the 1960s and 1970s took place largely within the social sciences (eg, economics, sociology and psychology). However, in the 1980s, under the influence of TVEI, more applied courses were developed for which there was no accreditation. A-levels in subjects such as business, leisure studies, photography and accounting were developed in response to this lack of accreditation. There appear to have been few content criteria for new subjects, provided they complied with the agreed criteria on syllabus design and assessment, though, as with general studies, this did not mean that all the new subjects were accepted by universities.[6]

New half subjects (AS)

Unlike the introduction of new subjects, which arose from a demand from schools and colleges, the introduction of the AS examinations in 1987 was initiated by the government, which hoped it would satisfy the demands for additional breadth and flexibility. However, in a voluntarist system, an innovation such as the AS exam depends for its success on more than government approval; it depends on the choices and decisions of teachers, students and higher education admissions tutors. The take up of AS examinations was poor; it has never reached above 7 per cent of all A-level entries. University admissions tutors preferred A-levels and students saw A/AS combinations as more demanding than three A-levels.

The fate of the AS examination is a good example of how an incremental change designed to increase the flexibility of the curriculum can have potential structural implications for the A-level system. As long as AS examinations remained additions to the A-level curriculum, they were accepted without question. As soon as there was a suggestion that the smaller AS exams could be used as building blocks in place of A-levels, as a way of making the system broader and more flexible there was opposition. In 1991, a SEAC Committee came up with a proposal to reverse the relationships between AS and A-levels. They suggested that a student might take five or six AS exams in her or his first year and continue with two or three of the subjects as A-levels in the second year. This was perceived by the Headmasters Conference (HMC) as a way of changing the A-level system (Mathieson, 1992). HMC was influential enough for the proposal to be immediately rejected.

Modular syllabuses and coursework assessment

These two changes are taken together despite the fact that not all coursework-based assessment schemes were modular. However, both represented efforts on the part of teachers to make A-levels more relevant and accessible to the wider range of students who were now staying on in sixth forms (Young, 1994).[7]

Three-hour written examinations at the end of a course have been one of the defining features of A-levels since they were launched; it linked them closely to the typical final exam of the English honours degree. However, in the 1980s A-level syllabuses began to allow a proportion of teacher-assessed coursework; the amount varied from 25 per cent to 100 per cent. It was not until the beginning of the 1990s that these changes in assessment, as well as in syllabus design, were challenged. In the new and more ideological political climate of the time criticism of modular courses and teacher-based assessment became part of the government's attack on teachers and what it saw as falling standards. There was no actual evidence that modular syllabuses or coursework assessment led to lower standards. However, it was a time when pass rates in A-levels and the number of students achieving higher grades were rising steadily. Some members of the Right-wing think tanks appeared to doubt that more than a very small number of students could possibly do well at A-levels. It followed that if they did, it must be because the assessment system had made it easier to get high grades or that the new A-level subjects were easier than the old. From then on, coursework assessment and modular A-levels became not only issues for professional debate but political issues.

Core skills

Core skills were proposed in 1990 as a way of broadening A-levels and even of unifying academic and vocational qualifications. However, the first attempt to bring core skills into the A-level curriculum collapsed soon after, with a change of Secretary of State (Mathieson, 1992). There were clearly technical difficulties that were due partly to confusion about what was meant by core skills and partly to uncertainties as to whether a common system of assessment could be devised for all A-level subjects. However, over-riding the technical issues was the question of ideology. It was difficult to combine the idea of A-levels as the 'gold standard' with the view, strongly supported by the CBI (1993), that even those with A-levels could lack core skills. In retrospect, the core skills initiative can be seen, despite all the efforts of the Further Education Unit and others, as another half-hearted attempt to make A-levels more 'relevant'. Inevitably, the A-level system and its selective function won.

The Higginson Committee's proposals

The Higginson Report (DES, 1988) stands apart from the other A-level developments of the time. The Committee was set up to clarify the principles on which A-level syllabuses should be based. It seemed to have gone well beyond its brief in the report, which endorsed the arguments for broadening A-levels and proposed a five-subject examination of 'leaner' and 'tougher' A-levels. Despite the radical character of the Higginson Committee's proposals, they were still a compromise with the A-level tradition. A five-subject grouped award was clearly a break from A-levels as an elective curriculum. However, in keeping with the A-level tradition, the Committee refused to prescribe which subjects a candidate should take, leaving it to schools and colleges to help students to choose. The Report represented continuity with the past in another way: it assumed a broader curriculum was a 'good thing' and that all this involved was doing more subjects. It did not consider different forms of breadth or how breadth might enhance or subtract from a student's specialist studies. The professional climate of opinion towards A-levels had changed since the 1970s and there was virtually unanimous support for the Higginson proposals. The fact that the proposals were summarily rejected by the government means that we cannot tell whether this professional support might have changed if the proposals had actually been implemented.

From this review of the main examples of internal A-level reform in the period 1979–1991, three conclusions can be drawn. First, content criteria for new A-level subjects are flexible; it is the A-level system that is so resistant to change. Second, incremental changes, some hardly noticed when they were introduced, built up pressures which were ultimately perceived as challenges to the A-level system itself. The third conclusion is the extent to which, in contrast to the 1970s and early 1980s, A-level debates from the end of the 1980s have become polarized and politicized. This has had the effect of minimizing the professional and technical debates and masking the differences within the education community.

Phase 3: Reforms within a framework approach (1991 – present)

The period between 1991 and the publication of the Dearing Report in 1996 began with the government's 1991 White Paper laying down the triple-track qualification system. Most of the developments during this period have been attempts to establish some kind of framework to include all qualifications, thus mitigating the divisiveness of the three-track system. Two proposals for diploma frameworks were initiated by the government but were quickly dropped.[8] Other attempts at frameworks were the FEU's Credit Framework Initiative (FEU, 1992),[9] the Joint Statement (AFC et al., 1994) and the CBI proposals for an overarching Diploma (CBI, 1993). All were designed to include A-levels, but all focused more on 'collecting' existing qualifications rather than trying to change them. The most radical proposals from the point of view of A-levels were the FEU Credit Framework and the Joint Statement. They both suggested that all qualifications could be unitized according to a common set of criteria. Only in Wales was this proposal taken up systematically (Fforwm, 1995).

The idea of a framework for bringing qualifications together culminated in the Dearing proposals for National Certificates and an Advanced National Diploma. However, Dearing stepped back from the Joint Statement in two ways. First, he did not propose unitizing qualifications; the AS or half GNVQ was to be the smallest block in his framework. Second, the framework was to be voluntary; existing qualifications would remain for those who wanted them.

Dearing's strategy on A-levels

Dearing endorses the familiar features of A-levels considered earlier in this chapter – the collection of insulated subjects, the emphasis on terminal examinations to underline 'rigour', and the preference for linear rather than modular syllabuses.[10] His approach to A-levels involved four elements: making A-levels more distinctive, establishing the Advanced Diploma as an option for those students who want a broader curriculum than is possible with three A-levels, introducing a one-year AS examination and aligning A-levels and GNVQs within six-unit blocks. Of primary significance here are the first two proposals.

Dearing begins by claiming that there are 'difficult', 'average' and 'easier' A-level subjects. He then considers the implications of making 'easier' subjects more 'difficult' and how this would be likely to lead either to fewer candidates or to more failures. His answer is that students likely to fail A-level should be guided to take the GNVQ or the Modern Apprenticeship route where they might, he suggests, stand a better chance of achieving a level 3 qualification. Unwilling to consider any structural reform of A-levels, Dearing is trapped in the familiar and characteristically English assumption that slower learning students are better on vocational courses.[11]

His second approach to strengthening A-levels was to consider the overlap of subjects between A-levels and GNVQs. His argument is that, from the point of view of students making choices and employers assessing the worth of qualifications, there is much to be gained by making A-levels and GNVQs more distinct. Dearing links the distinctiveness of A-levels to subject content. He recommends that examining boards[12] should re-examine the appropriate qualification for subjects such as science, which for him should be an A-level not a GNVQ, and A-levels such as media studies and photography, which for him are applied and so should be GNVQs and not A-levels. If taken literally, his proposal would rule out most of the 12 per cent of current entries in applied A-levels.

Dearing's second strategy is concerned with breadth. He started not by asking how A-levels could be broadened but how A-level students might broaden their curriculum while, at the same time, A-levels remained unchanged. His proposals have two parts: a reformulated one-year AS (effectively a Part One of an A-level) and a four-domain Advanced Diploma.[13] To obtain the Advanced Diploma a candidate would have to take an A-level in two of the four domains, an AS in the other two and be assessed in core skills through a new AS exam.[14] The Diploma does not replace A-levels; it is additional to them. Dearing leaves it up to schools and colleges to decide whether or not to take it up.

There is a pragmatic advantage in his proposals, in contrast to earlier attempts like Higginson's 'five lean A-levels'; Dearing uses existing A-levels. However,

A-levels were not designed to be part of a broader-based overarching qualification; they are too rigid and inflexible. The four-domain proposal, based on A-levels and ASs, appear very difficult to deliver. It seems likely that, if it remains voluntary, the Diploma will go the same way as AS examinations. It might be offered by a few innovative schools and colleges who have high A-level success rates. A student could take three A-levels plus two ASs and core skills; then if the Diploma requirements become too demanding, she/he would have the 'insurance' of three A-levels. Such evidence as we have suggests that although schools like the idea of the Advanced Diploma, they would need a cast-iron guarantee from the universities that it would be accepted in preference to three A-levels (Spours, 1996). The key issue for university admissions tutors is whether or not the Diploma remains voluntary; if it does, it seems likely that they will still go for high A-level grades in degree-related subjects, regardless of whether a candidate has the Diploma.

Dearing's Advanced Diploma raises a number of important new issues about advanced level qualifications. It is the first attempt, in England, to link breadth to high achievement. It is the first attempt to offer a content-based definition of breadth. It raises the issue, though not explicitly, that a broader qualification than A-levels will inevitably mean longer teaching hours and more work on the part of students. However, if the Diploma remains voluntary, the message to the schools and colleges about valuing breadth is unlikely to be strong enough to outweigh the risks and the additional resources that would be needed to run it. Furthermore, it does not take into account the inter-locking system that binds schools and colleges, universities and examining boards to A-levels as reliable selectors for the universities.

Frameworks and the reform of A-levels: some lessons

The Dearing proposals for an Advanced Diploma are an example of a 'weak framework' overarching a strongly track-based system (Spours and Young, 1996). However, it is probably too big a step from existing A-levels when they are not yet modularized or part of an effective framework. The crucial barriers to its take-up are that it is not mandatory and that it makes additional demands on students and staff at a time when course teaching hours are being reduced rather than increased.

However, Dearing's strategy could be built on by a government looking for a way of broadening A-levels as part of a more unified system. First, Dearing's proposals for making A-levels more distinctive seem impractical as well as backward-looking and could be dropped. Second, his proposals that GNVQs and A-levels are aligned in six-unit blocks could be extended by creating three-unit blocks to provide greater flexibility. Third, the concept of domains could be developed and applied to both tracks. Finally, the modularizing of both A-levels and GNVQs together with the unitizing of their assessment would create greater flexibility and make it more likely that the Diploma would be taken up, even if it remained voluntary.

Dearing's Advanced Diploma is the most recent of a series of attempts since 1991 to construct a framework to bring A-levels and GNVQs into closer relationship with each other. The examples highlight the weakness of a framework approach which is voluntary and does not unitize all qualifications and develop common approaches to assessment. Dearing's is the most ambitious of the framework proposals, but it still remains· voluntary. It represents a small step beyond a rigidly track-based system, but six-unit blocks make it difficult to see much scope for combinations across the tracks.

Towards a new conceptualization of an advanced level curriculum

To develop a curriculum rationale for an advanced level curriculum of the future it is necessary to go back to first principles and to consider what an advanced level curriculum is trying to do. First, it must be a way of developing the knowledge and skills that young people are going to need in the next century. This means it will need, as part of a core programme, to build in the skills and knowledge that young people require as citizens, workers and parents. Second, an advanced level curriculum will need to develop specialist areas of knowledge and interest and a way of linking a student's specialist studies to the aims of the curriculum as a whole.

In realizing these aims, any new curriculum will need to build on the strengths of what we have – A-levels. A-levels enable students to gain unrivalled access to bodies of specialized knowledge in a small number of knowledge areas and to the concepts which go with them. Depending on the subjects they choose, A-level students either learn to solve complex and abstract problems in mathematics and the sciences or to process large amounts of text in clear prose in the humanities and social sciences. However, there is a price to pay for these advantages of A-levels; the A-level curriculum is both socially and intellectually selective. Some of the ways these processes of selection occur are listed below. The list distinguishes between the socially and intellectually exclusive features of the present A-level curriculum and the socially accessible and intellectually inclusive features of an advanced level curriculum of the future. The two lists in the table represent models only. They are presented to indicate the kind of ways in which A-levels need to be reformed.

A-level curriculum	**Advanced level curriculum of the future**
socially selective	*socially accessible*
linear syllabuses	modular syllabuses
terminal assessment	continuous assessment

intellectually exclusive	*intellectually inclusive*
academic; knowledge for its own sake	educational; knowledge for specific purposes
purposes implicit; subjects taken as given	purposes explicit and debated; subjects interrogated from the point of view of learner's purposes, one of which may be knowledge for its own sake
prioritizes reproduction of given knowledge	prioritizes production of new knowledge
disciplinary concept of knowledge; knowledge and skill combined in only a few areas of specialization	inter-disciplinary concept of knowledge; knowledge and skill combined in all areas of specialization

A-levels represent a highly insulated form of subject specialization which directs learners' attention entirely to individual subjects, treated separately. However, new knowledge is more and more being produced at the interface of subjects and disciplines, not in subjects in isolation from each other (Gibbons *et al.*, 1994). It follows that the A-level curriculum, which allows students to collect any group of subjects together with no rationale other than personal interest, is no longer an adequate preparation for working life or for the new kinds of inter-disciplinary degrees being offered at universities. What is needed is an advanced level curriculum that treats the relationships between subjects as having as much importance as the individual subject content itself. Elsewhere, the principles of such a curriculum are referred to as 'connective specialisation' (Young, 1993).

A curriculum based on connective specialization reverses the relationship between subjects and the curriculum as a whole that is found in A-levels. Instead of subjects as ends in themselves, defining the purposes of the curriculum, as in the case of A-levels, the curriculum defines the learning purposes. Subjects are then drawn on to realize the overall purposes of the curriculum. Subjects thus become 'tools for learning' (Holt, 1979). An advanced level curriculum would need to create a balance between specialist studies, both discipline- or subject-based, and applied and core studies which would help lead students from their particular interests and specialization to the wider concerns expressed in the curriculum as a whole.

The basic elements of such an advanced level curriculum would therefore be of two types: a set of general and specialist curriculum purposes and outcomes; and two kinds of tools for learning – subjects, disciplines and domains and connective skills and knowledge to provide ways of making the connections between subjects. One initial attempt to show how a curriculum might be constructed on the basis of connective specialization is found in Young and Spours (1995). This, however, is very much a beginning. Much collaborative research is needed, undertaken by various kinds of subject specialists and curriculum analysts.

The most unfamiliar part of shifting from an A-level curriculum based on subject specialization to an advanced level curriculum based on connective specialization, would be to accept that subjects do not equate to ends in themselves; curriculum purposes become the ends and subjects the means.

Conclusion

In this discussion of A-levels, emphasis has been placed on the importance of two distinctions: that between the ideological and educational roles of A-levels, and that between two types of specialization. The first distinction reminds us that even if the political ideology of the 'gold standard' is no longer dominant, changes from A-levels to an advanced level curriculum of the future will not be easy. Professional and other sectional interests in preserving A-levels will undoubtedly become more visible, as they were in the 1970s. The second distinction is between subject and connective specialization as curriculum principles. The practical implications of this distinction could begin to be explored through the Dearing proposals for an Advanced Diploma.

A-level reforms failed in the 1960s and the 1970s because people did not have a clear idea of what the alternatives to A-levels might look like. Reforms have failed since 1979 because we have had governments which have had both political and ideological interests in preserving A-levels. From 1997, we could have a new government with different priorities. This may create a new context for extending the debate about A-levels and how they might be transformed into an advanced level curriculum of the future.

Notes

1. O-levels were, of course, also used as a means of selection for apprenticeships.
2. The characteristics of the Continental curriculum do not refer to a particular country, but are an amalgam of different national systems designed for the purpose of illustration.
3. This legal right is of course limited in two ways. First, through what has become known as the *numerus clausus* which applies to such over-subscribed courses as veterinary science; second, legal right does not always mean substantive right when lecture rooms are full and overcrowded.
4. These are usually seen as English literature, history, geography, maths, French or German, physics, chemistry or biology. In 1979, three-quarters of A-level entries were in these nine subjects (Mathieson, 1992).
5. Except in the north of England where there was an agreement between NEAB (then NUJMB) and the northern universities to accept General Studies.
6. The proportion of entries in what used to be seen as the traditional A-level subjects has been falling since 1979 when they accounted for three-quarters of all entries (Matthieson,1992) (see Note 4).
7. The scope and possibilities of modular A-levels are discussed fully by Hodgson and Spours in Chapter 6.

8. The government's two versions – Advanced and Ordinary Diplomas – were launched publicly in 1991 and 1994.
9. This created considerable interest among further education colleges. Some saw it as a way to unify the post-16 curriculum 'by the back door' and others, less ambitiously, as a curriculum management tool (Young *et al.*, 1994).
10. Despite the very strong support for modularization that he reports from his consultations (Dearing, 1996).
11. The existence of GNVQs masks the case for an intermediate level of general education between GCSEs and A-levels. However, the problem of an intermediate level may not be primarily a qualification problem. The opportunity for lower achieving students to take an extra year to reach Level 3 and, in some cases, Level 2 might be solved by changes in funding and a reorganization of sixth forms. With 70 per cent and, in many areas, 80 per cent of the cohort remaining in full-time education after 16, it is more likely and more realistic to see three years to A-level rather than two as the norm.
12. The merging of examining and validating bodies does, of course, make this easier, as it will not involve them in 'loss of business'!
13. Dearing's four domains of knowledge are science, technology and mathematics, humanities, social sciences and languages.
14. Dearing also suggests a GNVQ route to the Advanced Diploma, but the proposals are less developed than for A-levels and will not concern us here.

References

Association for Colleges, The Girls' School Association, The Headmasters' Conference, The Secondary Heads Association, The Sixth Form Colleges' Association and The Society for Headmasters and Headmistresses in Independent Schools (1994) *Post-Compulsory Education and Training: A Joint Statement*, London: AfC.

Confederation of British Industry (1993) *Routes for Success. Careerships: A Strategy For All 16–19 Learning*, London: CBI.

Dearing, Sir Ron (1996) *Review of Qualifications for 16–19 Year Olds*, London: SCAA.

Department for Education/Employment Department/Welsh Office (1991) *Education and Training for the 21st Century*, London: HMSO.

Department of Education and Science (1968) *The Dainton Report*, London: HMSO.

Department of Education and Science (1988) *Advancing A-levels, Report of the Committee chaired by Professor Higginson*, London: HMSO.

Finegold, D, Keep, E, Miliband, D, Raffe, D, Spours, K and Young, M (1990) *A British Baccalaureate: Overcoming Divisions Between Education and Training*, London: Institute for Public Policy Research.

Fforwm (1995) *An Interim Report on the Wales FE Credit Framework*, Fforwm Wales Modularisation and Credit Based Development Project, Cardiff: Fforwm.

Further Education Unit (1992) *A Basis for Credit? Developing a Post-16 Credit Accumulation and Transfer Framework*, London: FEU.

Gibbons, M, Limoges, C, Nowotny, H, Schwartzman, S, Scott, P and Trow, M (1994) *The New Production of Knowledge*, London: Sage.

Holt, M (1979) 'Why N and F Had to Die', *Education*, 6 July.

Mathieson, M (1992) 'From Crowther to Core Skills', *Oxford Education Review*, **18**, 3.

Ministry of Education (1959) *15 to 18: Report of the Central Advisory Council for Education – England (Vol. 1)*, London: HMSO.

Smithers, A (1994) 'The Paradox of A-levels', *The Curriculum Journal*, **5**, 3.

Spours, K (1995) *Post-Compulsory Education and Training: Statistical Trends*, Working Paper 7, Post-16 Education Centre, Institute of Education, University of London and the Centre for Education and Industry, University of Warwick.

Spours, K (ed.) (1996) *Institutional Responses to Dearing and Aiming Higher*, Report of Research and Development Work for Essex LEA, Post-16 Education Centre, Institute of Education, University of London.

Spours, K and Young, M (1996) 'Dearing and Beyond: Steps and Stages to a Unified System' *British Journal of Education and Work*, December.

Walden, G (1996) *We Should Know Better*, London: Fourth Estate.

Watson, J (1991) *The French Baccalaureate Professionale*, Working Paper 9, London: Post-16 Education Centre, Institute of Education, University of London.

Young, M (1993) 'A Curriculum for the 21st Century: Towards a New Basis for Overcoming Academic/Vocational Divisions' *British Journal of Educational Studies*, **40**, 3.

Young, M (1994) 'Modularisation and the Outcomes Approach: Towards a Strategy for a Curriculum of the Future' in Burke, J (ed.) *Outcomes and the Curriculum*, London: Falmer Press.

Young, M and Spours, K (1995) *Post-Compulsory Curriculum and Qualifications: Options for Change*, Learning for the Future Working Paper 6, Post-16 Education Centre, Institute of Education, University of London and the Centre for Education and Industry, University of Warwick.

Young, M, Hodgson, A and Morris, A (1995) *Strategies and Organisational Change in Post-16 Education*, Post-16 Education Centre, Institute of Education, University of London.

CHAPTER 4

GNVQs and the Future of Broad Vocational Qualifications

Ken Spours

The problem of broad vocational qualifications in the English system

Vocational qualifications in the English education and training system have been in a state of constant flux since the late 1970s. This has been due to two interrelated factors: changing patterns of participation and an ideological approach to reform. Responding to the collapse of the youth labour market, broad vocational qualifications have been used primarily to absorb rising levels of full-time participation. The Certificate of Pre-Vocational Education (CPVE) was introduced in the early 1980s, for example, for low-achieving and vocationally undecided students who could not immediately enter the labour market. By the early 1990s, GNVQs were developed as an alternative pathway of progression both to jobs and to higher education.

At the same time, the design of vocational qualifications was also being reformed. They became the focus of experimentation aimed at establishing 'standards of a new type' (MSC, 1981). The creation of NCVQ in the mid-1980s saw the start of a process to convert all vocational qualifications to an outcome- and competence-based model. The NVQ approach to competence was designed to be accessible to those who were outside the mainstream qualifications system and, at the same time, to meet employers' immediate job-related training needs. The development of NVQ-type competence methodology (which will be referred to throughout this chapter as 'NVQ methodology') was conducted with a missionary zeal and took on an ideological character (Gleeson and Hodkinson, 1995; Hyland, 1994).

The effects were paradoxical: the pursuit of NVQ methodology succeeded for a time in intellectually dominating debates about vocational education, but it did not succeed in transforming all vocational qualifications. At present, over 60 per cent of all vocational qualifications lie outside the NVQ and GNVQ tracks (FEFC, 1996) and the continued presence of traditional vocational qualifications, such as BTEC and City & Guilds awards, was certainly not intended in the original NCVQ plan. The vocational qualifications most affected by NVQ methodology have, in fact, failed to secure a broad consensus amongst those either in education or in employment. They have been most successful in polarizing opinion: both NVQs and GNVQs have their ardent supporters and their vitriolic critics. But it is also increasingly recognized that NVQ-type competence-based qualifications suffer inherent design problems, reflected in the low take-up of NVQs by employers or by low successful completion rates in GNVQs (Robinson, 1996; Spours, 1995a). Not surprisingly, both qualifications have also been under review (Beaumont, 1995; Capey, 1995) and the debate about their future role shows no signs of abating.

Five weaknesses of broad vocational qualifications

This chapter will focus on the future of what have been termed 'broad vocational qualifications' which have become associated almost exclusively with the full-time education route. These include various BTEC, City & Guilds and RSA qualifications and, more recently, GNVQs. It will be argued that all vocational qualifications in the English system suffer from several related weaknesses. The principle causes are their location in a divided qualifications system, the ways in which they have been used to respond to participation and low achievement and the lack, until quite recently, of a quality work-based route. It will also be argued that these weaknesses have been exacerbated by the development of GNVQs.

First, and most obvious, is the association of broad vocational qualifications, at least at NVQ Levels 1 and 2, with low achievers. Most vocational provision in schools is below Level 3 and, combined with post-16 GCSE, is offered as an alternative to A-level courses. Despite the recent growth of Level 3 courses (DfEE, 1996), more mixing by students of academic and vocational qualifications and a different balance of provision in further education colleges, the cultural perception that 'vocational equals second best' remains very strong.

Responsiveness to growth in full-time participation has meant that vocational courses have tended to become less vocational and more core skills oriented. This can be seen both as a strength and as a weakness. If the main aim of vocational education is to create more flexible learners for an uncertain future, then generic forms of learning – problem-solving, team-work and exercising greater control over the compilation of portfolios – can be seen to be producing 'deep learning' (Oates, 1994).

GNVQs in particular have been recognized as being highly motivational because of the way in which they involve students in assessment (OFSTED, 1994). But at the same time a process-based approach has been accused of robbing vocational education of its vocational identity and of not producing sufficiently high levels of technical skill and core knowledge (Smithers, 1993; Wolf, 1995). Implementation studies have suggested that GNVQs have been neither sufficiently educational to provide a strong progression route to higher education nor sufficiently vocational to be an adequate preparation for certain specialist areas of employment (FEU/Institute of Education/Nuffield, 1994; Green, 1996).

The weaknesses of broad vocational qualifications are not only the result of their association with low achievement and changing patterns of participation but also their relationship to the academic track. Despite the growing numbers involved in full-time advanced level vocational courses, they are still outnumbered by those taking A-levels by more than two to one (Spours, 1995b). Low status is not simply confirmed by low volume of participation but also by low prestige linked to selection and progression. A-levels (at least the upper grades) are more highly regarded because their selective role has provided a clear progression route to traditional universities. Vocational qualifications also now provide an alternative route to higher education, in numbers proportionate to A-levels, but overwhelmingly to the new universities. The increased presence of GNVQs alongside A-levels has intensified rather than reduced the debate about 'parity of esteem' and the relative status of vocational qualifications.

Despite the fact that they are meant to provide a route to employment, broad vocational qualifications have suffered from a lack of recognition in the labour market. Employers have tended to use academic qualifications as a means of selecting employees or have used occupationally-specific qualifications, such as NVQs, for training purposes (Raffe, 1988). In this context, broad vocational qualifications could be seen to be caught between two stools.

The fifth weakness, and arguably the most significant, has been the role of a competence-based approach to skill and knowledge in the design of vocational qualifications. For nearly a decade, vocational qualifications have been dominated by competence-based ideas, reflected in their most pure form in NVQs (Hyland, 1994; Taubman, 1994). NVQs have been most successful in providing accreditation for adults in work, particularly for those in less skilled employment. They have also been used by some companies for internal training purposes and have been regarded to be highly motivating for trainees (Beaumont, 1995).

However, the shortcomings of NVQs have had a significant effect on broad vocational qualifications. By the early 1990s, NVQs had failed to take root in full-time 16–19 education (Watson and Wolf, 1991). This failure was one of the main factors in the emergence of GNVQs as the full-time middle route of what would become known as a national triple-track qualifications framework. By 1991, NCVQ was asked to oversee the development of GNVQs and proceeded to apply NVQ assessment methodology to the new qualification (Spours, 1995a).

We can see, therefore, that the weaknesses of broad vocational qualifications are due to a combination of factors – their position within a divided qualifications system, their responsiveness to low participation and achievement outside that of the academic track and the way in which their more generic path of development has been ignored by employers. Most significant, however, was the transfer of NVQ methodology to the broad vocational track and the effect it was to have on the design of GNVQs.

GNVQ qualification design and its effects

A hybrid, a contradiction and a paradox

GNVQs are a hybrid, based on qualification design features borrowed from NVQs, CPVE and BTEC awards (Spours, 1995a). The GNVQ design model has been built on six main features: assessment outcomes, knowledge coverage, complex assessment procedures, groupings of units, core skills development and active learning through portfolio compilation.

GNVQs are also a contradiction because their relationship with the academic and occupationally specific tracks means that they are being pulled in different directions. They were designed using an NVQ methodology originally conceived for work-based qualifications and for an adult population. This design was then deployed in a full-time vocational qualification for younger learners, which has been compelled to seek parity with a more traditional subject-specialized, knowledge-based and terminally examined qualification – A-Levels. The contradiction lies in the desire to make GNVQs 'distinctive' at the same time as encouraging the mixing of vocational and academic qualifications. The stark differences between GNVQs and A-levels has inhibited students from creating mixed programmes (FEU/Institute of Education/Nuffield, 1994; Mudd, 1994).

GNVQs are not only a hybrid and a contradiction; they are also a paradox. Their curriculum strengths are also their weaknesses. The following analysis of the GNVQ qualification design suggests that the process-based approach to assessment, while motivating some learners, undermines the capacity of the award to produce good technical outcomes in areas such as mathematics and vocational knowledge and, in doing so, compromises the ability of GNVQs to achieve parity of esteem with the academic track or successfully to fulfil a vocational role.

Features of GNVQ qualification design prior to the Capey Review

The NVQ outcomes and assessment

The NVQ competence-based approach to assessment of learning outcomes is at the heart of the GNVQ model (Oates, 1994). The NVQ model stresses the separation of learning and assessment in terms of classroom delivery, but a close relationship between individual learning and assessment. This is seen as evidence of the openness of a model that stresses flexibility of delivery by the local centre (Jessup, 1993). The main focus in the learning process is on students collecting evidence of activity, relating this to the assessment specification and submitting this in their portfolio for final grading. Many practitioners have welcomed this approach because they felt that it could improve learning and empower the student. However, the particular GNVQ approach to outcomes has been subjected to constant criticism for fragmenting understanding, being bureaucratic, paper-heavy (Hyland, 1994; Smithers, 1993; Wolf, 1995) and ignoring knowledge development (Young, 1995). This has meant that schools and colleges have found it difficult to design courses which allow students effectively to cover all the required units and to provide opportunities for the integration of core skills (OFSTED, 1994). The emphasis on outcomes at the expense of inputs has meant that structures of delivery have been regarded as a second-order issue and the responsibility of the institution. The effect has been to produce an enormous variability of approaches to GNVQs and the resourcing of courses, as well as confusion about course design (FEU/Institute of Education/Nuffield, 1994; OFSTED, 1994).

Coverage of broad vocational knowledge
The concept of 'coverage' is directly related to the NVQ notion of 'mastery-based' assessment of competence and the minimum requirement of 'industry-defined standards'. The adoption of this approach points to an NCVQ assumption that GNVQs are basically a preparation for NVQs. The Further Education Unit/ Institute of Education/Nuffield implementation evaluation study showed, however, that GNVQs are being used principally as a means of progression to higher education. So why the central role for coverage?

At one level it reflects the historical desire of NCVQ to apply NVQ methodology to all vocational qualifications. But in an era of increasing concern about qualification standards, the concept of coverage has become more related to a critique of academic courses and a concern for transparency of achievement without recourse to external examinations (see Oates in Chapter 9).

This approach to knowledge, while purporting to improve transparency, can have several negative effects, including the lack of theoretical inquiry (Sparkes, 1994). The concept of coverage, in its extreme form, has meant recording minute elements of the curriculum and has made GNVQs difficult to deliver. In the last two years there has been a gradual retreat from the principle of coverage, signalled by the *GNVQ Quality Framework* (NCVQ/BTEC/CGLI/RSA, 1995) and the Capey Review (1995), but it still lingers within the GNVQ design model.

Complex assessment procedures
GNVQs probably have had the most complicated assessment procedures in the history of vocational qualifications. They have combined the assessment of vocational outcomes on a pass/fail basis with the application of grading criteria to the portfolio to determine the overall grade for the award and external tests of mandatory units. The pass/fail approach to vocational outcomes reflects NVQ methodology, but the lack of grading for all parts can be interpreted as not taking the vocational element seriously. The application of grading criteria to the final portfolio involves students directly in assessment and can be motivational and

skill-building, but it has also contributed to low rates of successful completion (Spours, 1995b). The most controversial feature of GNVQ assessment has been external testing. NCVQ did not want external testing because it was considered anathema to the NVQ model, but the government insisted because they saw it as a means of securing parity of esteem with academic qualifications. The external tests, in pre-Capey form, have been based on multiple-choice questions. They have few supporters. This form of testing does not utilize essay-writing skills and the marshalling of ideas and facts or concepts – valuable skills demanded by academic examinations. The external tests have not influenced the unit grade because of the decision, in line with NVQ methodology, that grasp of knowledge should not be graded. In essence, the external tests have been a bureaucratic compromise. It is not surprising, therefore, that assessment has become an area of crisis for GNVQs and the focus of the Capey Review.

Grouped structure and low flexibility
GNVQs follow the BTEC tradition of grouped integrated awards. Prior to the Dearing Review recommendations, the rule of combination in GNVQs at Advanced Level was based on a minimum of eight mandatory units and four optional units. Its lack of flexibility in relation to the six units of an A-level was the main reason for the Dearing proposal of a GNVQ based on a six-unit building block, or even a three-unit block.

The inflexible grouping of units affected not only the relationship of GNVQs with the academic track but also the development of the award in specific vocational areas. BTEC has continued to offer its National Diplomas in order to cover these requirements (BTEC, 1995). There has been an assumption by NCVQ that specialized vocational study would be provided by NVQ units. This has not always taken place, with many leading companies looking to existing BTEC National awards for technical specialization in areas such as design and engineering. There is also an imposed limit of 15 broad vocational titles for GNVQs, leaving little room for specialist 'sub-lines' to include an in-depth range of specialist units in particular vocational areas.

Core skills and breadth of learning
Core skills have a fundamental role in GNVQs and perhaps are the feature that most distinguishes them from NVQs. The approach to core skills is essentially that followed by previous BTEC awards – core skills are meant to be 'embedded' in vocational situations, but are separately recorded as core skill units. This makes them appear more relevant to the learner and also more transparent to the employer.

In practice, however, there is little consensus on how to deliver core skills. Implementation studies have highlighted the variation in schools' and colleges' approach to the delivery of core skills, some favouring embedding, others stand-alone strategies (FEU/IOE/Nuffield, 1994). The embedded approach was also criticized by the schools' inspectorate for providing very few examples of good work (OFSTED, 1994). The response of higher education admissions tutors has been to demand that Advanced GNVQ graduates also attain GCSE maths and English with A–C grades. It has been persistently argued in recent years that whatever its pedagogic strengths, the embedding of core skills does not allow for the systematic development of mathematical and language skill. Moreover, this approach differs dramatically from the type of stand-alone delivery practices prevalent in European systems, which have provided greater levels of attainment in these core skills areas (Green and Steedman, 1993; Wolf, 1995).·

Active learning and portfolio development

The GNVQ emphasis on active learning and the creation of portfolios has been borrowed directly from CPVE. Collaborative and active styles of learning which have flowed from these features are arguably the strongest element of the award, a strength recognized in inspection reports (FEFC, 1994; OFSTED, 1994).

A critical weakness of portfolio development is that, combined with the NVQ approach to coverage, it also demands a great deal of record-keeping both for students and for teachers. Student involvement in assessment may also become a form of control and exclusion. When they are having to busy themselves covering multiple criteria and aligning these with assessment specifications for the portfolio, students have little time to do anything else. When teachers are tackling the demands of this complex range of individualized activities, they cannot be concentrating on specific skill and knowledge development. With this density of activity, something has to give and it appears to have been fundamental skill development and theoretical understanding (Young, 1995).

The combined effects of these components of the GNVQ design model demonstrate the extent of the paradox. GNVQs have motivated many students who were turned off by a more academic curriculum, but at the same time GNVQs have produced a one-sided approach to achievement with an emphasis on process skills rather than on technical knowledge and skill. At a time when A-levels have become more externally assessed, the divisions between the broad vocational track and the academic track have, in many respects, become deeper with far-reaching implications for the status of GNVQs and their progression capability. The issue of most immediate concern has been the effect of the GNVQ curriculum design on student performance.

The effects of GNVQ design on participation and attainment

Because of the current government policy to restrict participation in A-levels (Dearing, 1996) GNVQs have been given an enormous responsibility to fulfil the revised Foundation Target of 60 per cent of those under 21 years reaching Level 3 by the Year 2000 (NACETT, 1995). In this respect, the performance of GNVQs has been very uneven.

The participation role of GNVQs has been a mixture of successes and failures. By 1996 GNVQ registrations exceeded 180,000. This represents a growth from

0.2 per cent of the cohort in 1992 to over 20 per cent in 1996 (DfEE, 1996). However, the levels of full-time participation at 16+ have not risen between 1995 and 1997 and, in this sense, GNVQs have not succeeded in boosting overall staying-on rates. They have, on the other hand, succeeded in changing the composition of participation. Participation in Advanced GNVQ at 16 now out-numbers that of other advanced vocational qualifications by three to one. However, this expansion has not come about as an alternative to the academic track. Participation in A-levels has only declined·by 1 per cent in the last two years and post-16 GCSEs by 2 per cent. The growth of GNVQs has been largely the result of schools and colleges converting from traditional vocational qualifications rather than enticing students away from A-levels (DfEE, 1996; Robinson, 1996).

Moreover, this success has not been matched by student achievement. GNVQ successful completion rates still hover around 55 per cent, compared to over 70 per cent for BTEC National and A-levels (Spours, 1995b). A major factor in GNVQ non-completion has been the failure of students to finish their portfolio, upon which the GNVQ overall grade has depended. The effect of a low successful completion rate in GNVQs at both Advanced and Intermediate Levels has been adversely to affect progression rates, which are also lower than those of equivalent BTEC vocational awards (Robinson, 1996; Spours, 1995b).

At the heart of the performance problems of GNVQs lies the issue of assessment. By 1995, following three years of implementation, this was finally recognized by NCVQ. What followed was the Capey Review of GNVQ Assessment, which also contributed to the Dearing Review of qualifications.

The Capey Review of GNVQ Assessment: adjustment or a fundamental rethink?

The Capey and Dearing Reviews can be seen as ways of stabilizing the role of GNVQs at a time when they could have failed as a viable qualification. The major question is whether these Reviews and the most recent GNVQ inspection reports are responding to problems of implementation or to more fundamental design issues?

The GNVQ design model has, in the last year or so, come under increasing scrutiny. In its early years, 1992–94, it was argued that implementation, not design, was the main problem (FEFC, 1994; OFSTED, 1994). The most recent OFSTED report, however, is far more critical than its 1994 version and appears to be responding to design rather than to implementation issues, because of its preoccupation with assessment (OFSTED, 1996).

The Capey Review of GNVQ assessment, carried out during 1995 (Capey, 1995), covered five areas: assessment, the grouping of GNVQ units, core skills, portfolio development and external tests. In September 1996 NCVQ submitted proposals to the Secretary of State for Education and Employment for a revised GNVQ assessment model (NCVQ, 1996). The NCVQ document reflects the main emphasis of both the Capey and Dearing Reviews with proposals to simplify assessment procedures and to make GNVQ assessment more standardized and external. The main aspects of the revised model are: a simpler approach to the assessment of each of the GNVQ units, involving one or two assignments per unit; more open-ended cross-unit external tests (each test covers two units) which also influence the grade; a set assignment for each vocational unit and externally tested key skills through set assignments. The set assignment in key skills will also include an arithmetical skills test under controlled conditions. There will, in addition, be a new model of 'standards moderation' which focuses more on the standard of students' work.

At first glance, the proposals in the document *The Revised GNVQ Assessment Model* (NCVQ, 1996) represent the most significant departure from the NVQ model to date. Gone are the exhaustive assessment of 'elements', the grading of the award by one third of evidence in the portfolio and the machine marking of tests. NVQ methodology has been replaced by an external approach to assessment which may substantially reduce the assessment burden on teachers. The approach is reminiscent of the Dearing Review of assessment in the National Curriculum, which moved the focus more externally and to the end of each key stage.

The Capey Review could have significant consequences for the future reform of the 14–19 qualifications system as a whole. It reduces, if not removes completely, the effect of NVQ methodology on GNVQs, which opens the way for a potentially closer relationship with the academic track. The 'unitization of assessment' is the most fundamental change in this respect. At the same time, SCAA and NCVQ are working on a three-unit component of GNVQ to parallel the proposed lateral AS-level.

On the other hand, the shift to more standardized and external assessment could make GNVQs more difficult for some students and could keep successful completion rates depressed, though for different reasons than at present. The obvious benefit of more external testing could be a rise in the status of GNVQs in the eyes of both university admissions tutors and employers.

It is hard not to conclude that, despite all the discussion about 'distinctiveness' of the tracks in the Dearing Report, what we are now witnessing, in late 1996, is a move towards some form of convergence between the tracks, based on external assessment. It is also apparent that Capey has addressed GNVQ design, not just implementation issues. The changes also go some way to answering the critics of GNVQs, who have argued that these qualifications are not sufficiently rigorous (Green, 1996; Labour Party, 1996; Smithers, 1993; Wolf, 1995). However, *The Revised GNVQ Assessment Model* (NCVQ, 1996), while promoting a simpler, less bureaucratic and more externally rigorous approach, may represent a strategy for raising the status of GNVQs, without producing all the conditions for convergence. This requires a more fundamental review, not only of the internal design of GNVQs but of its relationship to the academic track, to employment and to institutional implementation strategies.

The future of broad vocational qualifications: distinctive tracks or part of a unified system?

GNVQs and the role of broad vocational qualifications

The intense contradictions of GNVQs have highlighted the deeper problems of a broad vocational track and how it relates to other qualifications. The root of the problem has not only been lack of technical rigour and increased bureaucratism, but an inability to play an effectively flexible role in relation to the academic track, in relation to specialized vocational study or to combined full-time and part-time study. The result has been a proliferation of qualifications and increased confusion as traditional vocational qualifications continue to meet more specific vocational needs and the requirements of part-time students (BTEC, 1995). This has been particularly the case in certain vocational areas, such as Leisure and Tourism and Land and Environment, where the GNVQ vocational area has been drawn too broadly. There is also growing evidence that by 1996 some further education colleges are converting back to BTEC provision and away from GNVQs.

The problem of the vocational role of GNVQs will be highlighted further by the development of the Modern Apprenticeship (MA) and any future attempt to up-grade the work-based route. Currently, GNVQ units are supplemented by NVQ units in many MA programmes, but this qualification combination has been criticized by employers because of the weight of the recording and assessment bureaucracy (see Chapter 5). Traditional vocational qualifications, tailored for the purpose, might provide a better qualification base for MAs.

The problem of the indeterminate role of GNVQs, arising from its inherent design, has been reinforced by market forces, causing further fragmentation within the vocational route. The vocational awarding bodies have responded to rising levels of full-time participation by competing with each other to meet new market demands. During the 1980s this resulted in a lack of cooperation over pre-vocational education, such as CPVE, and more recently in competition over the development of GNVQs and support for the continuation of other vocational qualifications such as BTEC National. As a result, vocational qualifications have proliferated into three different types: GNVQs, traditional vocational qualifications and NVQs. This is causing confusion and the inability of any form of vocational qualification to establish a dominance in the minds of the public or end-users. At a local level, market competition between schools and colleges has meant that some schools have rushed to offer the award in order to boost staying-on in sixth forms. GNVQs were deliberately designed to make it easy for schools to offer vocational qualifications as an alternative to the academic route. In addition, there has been a very hasty implementation programme and some schools were quite clearly not ready to offer these new awards, a fact that was picked up in the early inspection reports in 1994 (OFSTED, 1994).

GNVQs have suffered from fundamental design, role and function problems due to their uneasy position between the academic and the occupationally-specific qualifications tracks. The policy of creating more curriculum distinctiveness cannot possibly work at a time when more students need more not less general education and when it is increasingly recognized that vocational education needs to become more rigorous. The Capey Review of assessment has, it appears, reduced one of the main contradictions – the distinctiveness of GNVQ assessment – but others remain. The contradictions faced by the broad vocational route are not confined to GNVQs: they are system-wide and include this route's relationship with the academic track and with more vocationally-focused qualifications. Capey may have unlocked one of the doors with GNVQ assessment reform, but others remain firmly closed.

The preceding analysis suggests that GNVQs, as broad vocational qualifications, have reached a watershed. They are assuming a more important strategic role in terms of qualifications outputs, but they have been in a state of crisis due to their complexity and poor performance. At the same time, broad vocational qualifications are increasingly becoming a parallel route to A-levels as participation in Advanced GNVQs expands. The Capey and Dearing Reviews are pushing GNVQs and A-levels into an ever closer relationship, though arguably on terms dictated by the assessment approach of A-levels. In this context, parity of esteem will be a constant issue.

Directions of development and parity of esteem

At this point, the broad vocational track could develop in three directions, each with its own version of parity of esteem (Raffe *et al.*, 1996).

Option 1: Curriculum distinctiveness within the National Qualifications Framework

The first option would be to emphasize the distinctiveness of both the academic and the broad vocational routes by preserving sharp differences in assessment and learning styles. This could be accompanied by an attempt to clarify the role of vocational and academic qualifications, by placing different subjects or areas of study into either the academic or the vocational track. This was recommended in the Dearing Report (1996), but has subsequently been dropped.

Those who wish to accentuate the distinctiveness of vocational education will tend to see parity of esteem in terms of being 'separate but equally valued'. It is argued that vocational education and training (more the latter) have different purposes from academic learning and that both would benefit from separation – the academic track could retain its 'integrity' and the vocational track could become more vocational and avoid being constantly compared to its more prestigious counterpart.

The main problem with this position is that the realities of the qualifications tracks in the 1990s suggests that they cannot be separated. Knowledge refuses to be placed neatly in one track or another and both academic and vocational courses are offered alongside each other, rather than being separated by mode of participation or by institution. The German Dual System, often used as a model to justify this kind of separation, is also changing and becoming less internally distinctive (Lasonen, 1996). The aftermath of the Capey Review and the decision not to allocate different subjects to the qualifications tracks constitutes an admission that parity, based on assessment and content distinctiveness of qualifications, is no longer viable.

Option 2: Academic and vocational equivalences within the National Qualifications Framework

A second position on parity, and one which is most concerned with the concept itself, argues for the equivalence of academic and vocational learning and qualifications. This can be approached through a variety of strategies, ranging from the alignment of units from academic and vocational qualifications to level and grade equivalences and the building-in of common curricular elements in both tracks.

The equivalences approach has its weak and strong variants (Spours and Young, 1996). The development of equivalences, while at the same time pursuing track distinctiveness (the Dearing strategy), can be considered as 'weak parity', whereas the idea of creating parity by building common elements (or a common core) in different pathways can be termed 'strong parity' and is more typical of continental education and training systems (Green, 1996).

The first strands of evidence emerging in the implementation of the Dearing agenda suggest that 'parity through equivalences' is the main strategy being pursued. The strength of parity will be determined by the balance of commonality or distinctiveness.

Option 3: Enhancement of vocational education within a unified system

A third option would be to try to enhance vocational education within a unified qualifications system by redefining what constitutes both academic and vocational learning. It adopts the premise that the broad vocational track cannot be redefined and reformed without the other tracks also being brought into the equation, whereas Option 1 and the weaker version of Option 2 assume that vocational education can be reformed on the basis of an unchanged academic track.

This strategy goes beyond the idea of 'linkages' and 'equivalences' and promotes a process of 'mutual enrichment' in which the strongest approaches from both tracks are fused (eg, the fusion of theoretical and applied learning within a single framework). In this model the inter-dependence of the concepts of parity and tracks becomes apparent. As the qualifications tracks are eroded in the development of a unified system, so the concept of parity itself begins to wither. There is a shift away from the comparison of separate qualifications and a growing focus on a common core curriculum and the relative status of 'specialist pathways'. This is now beginning to happen in the less track-like French and Swedish systems (Lasonen, 1996).

Reconceptualizing broad vocational education

Elsewhere is this book (Chapters 1, 2 and 13) it is observed that the 14–19 qualifications system in England is moving, albeit in a hesitant and contradictory way, from a track-based system to a 'weak framework' position. The relationship between tracks and frameworks and what it means for future reform is a major issue of the Dearing review process. In this chapter it has been argued that the function and definition of the broad vocational track cannot be seen in isolation from its relationship to other tracks. If this relationship is now changing, it is logical to assume that the definition of what constitutes broad vocational education will also change.

Since the 1991 White Paper, broad vocational education, as defined by GNVQs, has been track-based because of the emphasis on curriculum distinctiveness but this was not always the case. In the late 1980s broad vocational qualifications, represented by BTEC National Diploma, began to establish a potentially close relationship with modular A-levels through the creation of common core modules in the first year of study in areas such as Business and Science (Rainbow, 1993). These became known as Y-models (Burgess, 1993). This formation of core learning in different areas of study suggested that aspects of broad vocational education were, in fact, part of general education. Despite the government's insistence on curriculum distinctiveness in GNVQs, students themselves treat this new award as an applied form of general education (FEU/IOE/Nuffield, 1994).

Any future attempt to bring different qualifications into a closer relationship will therefore directly question the very concept of a broad vocational track. Moreover, the development of more common elements and linkages between qualifications will tend to lead to a broadening rather than a narrowing of the definition of the academic. This could happen in two ways. First, the emphasis on core skills and processes, such as mathematics or languages, problem-solving and student involvement in assessment practices, will mean promoting aspects of the curriculum that both academic and vocational tracks can share. Second, such a process could also embrace theoretical and applied learning in areas such as technology, media, art and design, business and engineering. These areas of knowledge, which are theory/application combinations, have expanded historically. Such developments would represent the formation of different elements of a 'post-14 core curriculum' and the definition of broad vocational education as general education.

But, if broad vocational education becomes in fact an aspect of general education, what about the role of 'vocational specialization'? Vocational education is ultimately defined by its relationship to working life, both preparation for it and on-going training at work. Rather belatedly, there has been a recognition that the work-based route has suffered from low-quality training schemes and needs to be up-graded (see Chapter 5). The development of Modern Apprenticeships could provide a vehicle by which vocational qualifications fulfil not only a general education role but also encourage vocational specialization (Richardson *et al.*, 1995). At present NVQs provide a type of vocational specialization, though in their current design cannot satisfy all aspects of this concept of learning. The future of vocational specialization, therefore, could lie in incorporating NVQ-type units into a vocational qualifications framework which combined 'general education units', 'vocational knowledge units' and 'units of vocational practice'.

What this process represents is the development of vocational qualifications which are both educationally broad and vocationally specialized. Broad vocational qualifications would no longer constitute a separate track, but would explicitly incorporate both general education and vocational education and training. It would mean the dissolution of the broad vocational track as we know it. There would be no need for a middle route in a system which placed emphasis on integration rather than on division. Current qualifications for younger learners would be replaced by a single qualification encompassing A-levels, GNVQs, traditional vocational qualifications and NVQs, which would allow different modular combinations of broad general education and various forms of specialization that encompass what has been traditionally seen as 'academic' or 'vocational' learning. This system could be contained within a common Diploma framework. Design issues would focus on how to build both breadth and specialization into a common framework, rather than on pursuing distinctiveness and division between academic and vocational learning.

Enhancing broad vocational education within a single framework

The reconceptualization and reform of the broad vocational track within a unified system approach can be seen in strategic 'steps and stages', originally outlined in the *Learning for the Future* report (Richardson *et al.*, 1995). The two aims of this approach would be to introduce into the reform process a more technical and curriculum oriented approach to change, rather than ideologically inspired change, and to combine visions and blueprints with a gradualist change strategy.

Stage 1: Creating stronger linkages and equivalences in the Framework Stage

The creation of stronger linkages between academic and vocational qualifications could be pursued by a strategy of common assessment, unitization/modularization and the introduction of elements of a common core. The first step would involve removing those curriculum features which promote an ideological approach to distinctiveness (eg, NVQ assessment methodology in the broad vocational track and the emphasis on external and terminal assessment in the academic track). This would make possible a common design for full-time vocational qualifications to resolve the current division between GNVQs and BTEC traditional qualifications. The proposals flowing from the Capey Review have removed or reduced the influence of NVQ ideology within GNVQs but Dearing's refusal to look at assessment in A-levels still means that there is assessment inflexibility in the academic track.

A vital reform in the Framework Stage would be the introduction of a fully unitized system to both the academic and vocational tracks so as to create a more common structure between the two. The Dearing and Capey processes go some way towards this with the unitization of assessment in GNVQs and the development of a three-unit GNVQ and Lateral AS-level, but the Reviews have still held back on modularization of A-levels. On the basis of current proposals emerging in the Dearing implementation phase, it would also be possible to move further to a 'common assessment framework' and the construction of a credible equivalence of grades and levels.

One final feature of the Framework Stage would be the introduction of limited process-based learning that would be common to both tracks (eg, portfolios or integrated assignments as synoptic units within a more modular system). The creation of core skill units could be the basis for the development of a common applied approach, but the emerging emphasis on external assessment of these units within GNVQs could create a lack of symmetry with a lateral AS-level in core skills, which appears likely to contain a balance between internal and external assessment. It is ironic to observe GNVQs becoming more externally assessed and the lateral AS apparently becoming more internally assessed, with the resulting possibility that they might well not meet in the middle!

Overall, it appears that the Dearing implementation process is now taking the 14–19 qualifications system tentatively into the Framework Stage. What is still missing is the modularization of the academic track and a strategy of balanced assessment. These would represent both an 'improvement' in the qualifications themselves and a strengthening of the framework.

Stage 2: The broadening of general education and the creation of new forms of vocational specialization

The second stage of development would be to build on the first and corresponds to the Learning for the Future Project's stage of 'unification'. This stage attempts to redefine academic and vocational education by bringing both of these into a structure which combines breadth and specialization. This is the stage at which there is a Diploma system, which has general educational and vocational variants, according to the needs of individual learners and the needs of end users. There would be no such thing as a broad vocational qualification per se.

In terms of design, this stage could include the introduction of a core curriculum for all modes of study, together with a unitized common assessment framework. It would extend the process already started by the Dearing Review and the strategies put in place to strengthen the framework. Beyond the core, specialist study would be defined by 'pathways' of unit groupings rather than by separate qualifications. A common Diploma structure could be designed to encompass general and mixed patterns of study or highly specialized combinations.

These basic components of a new Diploma structure would aim to overcome the design deficiencies of existing vocational qualifications by having enough breadth to promote progression to higher education and by giving sufficient room for specialization by grouping units to meet employment needs. The development of new forms and combinations of vocational specialist study will be essential in a newly forged unified system. Without a strong strand of vocational education which has clear links to the labour market, a unified system which promotes personal choice of study could inadvertently promote 'academic drift'. Students might then increasingly choose to study more prestigious and more general educational pathways at the expense of vocational specialist ones.

Conclusions

Developing stages of qualification design is just one part of the reform equation. The future of vocational education would not only be determined by the issues of design but also by the context of changes in vocational training. Central to this is the development of a more robust work-based route with 'alternance-based' qualifications, which increasingly would be entered directly from full-time 16–19 education, rather than being seen as alternatives to full-time participation. This will mean securing more employer collaboration, with the recognition that the reform of vocational qualifications has to be accompanied by reforms of the labour market (Finegold et al., 1990)

Equally important will be the context for implementation. At both the national and local levels there will have to be a unified and collaborative structure of regulation to create a combined general education and vocational education culture. The proposed merger of SCAA and NCVQ can be seen as the first step in this process. At an institutional level there would have to be extensive collaboration between schools, colleges and employers to deliver a curriculum which spans both general education and vocational specialization.

Another contextual factor would be the size of a curriculum which attempts to combine, albeit in many different ways, both general and vocational education. The unavoidable conclusion is that it will involve the expansion of student contact hours, which have declined dramatically in recent years. There would also be significant implications in terms of funding the reform, persuading students that working longer hours is worthwhile and supporting schools and colleges with timetabling issues.

A unifying reform strategy must start with the historical problems of the broad vocational route, of which the most important is the academic/vocational divide. The basic argument of this chapter is that the reform of vocational and academic tracks must go hand-in-hand. This means taking the broad vocational knowledge content and diverse learning and assessment styles of vocational education and merging them with the academic track. In this sense the world of the vocational becomes an instrument through which to reform and to strengthen academic education. What has stood in the way of this strategy has been not only the obstruction of unreformed A-levels but the barrier of NVQ methodology. Some of these barriers are being dismantled in a hesitant way in the vocational track. The real battleground still is, and has always been, the academic track.

References

Beaumont, G (1995) *Review of 100 NVQs and SVQs*, A Report submitted to the DfEE, London: DfEE.

Burgess, M (1993) 'Linking BTEC and A/AS Levels', in Richardson, W, Woolhouse, J and Finegold, D (eds) *The Reform of Post-16 Education and Training in England and Wales*, Harlow: Longman.

Business and Technician Education Council (1995) Letter to Principals and LEAs regarding the continuation of BTEC National Diplomas, London: BTEC.

Capey, J (1995) *GNVQ Assessment Review*, London: NCVQ.

Dearing, Sir Ron (1996) *Review of Qualifications for 16–19-year-olds*, London: SCAA.

Department for Education and Employment (1996) *DfEE News 213/96 Participation in Education and Training by 16–18-year-olds in England: 1985–1995*, London: DfEE.

Finegold, D, Keep, E, Miliband, D, Raffe, D, Spours, K and Young, M (1990) *A British Baccalaureate: Overcoming Divisions Between Education and Training*, London: Institute for Public Policy Research.

Further Education Funding Council (1994) *General National Vocational Qualifications in the Further Education Sector in England National Survey Report*, Coventry: FEFC.

Further Education Funding Council (1996) 'Student Numbers at Colleges in the Further Education Sector in England in 1994–95', Press Release 23 January, Coventry: FEFC.

Further Education Unit, Institute of Education and Nuffield Foundation (1994) *GNVQs 1993–94: A National Survey Report; An Interim Report of a Joint Project 'The Evolution Of GNVQs: Enrolment and Delivery Patterns and Their Policy Implications*, London: FEU.

Gleeson, D and Hodkinson, P (1995) 'Ideology and Curriculum Policy: GNVQs and Mass Post-Compulsory Education in England and Wales', *British Journal of Education and Work*, **8**, 3, 5–19.

Green, A (1996) 'Breadth, Core Skills and the Reform of 16–19 Education', MA VET Open Lecture, Institute of Education, University of London.

Green, A and Steedman, H (1993) *Education Provision, Education Attainment and the Needs of Industry: A review of the Research for Germany, France, Japan, the USA and Britain*, National Institute of Economic Research, Report No. 5, London: NIESR.

Hyland, T (1994) *Competence, Education and NVQs: Dissenting Perspectives*, London: Cassell.

Jessup, G (1993) 'Towards a coherent post-16 qualifications framework: the role of GNVQs' in Richardson, W, Woolhouse, J and Finegold, D (eds) *The Reform of Post-16 Education and Training in England and Wales*, Harlow: Longman.

Labour Party (1996) *Aiming Higher: Labour's Plans for Reform of the 14–19 Curriculum*, London: Labour Party.

Lasonen, J (1996) *Reforming Upper Secondary Education in Europe: Surveys of Strategies for Post-16 Education to Improve the Parity of Esteem for Initial Vocational Education in Eight European Educational Systems*, Finland: University of Jyväskylä.

Manpower Services Commission (1981) *NTI – An Agenda for Action*, Sheffield: MSC.

Mudd, R (1994) Interview with Bob Mudd, Science coordinator, GLOSCAT, by K Spours, January.

National Advisory Council for Education and Training Targets (1995) *Report on Progress*, London: NACETT.

National Council for Vocational Qualifications (1996) *The Revised GNVQ Assessment Model*, Proposals Submitted to the Secretary of State for Education and Employment, September, London: NCVQ.

NCVQ, BTEC, CGLI and RSA Examinations Board (1995) *GNVQ Quality Framework*, London: NCVQ.

Oates, T (1994) 'Fair assessment and candidate's self-perception', *The NVQ Monitor*, Autumn, London: NCVQ.

OFSTED (1994) *GNVQs in Schools 1993/4: Quality and Standards of General National Vocational Qualifications*, London: HMSO.

OFSTED (1996) *Assessment of General National Vocational Qualifications in Schools in 1995/96*, London: HMSO.

Raffe, D (1988) 'The Story So Far: Research on Education, Training and the Labour Market from The Scottish Surveys' in Raffe, D (ed.) *Education and the Youth Labour Market*, London: Falmer Press.

Raffe, D, Howieson, C, Spours, K, and Young, M (1996) 'Unifying Academic and Vocational Learning: English and Scottish Approaches', paper presented to the British Association Annual Festival, University of Birmingham, 11 September.

Rainbow, R (1993) 'Modular A and AS levels: The Wessex Project', in Richardson, W, Woolhouse, J and Finegold, D (eds*) The Reform of Post-16 Education and Training in England and Wales*, Harlow: Longman.

Richardson, W, Spours, K, Woolhouse, J and Young, M (1995*) Learning for the Future – Interim Report*, Institute of Education and University of Warwick.

Robinson, P (1996) *Rhetoric and Reality: Britain's New Vocational Qualifications Centre for Economic Performance*, London: London School of Economics.

Smithers, A (1993) 'All Our Futures: Britain's Education Revolution', A Dispatches Report on Education London: Channel 4 Television.

Sparkes, J (1994) *The Education of Young People aged 14–18 Years: Learning for Success*, London: Royal Academy of Engineering.

Spours, K (1995a) *The Strengths and Weaknesses of GNVQs: Principles of Design*, Working Paper No 4, Learning for the Future Project, Institute of Education, University of London and University of Warwick.

Spours, K (1995b) *Post-compulsory Education and Training: Statistical Trends*, Working Paper No 7, Learning for the Future Project, Institute of Education, University of London and University of Warwick.

Spours, K and Young, M (1996) 'Dearing and Beyond: Steps and Stages to a Unified System', *British Journal of Education and Work*, December.

Taubman, D (1994) 'The GNVQ Debate', *Forum*, **36**, 3.

Watson, J and Wolf, A (1991) 'Return to Sender', *TES*, 6 September.

Wolf, A (1995) 'Awards that Pay Lip Service to Flexibility', *TES*, 3 February.

Young, M (1995) 'Modularisation and the Outcomes Approach: Towards a Strategy for a Curriculum of the Future' in Burke, J (ed.) *Outcomes Learning and the Curriculum: Implications for NVQs, GNVQs and other Qualifications*, London: Falmer Press.

Young, M and Spours, K (1995) *Post-Compulsory Curriculum and Qualifications: Options for Change, Learning for the Future*, Working Paper No 6, Institute of Education, University of London and University of Warwick.

CHAPTER 5

Reforming the Work-based Route: Problems and Potential for Change

Lorna Unwin

Introduction

This chapter examines the problems associated with and the potential for the provision of a credible work-based route for young people in the UK. In doing this, the chapter will explore the historical evolution of the work-based route, coming up-to-date with the establishment of the Modern Apprenticeship programme. Alongside a discussion of the nature and scope of the work-based route, the chapter will also examine the role and relevance of vocational qualifications. The chapter questions whether the introduction of competence-based NVQs has proved to be an appropriate strategy for ensuring that the training and development needs of young people and their employers are met.

It is, perhaps, a testament to the continued failure of the UK system to develop and to embed a respected and attractive work-based route to say that parts of this chapter could have been written at any time since about 1851, when concerns about the level of the nation's technical skills and quality of vocational education began to be widely expressed. If the state could be put on trial charged with the crime of consistent neglect of vocational education and training (VET), much evidence could be called for the prosecution. Others have dealt with that evidence in depth elsewhere (for example, Finegold and Soskice, 1988; Keep and Mayhew, 1988; Raggatt and Unwin, 1991a), but it is worth noting that in 1996, the Dearing Report (Dearing, 1996) was still having to remind people of the importance of VET:

> In national terms, achievement in applied and vocational education ranks
> alongside the academic. Failure to recognise that is to do an immense disservice
> to today's young people. The nation needs to value good technicians and good
> graduates equally. A good share of our most able young people should choose to
> follow the applied and vocational pathways, confident that they are equally
> esteemed by society. (p.4)

Given that the number of young people choosing to stay in full-time education after the age of 16 in the UK appears to have stabilized at around 70 per cent of the cohort, as many as one-third of 16-year-olds could be opting for the work-based route. In addition, the work-based route has attractions for those young people, particularly boys, who are academically able enough to remain in full-time education but who want to continue their learning outside an education institution (Unwin and Wellington, 1995a). The work-based route, therefore, is not just an unavoidable way to house young people for whom the schools and colleges do not want to cater – the so-called 'disaffected' – but it is a route which should be governed by the same attention to quality, reliability, viability and, above all, credibility which governs 16–19 education in general. It should not be regarded as the least favourable route, but as a route which is of equal status to other post-16 options, leading to qualifications which have the same regard for issues of progression and rigour as their academic counterparts. There is a danger that in the movement towards a unified system of post-16 education and training reformers will neglect fully to explore the strengths and weaknesses of the work-based route. Now more than ever it is important to articulate how such a route can enhance the emerging post-16 landscape.

In examining the historical evolution of the work-based route, this chapter will try to show how in the UK we have lost sight of the real purpose of work-based learning by demonizing the role of employers, downgrading the concept of vocationalism, falsely elevating the worth of education institutions as sites of learning and underestimating the capacity of young people to develop as learners if they leave education after the compulsory stage.

Voluntarism and the encouragement of 'self-help'

Despite continued calls for a coordinated approach to technical education and training and the evidence of Britain's skill shortages, highlighted by two World Wars, the state concentrated its efforts on general schooling, leaving industry and commerce to bear the responsibility for improving the country's technical performance. Until the introduction of the Industrial Training Act in 1964, this policy of non-intervention by the state prevailed, as did the long-held view that academic education was vastly superior to vocational training. Typically, the state only intervened during times of particular stress, most notably during wartime and periods of unemployment such as the 1920s and 1930s.

The following comments from a paper on engineering education, given in 1868 to the Liverpool Engineering Society, would still find echoes in workplaces around the country today:

> Hitherto our workmen have been left to do for themselves... although engaged
> from 6am to 6pm at their daily work, they manage to attend evening classes
> where these are available, and where they are not, they tread their way along,
> picking up what scraps of information they can find in the nearest lending library

and by dint of their British pluck... get sufficient knowledge to fit them for foremen and managers. (Roderick and Stephens, 1982, p.23)

This tradition of self-help continues and, ironically, is thriving particularly well in institutions which provide education and training. School teachers, college and university lecturers and trainers are increasingly seeking professional development courses delivered via distance and open learning modes, as they find they must study out of working hours and in the most flexible way, given the considerable demands on their time. The influence of Samuel Smiles through his works on 'Self-help', 'Thrift' and 'Duty' lives on today in the British attitude to adult education, higher education and, in particular, to youth training (Strong, 1992).

Central to the development of VET policies in Britain has been and continues to be an argument between those in favour of voluntarism and those in favour of intervention (Rainbird, 1990). That VET policy has been a victim of these swings in ideological approach is possibly partly due to its lack of a permanent home in one government department. Rather like an orphaned child who is constantly being presented for adoption, VET policy has been shunted between a number of foster homes – Employment, Education, Trade and Industry, Environment – but has never been permanently claimed by one set of parents. The creation of the Department for Education and Employment (DfEE) in 1995 and the merger of SCAA and NCVQ to create an overarching qualifications council may provide greater stability for VET policy-making, but the historical divisions between the vocational and the academic will have to be tackled.

Unlike Germany, which consolidated a century of cooperation between education, government and industry in its 1969 Vocational Training Act, the first attempt at state intervention by a British government came with the 1964 Industrial Training Act, which introduced a grant/levy system administered through specially created, occupationally-specific Industrial Training Boards (ITBs). As early as 1972, however, a Department of Employment report, which laid the ground for the establishment of the Manpower Services Commission (MSC), attacked the ITBs for their inability:

- to cover the whole economy;
- to represent small firms;
- to represent job functions which cross occupational sectors;
- to provide a general advisory service on training for the whole country;
- to cope with local and regional labour markets;
- to provide a central focus for management training.
  (DE, 1972)

Other criticisms of ITBs centred around their bureaucratic behaviour, their failure to deal with skill shortages and their failure to meet the needs of young people in semi-skilled and unskilled jobs (Farley, 1985). Despite such criticisms, ITBs did win praise for their influence on training standards. Even the 1972 report recognized that the ITBs had emphasized the need for trained trainers and had formalized 'on-the-job' training by insisting on specified objectives (DE, 1972). The ITBs were cut back by the MSC and have since metamorphosed as some 126 Industrial Training Organizations (ITOs), but they attract some of the same criticisms that haunted the ITBs, notably that they should pay more attention to the needs of small firms, ensure they identify clearly with a specific industrial sector and play a full part in the national training infrastructure (Berry-Lound, 1994).

The 1964 Act could be said to have been flawed from the outset for, as Marsden and Ryan (1991) have asserted, the ITBs were only intended to correct the market in training rather than to replace it. Since the ITBs were abolished, report after report has shown that British employers invest very little in training compared to their foreign competitors and, when recession comes, training is often the first item to be cut. In 1996 just under 14 per cent of the working population of Great Britain was receiving some form of job-related training. Even taking into account the economic recession of the early 1990s, this figure has only risen by some 5 per cent since 1984 (LMT, 1996). Felstead and Green's (1993) research challenges the conventional wisdom that companies cut training during economic recession, suggesting that some companies actually increase their levels of training in order to stay competitive. They add, however, that the type of training being delivered tends to be short courses and that:

> Only a small proportion of those employees in training are working towards qualifications that would seem to equip them for the sorts of high-skill/technological frontier jobs upon which it is regularly said that future prosperity depends. (p.26)

This antipathy to investment in training has been translated into lack of status for the trainers themselves and poor management training in comparison to other countries.

The role of employers as defined by policy-makers

Despite the poor record of British employers *vis-à-vis* training, government intervention to improve employers' attitudes to and investment in a level and quality of training, which would have wider national benefits, has tended to take the form of what Coffield, in writing about the concept of 'enterprise education', has called 'a farrago of "hurrah" words' (Coffield, 1990, p.258). Since Callaghan's 1976 Ruskin speech, education and training White Papers have carried the explicit message that employers will play a major role in VET initiatives.

The influential 1981 White Paper, *A New Training Initiative* (NTI) (DE, 1981), outlined four key ways in which government was seeking the cooperation and commitment of employers in:

- providing better and more integrated training for those young people whom they employed straight from school;

- becoming the main sponsors for the new YTS programme;
- taking the main responsibility for training and re-training adults;
- supporting the shift away from qualifications and apprenticeships based on time-serving.

As well as being expected to provide placements for the new scheme, 'industry', acting as a collective whole, was also told that it would be expected to organize a complete transformation of the vocational qualifications system 'by 1985 at the latest' and, moreover, that 'Government will make financial support for skill training in industry at the enhanced levels... increasingly conditional upon steps towards implementation of these reforms' (DE, 1981, p.11).

In seeking to transform the country's VET system, NTI has the hallmarks of the 'dig for victory' campaign during World War II. Employers are referred to throughout the document as an homogeneous group, in the same way as colleges of further education, careers officers and voluntary organizations. There are hints that employers might need more than exhortation to play their part, for example, in the suggestions that training could be tax-deductible and that individual employees might contribute something to the costs of training, but the overall commitment of employers to the principles of the NTI is not debated.

Further evidence for the centrality of NTI in setting the employer-led agenda lies in its call for a system of vocational qualifications based on 'standards of competence', though an earlier document, the MSC's *A Programme for Action-training for Skills* in 1977, had first raised the concept of 'standards' (Raggatt and Unwin, 1991b). In 1988, two years after the establishment of the National Council for Vocational Qualifications (NCVQ), the White Paper *Employment for the 1990s* re-emphasized the employer-led nature of the NVQs:

> The standards must be identified by employers and they must be nationally recognised. Thus we need a system of employer-led organisations to identify and establish standards and secure recognition of them, sector by sector, or occupational group by occupational group. (ED, 1988, p. 33)

The inadequacy and inappropriateness of the competence-based model as a foundation for a system of vocational qualifications has and is being heavily criticized (for example, Beaumont, 1995; Hyland, 1994; Jones and Moore, 1995; Marshall, 1991). Here, however, it is the failure of the employer-led concept, supposedly underpinning the competence-based model, which is of primary interest. For, despite the establishment of industry lead bodies to identify sectoral standards of competence, research has shown that the vast majority of employers have not led this so-called 'skills revolution'. On the contrary, employers are rejecting NVQs *en masse* (Robinson, 1996). On the whole, NVQs have been taken up in government-sponsored training schemes, which demand that trainees work towards NVQs. If employers have introduced NVQs for their workforce it is usually in order to recognize existing skills levels or to motivate operative level employees (Unwin, 1991). From their roots in the MSC's attempts to impose a national training strategy, NVQs reflect what Field (1995, p.30) has called 'the ideas and aspirations of a small coalition of modernising civil servants and highly placed training professionals'.

It is ironic to note that, while the landscape of VET appears fractured and littered with discredited initiatives, those same 'modernizers' referred to by Field have demonstrated a continuity of purpose stretching back to the early 1970s and which still carries on today.

Vocational preparation as a panacea

Prior to the introduction of NVQs, the 'modernizers' reached their first mountain top with the Youth Training Scheme (YTS) which was designed around a complex mixture of ideas, both about what school leavers needed to make them employable and what the country needed its school leavers to be (Finn, 1987; Keep, 1986; Silver, 1988). The initial one-year scheme included, therefore, preparation for work, so-called 'core' and 'transferable' skills, on- and off-the-job training, guidance and counselling, and opportunities for tasting different occupational areas. By blurring the long-established demarcation lines between education and training, YTS enabled the Further Education Unit (FEU) to promote its work on vocational preparation and 'life and social skills'.

Here we see the direct influence of Callaghan's 1976 Ruskin Speech which, as Wellington (1993) suggests, brought into common parlance two concepts which have dominated government thinking about VET: that a key factor in the rise of unemployment is a shortage of skills; and that there exists a set of common skills which, if they have them, make young people more employable.

As Finn (1987) has pointed out, Callaghan's speech had been preceded by an outpouring of complaints from prominent business leaders that schools were failing to give young people even the basic skills needed in the workplace and that many school leavers were unemployable because they lacked the 'right' attitude to work. Despite the fact that economic and labour market studies in the 1970s were showing young people competing with older workers for jobs they would previously have gained, and that the nature of work was changing, the MSC's youth programmes took a decidedly 'educational' approach (see Jonathan, 1987). The problem was perceived as the mismatch between school leavers' skills and attitudes and the needs of industry: the solution was to be found in vocational preparation.

The history and development of vocational preparation has been extensively critiqued (for example, Bates *et al.*, 1984; Dale, 1985). On the whole, the critics have castigated the vocational preparation movement for being dishonest in its intentions. They argue that vocationalism uses jargon and rhetoric to dress up a curriculum which is chiefly concerned with getting young people to 'know their place' both at work and in society. Yet, as Watts (1983) has argued, the concept of employment has, for centuries, had a powerful influence on the education system, causing that system to perform four functions on behalf of employers:

1. selection (via the curriculum and qualifications);
2. socialization (school mirrors the world of work in terms of structure, ethos and culture);
3. orientation (through careers education and learning about the workplace);
4. preparation (employment-related skills and knowledge).

The young people (as well as the adults benefiting from access courses to the Training Opportunities Programmes) who poured into colleges of further education in the late 1970s and early 1980s presented a dilemma to lecturers and administrators. Unlike the generally cooperative day-release students, including apprentices who, of course, had been selected on academic achievement grounds, this new army of youth represented a considerable pedagogic and curriculum challenge.

At that time these students formed the majority of the school-leaving population. Their 'attitudes' in relation to work were, like most 16-year-olds', in need of some development, but their level of general educational attainment was more disturbing. In addition, their school experience had taught them that the academic curriculum was incapable of valuing their contributions.

To critique the MSC's attempts to provide vocational preparation programmes for young people without at the same time critiquing the experiences those same young people had had in school has produced a literature which is unbalanced. In addition, it has done little to advance the cause of a truly equitable curriculum for young people up to the age of 18. The emphasis on critiquing the concept of vocationalism drew attention away from valuable research emerging from adult education showing the range of learning experiences which are to be found both within the formal workplace and, informally, associated with the workplace. Most damaging of all, by concentrating on the desires of the politicians to confront the problem of mass youth unemployment, the often genuine concerns of employers in regard to young people's basic skill levels have been demonized as part of the ideological battle to put vocationalism on the agenda. Anyone who worked in further education in the 1970s and early 1980s knew that the numeracy and literacy levels of many young people were unacceptably low, yet there is nothing in the literature to suggest how allowing schools and colleges to remain 'untainted' by vocationalism would improve this situation.

The failure of employers to invest in workplace training and the lack of attention by government and the educational establishment to vocational education have both conspired to produce a situation in the UK in which vocational education and training is still having to fight for equal status alongside the academic route.

Casualization and the youth labour market

Finegold and Soskice (1988) have argued that the UK's inability to develop an effective vocational education and training strategy is partly a result of a failure to balance the needs and interests of employers, education and government – a tripartite balance which operates in some other developed countries. One of the consequences of that imbalance has been an unregulated market for youth labour, with some employers paying relatively high wages to 16–18-year-olds for jobs without structured training (Evans and Heinz, 1994).

The growth of part-time, temporary jobs, notably in the expanded retail sector, where the introduction of Sunday shopping and late-night opening is largely staffed by teenagers, is having a striking effect on the youth labour market. It is now possible, for example, for young people to earn the equivalent of the YT allowance by working a couple of shifts in a supermarket. Given that so-called full-time education students can spend as little as 18 hours a week attending classes in school or college, the availability of part-time work may be helping these young people to ignore the temptations of the full-time labour market (Fergusson and Unwin, 1996). In the late 1990s, these young people could be said to have taken the initiative, albeit by default, of putting into practice a dual system of post-16 experience.

We know, however, that this dual system does not work for all young people. Significant numbers of 16-year-olds who choose to stay in full-time education leave after one year and up to one-fifth of A-level candidates fail to get the required grades for entry to higher education. There is, therefore, a large pool of young people at 16, 17 and 18 for whom a credible and rigorous work-based route might prove to be a much more suitable alternative.

The potential of the Modern Apprenticeship

Before the 1970s, with its rise in government-sponsored programmes designed to contain youth unemployment, there was, in a sense, a collective national memory about vocational qualifications and training which, at the youth stage, was based upon an understanding and recognition of the concept of 'apprenticeship' (Unwin, 1996). In the last 20 years, and largely as a combined result of a lack of investment in training by employers and ineptitude by government, that collective memory has been gradually fractured – hence the distorted image of work-based learning in general.

In 1993, the government announced it was launching the Modern Apprenticeship (MA), a new initiative which, unlike previous apprenticeships, would be open to young women as well as to young men and would be available in non-traditional as well as traditional apprenticeship occupational sectors. The MA began life in September 1994, limited in its first year to 14 sectors. It is now available throughout the UK in over 50 sectors.

Based on training frameworks developed by ITOs in conjunction with TECs, the MA is open to young people between the ages of 16 and 24 and leads to a minimum NVQ Level 3, supplemented by GNVQ Core Skills units and, in some cases, by BTEC qualifications which lie outside the NVQ framework. Some apprentices, notably in engineering and chemicals, spend the whole of their first year studying full-time in a college, whilst others follow the traditional day-release pattern (Unwin and Wellington, 1995a). Although the involvement of trades unions is not a condition of the MA, the TUC has welcomed the initiative and is encouraging its members to play a part in the development of the MA frameworks.

For those with long memories and, given the adage that there is nothing new in education or training just a reinvention of wheels, the arrival of the MA might prompt the question: how does it differ from the concept of the two-year YTS scheme introduced in 1986? Under that scheme, trainees were expected to achieve four outcomes: competence in job-specific skills; competence in a range of core skills; the ability to transfer skills and knowledge; and personal effectiveness. When NVQs were introduced and YTS switched to YT, trainees were also expected to gain, at minimum, a Level 2 NVQ. Trainees could have employed status and some received wages above the YT allowance level direct from their employer. The advocates of the MA would argue, however, that there are significant differences between the old and the new.

Under the MA the role of the ITO is central in terms of developing an apprenticeship curriculum which both meets the needs of industry and offers a broad vocational education to young people. It is indicative of the widespread criticism of NVQs that simply offering an NVQ Level 3 as the content of that curriculum has been rejected by many ITOs. By including extra inputs on top of the NVQ, the MA frameworks are also reintroducing the notion of a common curriculum for apprentices as opposed to the individualistic curriculum produced under the NVQ model. The MA could, therefore, act as a test-bed for measuring the applicability and appropriateness of NVQs as the qualifications which should underpin the work-based route.

The emphasis on designing an appropriate and common curriculum for apprentices has brought further education colleges back into the part-time work-based route market, a role which many of them lost when NVQs were introduced as qualifications to be gained solely in the workplace. There is an explicit intention in the MA to integrate college and workplace learning and to revitalize a partnership approach to the design and delivery of the initiative. In addition, the reversion to the name 'apprenticeship' may signal an acknowledgement that effective and meaningful training takes time. The MA is not time-served, in the way that the traditional apprenticeships were, and the link to NVQs implies that time is an irrelevance, given that the competence approach advocates individual rates of achievement. However, there are indications that employers are signing up to a commitment of at least two years to their apprentices. The extent to which the

MA can embrace the developing holistic and empowering vision of workplace learning, as espoused by such writers as Engestrom (1990), remains to be seen (Fuller and Unwin, 1996).

Early research into the MA by Unwin and Wellington (1995a) suggests that young people are attracted to a work-based route which offers them the chance to train with a named, and hopefully reputable, employer, to achieve one or more nationally recognized qualifications, to have access to higher levels of education and training, including higher education, and to earn a reasonable wage. While the apprentices in the MA's first year could be said to be a self-selecting group, their comments in relation to schooling were illuminating. Many of these young people had done well enough at GCSE to enable them to take A-level courses or Advanced GNVQs, but they wanted to continue their learning in a different environment, one that offered new challenges and where they would be treated as adults. They were not rejecting education *per se* and many said they would eventually like to study for a degree.

Around one quarter of the apprentices surveyed in their first year of the MA had previously begun or completed A-level courses. The most common subjects taken were mathematics, physics, geography and chemistry. Apprentices were generally critical of A-levels, claiming that: they represented a return to didactic teaching, whereas GCSEs had been delivered using a variety of teaching and learning strategies; that they were not a good preparation for the world of work; and that the terminal examination would not enable them to demonstrate their true potential. The difference in level between GCSE and A-level, and in teaching and learning styles, had left some young people feeling they had been unprepared for the A-level route. In particular, they talked about the restrictive nature of A-levels, whereby a student can study for two years and fail to show their true potential. What the apprentices were looking for was a route that gave them 'the chance to shine' (Unwin and Wellington, 1995a).

If the MA can develop models of workplace learning which embrace well-integrated periods of learning in colleges or training centres, then full-time education in schools and colleges may find it can look to the MA for sources of inspiration and good practice.

The MA does, however, have the weight of UK policy failure behind it and, ultimately, it could be wrecked by two problems which have bedevilled previous work-based routes. The first relates to how far employers will commit themselves to long-term investment in the training and vocational education of young people. The second problem concerns the competitive market for young people constructed by policy-makers who have set schools, colleges and training providers against each other. This is a market which benefits no one. As the brokers in the training market, TECs have targets to reach for both YT and MA places and, in their rush to meet those targets, there is a danger that TECs will place young people with employers who cannot or do not intend to meet the full MA requirements. The following conversation between two MA retail apprentices indicates that the young people themselves are well aware of the target-driven climate:

> *Apprentice 1*: The apprenticeship should be delegated to certain places only because I mean this kind of thing wouldn't be any good in say a single department store where they'd limit you or in a place where people know the training's rubbish or they don't do training....
>
> *Apprentice 2*: If that happens, it will end up like YT...somebody will start taking people without any GCSEs and sacking them after two years and it's not going to do the apprenticeship any good. (Unwin and Wellington, 1995b)

The introduction in 1991 of Training Credits (since 1993, Youth Credits) was supposedly designed to empower young people by attaching the funding directly to them. The failure of this fundamentally flawed concept needs noting here, for it has done nothing to advance the cause of the work-based route (Hodkinson *et al.*, 1996; Unwin, 1993).

Conclusion

The creation of a sustainable, coherent and credible work-based route with parity of status remains a major challenge in the UK. Many young people want to continue their education beyond 16 in a route which combines the best of workplace and college-based learning. As has been noted here, the casualization of work has allowed a situation in which full-time students can spend as many hours in the workplace as they spend in the classroom, yet these two experiences remain completely separated, with the workplace element denied any formal recognition.

To create a work-based curriculum which develops sector-specific skills alongside a broader vocational education and which is capable of preparing young people to move across sectors and to continue their academic development, we need to acknowledge the powerful appeal and under-used potential of the workplace as a site for learning. We also need to recognize that the term 'work-place' can include sites of unpaid, as well as paid work, and the public as well as the private sector. The casualization of the labour market has been alluded to earlier in this chapter and there are those who would argue that the end of work is nigh, particularly as a result of new technologies. But there is a more compelling argument which recognizes the centrality of work, in the broadest sense of that term, in people's lives (Quicke, 1996; Spours and Young, 1988).

That we have allowed the vocational curriculum to be reduced to a series of tick-boxes is now, albeit very belatedly, being recognized as a disaster, but that does not mean that a credible and enriching alternative cannot be found. Teaching and developing skilled people has nothing to do with the tainted and rhetoric-bound crusade of vocationalism. It has everything to do with substantive and rigorous processes which bring together the best of on- and off-the-job experiences.

References

Bates, I, Clarke, J, Cohen, P, Finn, D, Moore, R and Willis, P (1984) *Schooling for the Dole?* London: Macmillan.

Beaumont, G (1995) *Review of 100 NVQs and SVQs: A Report Submitted to the DfEE*, London: DfEE.

Berry-Lound, D (1994) *ITO Non-members Survey*, Sheffield: Employment Department.

Coffield, F (1990) 'From the Decade of the Enterprise Culture to the Decade of the TECs', in Esland, G (ed.) *Education, Training and Employment, Vol.2: The Educational Response*, Wokingham: Addison-Wesley.

Dale, R (ed.) (1985) *Education, Training and Employment*, Oxford: Pergamon.

Dearing, Sir Ron (1996) *Review of Qualifications for 16–19 Year Olds: Summary Report*, London: SCAA.

Department of Employment (1972) *Training for the Future*, London: HMSO.

Department of Employment (1981) *A New Training Initiative: A Programme for Action*, London: HMSO.

Employment Department (1988) *Employment for the 1990s*, Sheffield: Employment Department.

Engestrom, Y (1990) *Learning, Working and Imagining: Twelve Studies in Activity Theory*, Helsinki: Orienta-Konsultit Oy.

Evans, K and Heinz, W A (1994) *Becoming Adults in England and Germany*, London: Anglo-German Foundation.

Farley, M (1985) 'Trends and Structural Changes in English Vocational Education', in Dale, R (ed.) *Education, Training and Employment*, Oxford: Pergamon Press.

Felstead, A and Green, F (1993) *Cycles of Training? Evidence from the British Recession of the Early 1990s*, Discussion Papers in Economics No. 93/3, Department of Economics: University of Leicester.

Fergusson, R and Unwin, L (1996) 'Making Better Sense of Post-16 Destinations: a Case Study of an English Shire County', *Research Papers in Education*, **11**, 1, 53–81.

Field, J (1995) 'Reality Testing in the Workplace: are NVQs "Employment-led"?' in Hodkinson, P and Issitt, M (eds) *The Challenge of Competence*, London: Cassell.

Finegold, D and Soskice, D (1988) 'The Failure of Training in Britain: Analysis and Prescription', *Oxford Review of Economic Policy*, **4**, 3.

Finn, D (1987) *Training Without Jobs*, Basingstoke: Macmillan.

Fuller, A and Unwin, L (1996) 'Reconceptualising Apprenticeship: Learning and Work', paper given to the Work and Learning Network Inaugural Conference, University of Sheffield, 14 November.

Hodkinson, P, Sparkes, A and Hodkinson, H (1996) *Tears and Triumphs*, London: David Fulton.

Hyland, T (1994) *Competence, Education and NVQs*, London: Cassell.

Jonathan, R (1987) 'The Youth Training Scheme and Core Skills: An Educational Analysis' in Holt, M (ed.) *Skills and Vocationalism: The Easy Answer*, Buckingham: Open University Press.

Jones, L and Moore, R (1995) 'Appropriating Competence: the Competency Movement, the New Right and the "Culture Change" Project', *British Journal of Education and Work*, **8**, 2, 78–92.

Keep, E (1986) *Designing the Stable Door: A Study of How the Youth Training Scheme Was Planned*, Warwick Papers in Industrial Relations No. 8, Industrial Relations Research Unit, University of Warwick.

Keep, E and Mayhew, K (1988) 'The Assessment: Education, Training and Economic Performance', *Oxford Review of Economic Policy*, **4**, 3, Autumn.

Labour Market Trends (LMT) (1996) *Labour Force Survey*, October, London: HMSO.

Marsden, D and Ryan, P (1991) 'Initial Training, Labour Market Structure and Public Policy: Intermediate Skills in British and German Industry', in Ryan, P (ed.) *International Comparisons of Vocational Education and Training for Intermediate Skills*, London: Falmer.

Marshall, K (1991) 'NVQs: An Assessment of the "Outcomes" Approach in Education and Training', *Journal for Further and Higher Education*, **15**, 3, 56–64.

Quicke, J (1996) 'Work, Education and Democratic Identity', *International Studies in Sociology of Education*, **6**, 1, 49–66.

Raggatt, P and Unwin, L (1991a) *Change and Intervention: Vocational Education and Training*, London: Falmer.

Raggatt, P and Unwin, L (1991b) 'Introduction: A Collection of Papers', in Raggatt, P and Unwin, L (1991a) *Change and Intervention: Vocational Education and Training*, London: Falmer.

Rainbird, H (1990) *Training Matters, Union Perspectives on Industrial Restructuring and Training*, Oxford: Blackwell.

Robinson, P (1996) *Rhetoric and Reality: Britain's New Vocational Qualifications and its Centre for Economic Performance*, London: London School of Economics.

Roderick, G and Stephens, M (eds) (1982) *The British Malaise*, London: Falmer.

Silver, H (1988) *Intentions and Outcomes, Vocationalism in Further Education*, London: Longman for FEU publications.

Spours, K and Young, M (1988) *Beyond Vocationalism*, London: Post-16 Education Centre Working Paper 4, Institute of Education, University of London.

Strong, M (1992) 'Self-help Learning: A Dual Concept', *International Journal of Lifelong Education*, **11**, 1, January – March.

Unwin, L (1991) 'NVQs and the Man-made Fibres Industry: A Case Study of Courtaulds Grafil Ltd', in Raggatt, P and Unwin, L (1991a) *Change and Intervention: Vocational Education and Training*, London: Falmer Press.

Unwin, L (1993) 'Training Credits: The Pilot Doomed to Succeed', in Richardson, W, Woolhouse, J and Finegold, D (eds) *The Reform of Post-16 Education and Training in England and Wales*, Harlow: Longman.

Unwin, L (1996) 'Employer-led Realities: Apprenticeship Past and Present', *Journal of Vocational Education and Training*, **48**, 1, 57–68.

Unwin, L and Wellington, J (1995a) 'Reconstructing the Work-based Route: Lessons from the Modern Apprenticeship', *Journal of Vocational Education and Training*, **47**, 6, 337–52.

Unwin, L and Wellington, J (1995b) 'Qualitative Research Data from a Study of Modern Apprenticeship funded by the DfEE Sheffield', University of Sheffield (unpublished).

Watts, A G (1983) *Education, Unemployment and the Future of Work*, Milton Keynes: Open University Press.

Wellington, J (1993) *The Work Related Curriculum*, London: Kogan Page.

CHAPTER 6

Core Skills, General Education and Unification in Post-16 Education

Andy Green

Introduction

The concept of 'core skills' – or 'key skills' as some now describe them (Dearing, 1996) – has become central to all policy debates around post-16 education and training. Exactly how these should be defined has been the subject of prolonged and, as yet, unresolved controversy. Different bodies, including the Confederation of British Industry (CBI), the Further Education Unit (FEU), the National Council for Vocational Qualifications (NCVQ), and the National Curriculum Council (NCC), have produced different inventories of core skills and there is still no definitive version. However, there is general agreement that competence in core skill areas, such as communication, numeracy, IT and problem-solving are important for individuals, both as learners in foundation education and training and as future employees in changing and flexible work roles. Beyond this, there is a common notion that core skills can act as a kind of catalyst for necessary reforms in post-compulsory education and training (PCET).

Critics of overspecialized A-levels (DES, 1988; FEU, 1990) have seen core skills as a way of introducing breadth and balance into the academic curriculum; advocates of competence-based vocational education have seen them as essential for promoting skills transfer and the portability of qualifications (Jessup, 1991); and supporters of the concept of a unified post-16 curriculum have seen them as a potential bridge between the academic and vocational tracks. Just about everyone recognizes that they are necessary building blocks for student progression to higher levels of education and training and for the achievement of the National Targets for Education and Training (NTETs). Some, like Nicholas Tate of the Schools Curriculum and Assessment Authority (SCAA), go even further and see them as a vehicle for reinserting moral values into the curriculum.

However, despite the almost totemic status that core skills have gained in specialist discourses around PCET, there is little evidence that core skills teaching is delivering the outcomes so frequently ascribed to it or hoped for it. Standards of attainment of students on vocational courses in maths and language are still widely held to be too low (Green, 1995; Green and Steedman, 1993; Smithers, 1993; Steedman and Hawkins, 1994; Wolf, 1992) – well below those achieved on comparable courses in countries like France, Germany and Sweden – and this is arguably one of the reasons for the low rates of completion and progression on many vocational courses (FEFC, 1994; Green and Ainley, 1995). Core skills have still not been introduced into A-level programmes and there is little evidence that their introduction into vocational qualifications has done much to bridge the divide between academic and vocational courses. Employers still frequently complain about the low standard of core skills amongst their young recruits (Brown and Scase, 1995) and there is, as yet, no evidence that the teaching of core skills has produced a generation of workers with more flexible skills. In fact, there is some evidence to the contrary, which shows that in certain areas of vocational training, such as NVQ Bricklaying, the introduction of competence-based approaches to core skills has actually reduced the generic competence of trainees, since they have only been taught to perform certain narrowly specified tasks without proper grounding in the core knowledge and skills that underpin these (Steedman and Hawkins, 1994).

Current concerns, such as those highlighted some while ago by the Smithers Channel Four documentary, 'All Our Futures', have led the Department for Education and Employment (DfEE) and the NCVQ to review the whole process of core skills learning on vocational courses. However, the remit of these reviews has been to investigate and improve the details of implementation, rather than to question the fundamental assumptions of the core skills approach. The 'Programme of Action' announced by the DfE in 1994 (OFSTED, 1994), for instance, called for actions to ensure greater quality and rigour through, *inter alia*, improvements in the external testing regime; more training of verifiers; clarification of knowledge required and grading criteria; clearer guidance for teachers and tightening of accreditation criteria. What the review has not done is to question whether a competence-based approach to the learning of core skills is at all adequate to the goals it has set itself, not least to the goal of creating a more unified post-16 curriculum and qualifications system.

The argument of this chapter is that this approach is fundamentally flawed and not amenable to piecemeal modification and improvement. Core skills teaching is essentially a surrogate for the kind of continuing general education that is taught on vocational courses in many continental countries and cannot be more than a poor substitute for it. Furthermore, it is only through a more concerted and rigorous approach to the latter that the worthy objectives associated with core skills teaching can be achieved. The peculiarly English emphasis on the concept of core skills is the product of a particular pedagogic history and it is only by unravelling this that we can understand the policy trajectory and inherent limitations of the approach.

The history of the core skills concept in England and Wales

Core skills have emerged out of an historical absence in the UK. Alone among the major European nations in the 19th century, England developed a technical and vocational education that had no inherent connection with general education and schooling. On the Continent, and particularly in France and the German-speaking states, the typical form of vocational training was the state-sponsored trade school, which combined workshop training with systematic instruction in vocational theory and general education. In England, with its voluntarist traditions, there were few such schools and vocational education, as opposed to skills training, had to evolve in an *ad hoc* and relatively unsupported fashion (Day, 1987; Green, 1995; Scott Russell, 1869; Thompson, 1897). The normative model of skills training in 19th-century England was provided by the apprenticeship, which was essentially practical, employment-based and marginalized from mainstream education (Green, 1990). It involved no general education and often little vocational theory (Thompson, 1897). Technical education grew up as an adjunct to this. It was voluntary in attendance, poorly supported by employers and often desultory and unsystematic in character (Roderick and Stephens, 1978; Sadler, 1979). For many decades it remained unintegrated with apprentice training – until, in fact, the 1964 Industrial Training Act made day-release to colleges a statutory part of most apprenticeships (Perry, 1976). While technical courses included vocational theory, they generally excluded general education and academic subjects.

What subsequently developed was a skills-based model of training, quite distinct from the general and technical education model dominant on the Continent. This peculiarity, apart from being a major factor in reinforcing the low status of technical education – particularly in England and Wales – also left another important historical legacy. Where general culture should have been in vocational education there was a gap: to put it bluntly, no one knew what to teach apprentices and other vocational students by way of general education. The tradition of the 'practical man' did not suggest any obvious way of embedding general culture in vocational education. Since then we have been struggling to invent something.

Core skills have emerged as the favoured but unrealized surrogate for general education through a series of failed experiments. During the 1960s, colleges started to include courses of Liberal Studies on City & Guilds apprentice programmes. Generally, these courses did not go down very well with students who were unlikely to take seriously a subject which was non-examined and which was generally not esteemed within the ambience of the technical department and by the vocational lecturers. The outcome was a good deal of cultural dissonance and frustration on the part of students and lecturers alike.

Later, during the early 1970s, Liberal Studies was gradually replaced by a new mandatory and assessed component of City & Guilds courses: Communications Studies. This fared somewhat better than Liberal Studies, being demonstrably more practical and occupationally relevant. However, it was probably never fully naturalized by the typical vocational student.

The concept of core skills developed out of these failures in a series of initiatives from the late 1970s onwards. The area of core skills was first opened up and promoted, not as a measure for apprentice students – since apprenticeships were now in decline anyway – but for the so-called pre-vocational students, who represented a new constituency of college students appearing as a result of the mass youth unemployment of the late 1970s. These students were deemed not yet ready to choose a vocational specialism and often lacked general social and life skills – to the extent, so it was believed, that it might make them unemployable (Holland, 1976). The Social and Life Skills course which had been developed for use on the Youth Opportunities Programme (YOP) and, in a more sophisticated version, in Unified Vocational Preparation programmes (UVP), was now recast into something much more ambitious in the way of a core programme of social knowledge and skills learning. The foundation for all this was, of course, the FEU's *A Basis for Choice* (1979). This seminal document not only developed the notion of a core skills curriculum for vocational students but also early versions of individualized student work programmes, profiling and criterion-based assessment. It also became the basis for many of the major innovations in college teaching in the 1980s, including the Certificate of Pre-Vocational Education (CPVE), the progenitor of the more recent Diploma of Vocation Education and, in some respects, GNVQ.

Since the FEU first developed these notions of a core skills curriculum, the agenda has been taken up and promoted in different ways by different bodies. In 1989 the CBI in its key document *Towards a Skills Revolution* advocated that all training and vocational education should include the following common learning outcomes as 'core elements': 'Values and Integrity'; 'Effective Communication'; 'Application of Numeracy'; 'Applications of Technology'; 'Understanding of Work and the World'; 'Personal and Interpersonal Skills'; 'Problem-Solving' and 'Positive Attitudes to Change' (CBI, 1989, p.27). The CBI has continued to be a major force behind the promotion of core skills and, with its encouragement, core skills are now being included within NTETs for which the CBI was itself initially responsible.

In 1989 John MacGregor, then Secretary of State for Education, invited SEAC, NCC, NCVQ and FEU to develop definitions of core skills in six areas: Communication, Problem-solving, Personal Skills, Numeracy, IT, and Modern Foreign Language (Avis, 1992). The following year, NCC published *Core Skills, 16–19* (NCC, 1990) and NCVQ, *Core Skills in NVQs* (NCVQ, 1990). The proposals for core skills at A-level were eventually rejected for two reasons. First, the examining boards felt that they would rather use the limited amount of coursework assessment available for assessing subject knowledge, rather than core skills and, second, the government feared the inclusion of core skills would in some way 'distort' A-levels. Core skills may also have involved unwanted additional costs, not least in the provision of large numbers of additional teachers for communications, maths and modern languages.

However, while the core skills train was decisively derailed on the A-level track, it continued at full speed on the vocational tracks. Out of the NCVQ proposals came 'Core Skills Units' at four different levels in: Communications, Problem-Solving, Improving own Learning and Performance, Working with Others, Application of Number and IT. These were subsequently introduced into the NVQ framework, although without separate mandatory assessment. Subsequently, with the inauguration of the broadly based GNVQs in 1992, core skills came into their own. All GNVQs included Communication, Application of Number and IT as mandatory units and Foreign Language, Problem-solving and Personal Skills (working with others and improving learning performance) as additional and desirable outcomes. NCVQ policy, in common with that of the awarding bodies, is that these core skills should be taught in an 'integrated fashion' through the vocational elements, although being separately assessed. This policy is based on the notion of relevance and acceptability to students (Oates, 1994).

Core skills have thus become enshrined in most vocational courses for young people, but continue to be absent from academic courses. This outcome conforms to the historical logic of their development. They have been seen precisely as an alternative – for vocational students – to the general education whose historic pedagogic form has been exclusively associated with academic subjects, taken by a minority, rather than a form of general culture necessary for all. They are a product of the divided academic and vocational culture. The underlying assumptions behind and problems with this approach can be seen more clearly by contrasting it with the alternative model, which we will call the 'general and technical education paradigm', which is represented in current vocational courses in France, Germany, Japan and Sweden.

The 'core skills paradigm' and the 'general and technical education paradigm'

The general and technical education paradigm is based on the precept that vocational learning rests on a common foundation of general education or *culture générale*, as it is termed in France (Wolf, 1992). Three assumptions are associated with this. First, there is the principle, derived from the radicals of the French Revolution, that there is a minimum of general knowledge and culture that all young people are entitled to and should attain as part of their initiation as citizens (Brubaker, 1992; Weber, 1976). Second, there is the belief that the learning of technology and technical mastery is an extension of applied science or *la science industrielle* and not just a matter of technical skills. Third, there is the assumption that the technical knowledge and theory which underpin vocational practice and skill are knowledge which should be explicit and thus capable of being articulated in oral and written form. Being able to handle abstract knowledge and theory is seen as part of the analytical capacity that enables students to develop flexible and transferable skills and which will allow them to adapt to new situations and learn new skills as they develop at work. The grounding they receive in general education subjects is part of the process of developing these skills in analysis and clear expression.

The core skills paradigm rests on different assumptions. There has, historically, been no concept of a minimum cultural entitlement for all as a precondition of competent citizenship, because there has been no strong notion of citizenship as a social contract. Rather than any concept of a necessary and universal cultural minimum, the cultural criteria applied to the education of vocational students have been particularistic and selective, based on concepts of 'suitability' and 'relevance'. Suitability has been defined in terms of pre-given assumptions about the limited 'cultural capital' of particular social groups and relevance has meant predominantly relevance to future work roles – as defined by employers – rather than relevance to future roles as citizens. In the English context, technical knowledge and skills have also embodied different assumptions. In the apprentice tradition, craft learning meant socialization into a particular work culture and the acquisition, through guided practice, of certain manipulative skills underpinned by a minimum of 'useful knowledge' which was often no more than rules of thumb. With the decline of the time-served apprenticeship, and the advent of competence-based learning, this already 'lean' notion of skill has become more minimalist, both culture- and theory-free. Competence-based learning, derived from behaviourist principles, defines skill as the ability to perform pre-given tasks with predictable accuracy (Ainley, 1993). Knowledge and theory are important only in so far as they are necessary to competent performance, and may be 'tacit' or non-articulated. So long as the student can 'do' there is little need to know 'why', or to be able to articulate 'how'. General education is only necessary to the extent that it 'underpins' competent performance in expected work tasks; it can therefore be reduced to core skills. It is assumed that the logical, analytical and expressive abilities, often associated with the acquisition of a good general education, can be delivered through core skills learning, which is generally 'embedded' in vocational skills.

The differences between these two models, and the limitations of the core skills approach, can be further illustrated through a comparative assessment of the 'content' and 'process' typical of a number of vocational courses in the UK and comparable courses in countries like France, Germany, Japan and Sweden which, broadly speaking, adopt the general and technical education paradigm. Vocational courses in the comparator counties vary considerably, of course, and there is no attempt here to explore the differences between them. However, what will be illustrated is that there are indeed common characteristics to these courses which are absent from those in the UK. Comparisons of content will concentrate on the range of general education subjects studied on vocational courses, the time devoted to them and the standards and levels of achievement expected in core skill areas. Comparisons of process will focus on modes of standard-setting and 'content' specification, modes of delivery and learning and forms of assessment. Courses compared will be those within or equivalent to the vocational Level 2 and 3 courses in the UK, including those which provide general vocational education and those providing occupationally specific training. For the UK, therefore, the focus will be on GNVQ and NVQ courses at Levels 2 and 3.

Content

The awarding bodies for the major vocational qualifications in England and Wales, now subsumed under the GNVQ and NVQ frameworks (SNVQs and SVQs for Scotland), do not specify the content of courses. According to NCVQ methodology, qualifications are based on the achievement of certain outcomes which are specified in terms of elements of competence, performance criteria and range statements. The content of what is taught is not detailed in terms of traditional syllabuses; rather it is inferred from these criteria by teachers and instructors. There are also no specifications as to the length and modes of learning. This makes it somewhat difficult to assess the precise range of what is actually covered by students who submit for assessment. Nevertheless, from the assessment criteria, which are specified in various units of competence, it is possible to gain some idea of what students would normally be expected to have done.

Neither GNVQs nor NVQs have any compulsory general education in the sense of the traditional subjects which come under that rubric in schools. Students may opt to take certain additional units, such as in a modern foreign language, which would appear similar to traditional general education subjects, but these are not required. What is required is that they demonstrate competence in the core skill areas of Communications, Application of Number and IT. In the case of NVQs these skills are not separately assessed, but their attainment is inferred from demonstration of competence in vocational skills which are deemed to require them. In the case of GNVQs, core skills are separately assessed, although not graded, but here also they may be acquired in the course of vocational learning without any separate teaching. It is impossible to say, therefore, how much time is spent on them, and this will vary from centre to centre. There has been concern, however, that whatever time it is, it is not enough (FEFC, 1994). Given that core skills only represent three out of 12 compulsory units on the GNVQ Advanced, and given that the average amount of class contact for students on these courses is typically between 10 to 20 hours per week (FEFC, 1994; Smithers, 1993), it can be assumed that the study of core skills per week is well below ten hours. According to the national survey of GNVQs in 1993–4 conducted by Alison Wolf and the FEU (FEU/IOE/Nuffield, 1994), the modal number of classroom hours timetabled for GNVQs was 12. About 80 per cent of the respondents indicated that they allocated three or fewer lessons per week to core skills and a third of subject team leaders said that they did not allocate any separate lessons for core skills teaching (FEU/IOE/Nuffield, 1994, p.46).

By comparison, students on similar vocational courses in France, Germany and Japan spend considerable time studying a wide range of general subjects. In France, students taking vocational baccalaureat programmes, which are broadly taken to be the French equivalent of the British Level 3 qualifications (Green and Steedman, 1993), have a very intensive and wide programme of general education. *Baccalauréat professionel* courses, which students take over three or more years, generally involve 30 to 35 hours per week in the classroom, 13 hours of which is spent studying general education subjects. These include: maths (2 hours); modern foreign language (three hours); contemporary studies (two hours) and art (two hours) (Young *et al.*, 1995).

In German vocational education there is the same concentration on general education. The *Abitur* in Business Studies, like the French *baccalauréat*, is a three-year academic/vocational course leading to vocational studies at university and involves 35 to 37 hours of class teaching per week, including general subjects such as German, maths, English, two sciences, history, geography and a second foreign language. Apprentice training courses in the Dual System, most of which reach standards judged equivalent to a Level 3 NVQ (Steedman and Green, 1996), normally involve two days per week studying at the vocational college, the *Berufsschule*, where the time is divided between vocational theory and general education.

The pattern is the same in the vocational high schools in Japan, whose graduates have been judged to attain standards similar to those on BTEC National Diplomas (Prais, 1987). Here students divide their three years of study almost equally between vocational studies, which are largely theoretical in nature, and general education subjects including Japanese, maths, social science and natural science.

We cannot make comparisons between the standards reached in most of these general education subjects by students in France, Germany and Japan and those reached by students in Britain since vocational students in Britain do not take them. However, comparisons are often made between the attainment level in the core skills areas of number/maths and communication/native language of British GNVQ and NVQ students and of comparable students abroad. Evidence from recent inspections and other surveys indicates that many students on vocational courses in England are experiencing difficulty in core skill areas such as number and communication (ALBSU, 1993; FEFC, 1994; Green and Ainley, 1995; OFSTED/Audit Commission, 1993).

Comparative studies conducted by the National Institute of Economic and Social Research in the 1980s on the attainments of craft students in France, Germany and England concluded that standards in maths in Germany and France were generally higher than in the UK (Steedman, 1988). There are particular weaknesses in mathematics within the English system and this has been borne out by a study by Steedman and Green for the Government Skills Audit (1996). Evaluations conducted by three English vocational experts and an FEFC

Inspector together with members of the French national and regional inspectorates responsible for vocational education suggested that: 'the gap between the general education base developed by the vocational bac students and the NVQ 3 students is a substantial one' (HMI, 1993, p.24).

It would appear, therefore, that not only are UK vocational students following a narrower course post-16 than their counterparts in France, Germany and Japan; they are also achieving lower standards of attainment in the core skills of communication and application of number.

Process

The second area of differentiation between the core skills and the general and vocational education paradigms relates to the theory and practice of learning and particularly to the processes of standard-setting, teaching and assessment. This is the area where, under the influence of the NCVQ, British vocational courses have been most innovative and where they have been most criticized (Smithers, 1993; Steedman and Hawkins, 1994; Wolf, 1992). It is also the area where they have most diverged from the more 'traditional' practices of courses operating under the general education paradigm in other countries. The differences are systematic and patterned and derive fundamentally from the divergent basic assumptions of the two paradigms, with the core skills paradigm starting from the position of competence and the general and vocational education model starting from the position of knowledge. Quite different principles of specification, learning delivery and assessment follow from these different starting positions.

Standard-setting

Under the core skills paradigm the overriding objective is that students or trainees should demonstrate competent performance of certain tasks. In the case of NVQs these tasks are derived by the lead bodies from a consideration of what is typically required now in particular occupations. GNVQs are also vocationally related but in a more general sense and here the NCVQ determines the attainment criteria with reference also to the requirements of higher level education and training courses. The purpose of standard-setting is to specify the criteria for competent performance, thus allowing the award to be assessed and certificated. How the competences are acquired is not thought to be the responsibility of the standard-setting bodies, ie, the NCVQ and the Awarding and Validating Bodies (AVBs): this is up to the individual learners and their instructors and teachers. In fact it is considered desirable that the process should remain as flexible as possible so that it can be adapted to the different needs of the learners and to their different circumstances. No stipulations are made for either NVQs or for GNVQs regarding the length or mode of learning, although assessment centres do, of course, have to be approved. Furthermore, since it is the performance outcomes that matter and not the acquisition of knowledge *per se*, specification of knowledge requirements remains low, being limited to whatever underpinning knowledge is deemed to be necessary for competent performance, much of which has to be judged by the instructors and assessors themselves (Jessup, 1991).

The effect of this 'outcomes' approach is a form of standard-setting that is radically unfamiliar to most practitioners and learners. There are no syllabuses laying down the detailed content of topics to be covered, no directives as to the amount of learning time that should be spent on them, and few directives as to appropriate learning methods.

This new methodology has caused considerable consternation amongst teachers who claimed they did not understand the jargon of the elements and criteria and who simply did not know what to teach (Spours, 1995). It has also invoked considerable criticism from commentators such as Smithers, who claim that the criteria lack clarity and rigour, as well as from the FEFC and OFSTED inspectors. Wolf has gone further in arguing that it is simply impossible to specify in words the precise standards of the performances to be demonstrated (Wolf, 1995). The NCVQ has not conceded that the principle of specifying performance outcomes rather than learning content and processes is wrong. However, after criticism by OFSTED (1994) and the FEFC (1994), they are now inserting into the range statements much more detail to indicate what should be taught. The fact that something like a syllabus with guidance notes for teachers is now beginning to reappear, albeit furtively, does suggest that the original principle of trying to specify outcomes, but not the process and content, was misguided.

By contrast to all this, in countries adhering to the general and vocational education paradigm the standard-setting and specification process has remained far more traditional. Standards for vocational courses are generally set by the national education ministries (or the *Bundesinstitut für Berufsbildung (BIBB)* and *Länder* ministries in Germany) with input from employer and teacher bodies. These tend to be laid out in mandatory courses of study which include detailed syllabuses and copious guidance for teachers (sometimes mandatory) on learning methods and forms of assessment. They are invariably accompanied by a range of textbooks required or at least approved by the ministries, which include exercises and other work material for students. Syllabus specifications will normally include 'can do' statements about tasks that students should be able to perform, but they will also contain detailed guidance on topics to be covered and knowledge to be acquired.

Delivery and the learning process

The second area of difference in the two paradigms relates to delivery or to the learning process itself. Again, the differences follow on from the divergent concepts of knowledge and competence that are embodied in the two paradigms. Under the core skills paradigm it is the performance that counts; the knowledge acquired is only important to the extent that it is essential for competent performance. Given that traditional subjects are based on knowledge definitions and boundaries, clearly under this principle even core skills such as Communication and the Application of Number cannot be taught as subjects, even if to the lay person they have more than a passing resemblance to the more traditional subjects of English and maths. NCVQ and the AVBs thus recommend that the learning of the core skills of Communications, Application of Number and IT are integrated with or 'embedded in' the process of learning vocational skills. Colleges, in fact, frequently offer extra support through workshops for those who need it.

It remains the case, however, that most of the core skills learning occurs within and as part of vocational learning. This is in sharp contrast to the practice in countries adopting the general and vocational education paradigm, where the native language and maths are invariably taught as separate subjects and by specialist teachers. In the best of this practice, teaching is related to the vocational specialism of the student, but nevertheless remains separately taught and assessed (Wolf, 1992).

The advantage of the integrated method of core skills teaching is said to be that it affords greater motivation for students who are 'turned off' by traditional school-type lessons in English and maths. This may well be the case, but the advantage may be gained at the expense of marginalizing the core skills to the point where they are not adequately learnt. Both FEFC (1994) and OFSTED (1994) have noted that there are often not enough specialist core skills teachers involved on teams delivering GNVQs and that the provision of support workshops is often poorly coordinated with the mainstream teaching for the units.

The approach adopted to the teaching of maths and language in France and Germany is often thought to have a number of advantages. The use of specialist teachers and the identifiable curriculum location of the subjects tend to underline their importance to both staff and students (Wolf, 1992). The maintenance of subject boundaries, traditionally derived from the defining methodologies, concepts and knowledge fields of respective disciplines, underlines the importance of coherent, sequential and accumulative approaches to learning. The frequent use of interactive whole-class teaching methods, as opposed to the individualized and resource-based learning often predominant on English courses, provides a structured approach to learning which reinforces norms regarding standards to be achieved and underpins the expected pace of learning (Reynolds and Farrell, 1996). Finally, and not least, the widespread use of textbooks and published materials not only frees the teacher from the labour of producing individualized learning materials but helps to ensure consistency of methods, coverage and standards across learning sites (Green and Steedman, 1993).

There are, of course, problems associated with the more 'structured' subject approach to the teaching of core skills. It generally involves teaching to a class norm which can cause difficulties in classes with very mixed attainments. This should not, however, be an overriding problem on courses such as GNVQ which normally have selected intakes. Students can also find it boring unless a very high level of interaction is maintained in the classroom and this requires considerable teacher skill and good class order. There are also, inevitably, complaints from French and German vocational students that much of what they learn in general education is not strictly relevant to their vocational goals, although one wonders if they may not think differently about this in retrospect when promotion at work has imposed greater demands on their core skills. These are perennial problems and, of course, precisely the ones which advocates of integrated core skills teaching would advance as justifications for their approach. Clearly there are arguments on both sides. However, given such evidence as we have about the low standards of core skills amongst many of the vocational students in England, there must be a case for asking whether the gains of the integrated approach have not been bought at too high a price.

Modes of assessment

The third area of difference between the two paradigms relates to modes of assessment. Much has been written about the problems of assessment on NVQs and GNVQs in terms of the cost, bureaucratic demands and reliability and consistency of the procedures. There is no need to reiterate this here. However, it is worth pointing to the essential differences between assessment methods on these courses and those in some of the other countries considered here. NCVQ philosophy emphasizes above all the importance of competent performance. Knowledge, as has been noted, is secondary. It follows from this that the major form of assessment is through the observation of performance, whether this be manipulative tasks or human interaction. Written evidence is, of course, used as a supplement in assessment for NVQs, and extensively so on GNVQs, but it is always in a sense a secondary or proxy kind of evidence for competent perform-ance. Under the general and vocational education paradigm, on the other hand, there are two things to be assessed: performance and knowledge. Performance is assessed through observation, as in the British case, but knowledge is also separately assessed, usually through a combination of externally set and marked written exams and internally assessed coursework assignments.

Neither system is perfect. Written exams are rightly said to have limited validity, even if they are relatively reliable. They mainly test people's ability to pass exams. Internally assessed coursework and performance observation can lack reliability and consistency, although they are closer to assessing what actually matters. There are at least three major advantages, however, of the traditional French and German method of assessment. First, it uses a mixture of assessment tools, which acts as a check against the major weaknesses of each. For instance, if there is a problem about the authenticity of student coursework and the consist-ency of internal marking, then the external written exams can, to some degree, compensate for this. Second, the combination of methods used ensures that theoretical knowledge is assessed as well as skilled performance. This is important, since assessment of performance by observation can never be so comprehensive as to cover all the situations in which competent performance is required. Assessment of theory ensures at least that students are assessed on their understanding of the principles underlying practice, from which it can be inferred that they can adapt their practice to different situations. Third, the mixed assessment regime takes account of the reality that all assessment methods are imperfect and to some degree subjective. NCVQ methodology involves the dangerously naïve assumption that standards can be articulated with a scientific rigour and precision which allows assessment to occur with minimum recourse to the judgement of the assessor. Assessment in France and Germany, on the contrary, recognizes the inevitable centrality of the experience and judgement of instructors and assessors. Standard-setting does not aspire to pseudo-scientific precision and accuracy. It indicates the knowledge, topics and skills which should be assessed and leaves the question of standards largely to the accumulated and, hopefully, consensual judgement of the teachers, instructors, juries and markers who are variously involved in the process.

Beyond this, and importantly, there is the strict regulation of the process, absent in NCVQ methodology, which acts in substantial part as a guarantor of the quality of student outcomes. It should be noted that in the German Dual System, widely regarded as the very hallmark of quality in training, the vast majority (over 90 per cent) of apprentices gain their certificates (Wolf, 1995). Assessment provides the final seal of approval: it does not act as the main definer of quality (Wolf, 1995). By contrast, in the British system, assessment and outcomes are not only a means of examination, they are also the primary instruments for course specification, quality control, teacher evaluation and, increasingly, funding. Too much has been laid at their door.

Conclusions and policy implications

The argument of this chapter has been that the core skills paradigm represents an impoverished form of general education, which is neither adequately delivering the minimum basic skills normally associated with an effective general education, such as verbal articulacy, logical skills and mathematical literacy, nor even attempting to impart a foundation of scientific and humanistic culture adequate to the demands of active citizenship in modern societies. This in itself, if true, represents a major indictment of the enterprise. However, the critique must go wider than this, since core skills fall short on another count central to the reform of post-16 education, which is that they fail to provide the basis for a workable unified curriculum.

A unified curriculum, containing different pathways within it, must have some principle of unification – there must be something holding it together over and above the formal structure, otherwise it will not be perceived as in any sense unified, even if it is notionally part of a single framework. There must be some unity at the level of the underlying aims and objectives. This unity palpably cannot be provided by core skills for a number of reasons. First, core skills were not originally designed with reference to the entire post-16 system of curricula and qualifications – they were essentially only for vocational courses. It is no wonder that they have not been introduced into A-levels since they rest on a notion of competence that is fundamentally at odds with the knowledge-based rationale of academic courses. Second, given their very narrow and particular aims, core skills cannot serve as the basis of a common core for both academic and vocational courses. Arguably no curriculum area derived from the world of work, with its minute division of labour and multiple social stratifications, can achieve the kind of universality which would allow it to serve as a common foundation for learning.

Only some notion of general culture, addressing the future needs of adults as both workers and citizens, can fulfil this function. Historically, in France, it has been precisely this concept of *culture génerale*, as a minimum entitlement of all French citizens, which has provided the cement that has held the academic and general education at least within talking distance of each other, if not exactly in unison. Without some mandatory core of general education, which is how this concept translates in educational practice, any plans for a unified curriculum will, in practice, turn out to be little more than technical fixes. They may allow 'mixing and matching', but they will provide no real commonality and no notions of a shared culture or of a common citizenship either. So how could we achieve this without unrealistically radical measures which go against the grain of the received culture?

The logic of the argument presented here is that there should be for all post-16 courses a mandatory minimum core curriculum of general education. This should include, at the least, English/communications, maths/numeracy, and some form of civic or citizen education which would have as its aim the cultivation of political literacy, environmental awareness, international understanding and social responsibility. Ideally, it would also include science and a foreign language although, given the great difficulties many students have in these areas, it would probably allow these as alternatives. In a modular system, these areas would occupy a discrete space, with the clear intention that they would be taught as separate subjects with specialist teachers, albeit with teachers encouraged to make connections across the curriculum.

A modular system, containing these subjects as mandatory core units, would have a clear basis of commonality across the different pathways and this would help to encourage parity of status between the pathways, as well as possibilities for student transfer and progression. Having said this, however, it would not be necessary for all students to study these areas in quite the same form. Maintaining some credibility of a minimum standard would be important for parity, but there is no reason why the core areas should not to some extent be customized to the requirements of different pathways within the system. For instance, students studying on a pathway which had engineering as its major component might be expected to take relatively demanding maths and science units, designed in relation to that major focus, as well as an English/communications unit that had a bias towards technical language.

Such an arrangement, with assessment attached to each module, would maintain the flexibility and motivational advantages associated with the modular system, but would begin to take on some of the characteristics of the linear curriculum models typical in countries like France and Sweden. In these countries the 'lines' are defined by reference to the major subject, with ancillary mandatory and optional subjects, customized to the requirements of the major subject, forming part of the 'cluster'. The advantages of such linear arrangements are that they tend to maximize coherence across the whole programme of study and to encourage accumulative learning.

There would no doubt be many objections raised to these arrangements. They would involve replacing the elective form of A-level examination with a form of grouped award which might be unpopular with some students; they would create difficult and possibly unpopular additional requirements for some students who are not confident with maths and languages; and they would incur additional costs in specialist teachers. However, these arguments can be met. Elective examinations are not an immutable part of our education culture. Until replaced by A-levels in 1951, matriculation used to be via a grouped award called the Higher National Certificate and this was not excessively unpopular. The cost implications of the changes are real, but they are not so great when set against the enormous wastage through drop-out on post-16 courses, general underachievement across the system and the additional costs to employers of training those with poor basic skills. The question of difficulty is the most serious and here their can only be a radical answer.

Many students in post-16 education find completion of both Level 2 and Level 3 courses difficult. The extra general education requirements proposed here would make them all the more so. However, the answer is not to avoid the problem, but to find ways of tackling it. One of these would be to increase the length and intensity of study for the Level 3 courses which it is hoped that the majority of the cohort would take and complete. Reaching world-class standards in post-16 education means competing against countries like France, Germany, Japan and Sweden where the majority of those completing compulsory schooling spend an additional three years in full-time study, involving upwards of 30 hours per week in the classroom and substantial amounts of homework. Students in England and Wales are typically expected to reach similar standards over two years with, in most cases, no more than 15 hours of tuition per week. It is no wonder that many have problems reaching the same standard. The answer is to increase the normal learning time on post-16 courses to a level comparable with these other countries, giving students a reasonable chance of reaching their levels of attainment. Now that staying-on has become the accepted cultural norm in the UK, this should no longer be a social problem. It would, of course, involve substantial costs. However, the social and economic costs of not doing this will ultimately be a great deal higher.

References

Adult Literacy and Basic Skills Unit (1993) *Basic Skills Support in Colleges: Assessing the Need*, London: ALBSU.

Ainley, P (1993) *Class and Skill: Changing Divisions of Knowledge and Labour*, London: Cassell.

Avis, J (1992), 'Social Difference and Antagonism Within the 16–19 Core Curriculum', *British Journal of Sociology of Education*, **13**, 3, 361–73.

Brown, P and Scase, R (1995) *Higher Education and Corporate Realities: Class, Culture and the Decline of Graduate Careers*, London: UCL Press.

Brubaker, R (1992) *Citizenship and Nationhood in France and Germany*, Cambridge, MA: Harvard University Press.

Confederation of British Industry (1989) *Towards a Skills Revolution*, London: CBI.

Day, C R (1987) *Education and the Industrial World: the Ecole d'Arts et Métiers and the Rise of French Industrial Engineering*, Cambridge, MA: MIT Press.

Dearing, Sir Ron (1996) *Review of Qualifications for 16–19 Year Olds: Summary Report*, London: SCAA.

Department of Education and Science (1988) *Advancing A-levels*, London: HMSO.

Further Education Funding Council (1994) *General National Vocational Qualifications in the FE Sector*, London: HMSO.

Further Education Unit (1979) *A Basis for Choice*, London: FEU.

Further Education Unit (1990) *The Core Skills Initiative*, London: FEU.

Further Education Unit/Institute of Education/Nuffield Foundation (1994) *GNVQs 1993–94: A National Survey Report*, London: FEU.

Green, A (1990) *Education and State Formation*, Basingstoke: Macmillan.

Green, A (1995) 'Core Skills, Participation and Progression in Post-Compulsory Education and Training in England and France', *Comparative Education*, **31**, 1, 49–67.

Green, A and Ainley, P (1995) *Progression and the Targets in Post-16 Education and Training*, Post-16 Education Centre Report No 11, Institute of Education, University of London.

Green, A and Steedman, H (1993) *Educational Provision, Educational Attainment and the Needs of Industry: A Review of the Research for Germany, France, Japan, the USA and Britain*, Report No 5, London: National Institute of Economic and Social Research.

Her Majesty's Inspectorate (1993) *Aspects of Vocational Education in France*, London: HMSO.

Holland, G (1976) *Youth and Work*, London: MSC.

Jessup, G (1991) *Outcomes: NVQs and the Emerging Model of Education and Training*, London: Falmer Press.

National Council for Vocational Qualifications (1990) *Core Skills in NVQs: Response to the Secretary of State*, London: NCVQ.

National Curriculum Council (1990) *Core Skills 16–19*, London: HMSO.

Oates, T (1994) 'Fair Assessment and the Candidate's Self-Perception', *The NVQ Monitor*, Autumn.

OFSTED (1994) *GNVQs in Schools 1993/4*, London: HMSO.

OFSTED/Audit Commission (1993) *Unfinished Business*, London: HMSO.

Perry, P J C (1976) *The Evolution of British Manpower Policy*, London: British Association for Commercial and Industrial Education.

Prais, S J (1987) 'Educating for Productivity: Comparisons of Japanese and English Schooling and Vocational Preparation', *National Institute Economic Review*, February.

Reynolds, D and Farrell, S (1996) *Worlds Apart? A Review of International Surveys of Educational Achievement Involving England*, London: OFSTED/HMSO.

Roderick, G and Stephens, M (1978) *Education and Industry in the Nineteenth Century*, London: Longman.

Sadler, M (1979) *Selections from Sadler: Studies in World Citizenship*, compiled by J Higginson, Liverpool: D&M International Publishers.

Scott Russell, J (1869) *Systematic Technical Education for the English People*, London.

Smithers, A (1993) 'All Our Futures', A Dispatches Report on Education, Channel Four Television.

Spours, K (1995) *The Strengths and Weaknesses of GNVQs: Principles of Design Learning for the Future*, Working Paper 3, Post-16 Education Centre, Institute of Education, University of London.

Steedman, H (1988) 'Vocational Training in France and Britain: Mechanical and Electrical Craftsmen', *National Institute Economic Review*, November, 49–62, London: NIESR.

Steedman, H and Green, A (1996) 'International Comparisons of Skills Supply and Demand: Report to the DfEE', unpublished.

Steedman, H and Hawkins, J (1994) 'Shifting the Foundations: The Impact of NVQs on Youth Training for the Building Trades,' *National Institute Economic Review*, August, 93–101.

Thompson, S (1897) *Apprentice Schools in France*, London.

Weber, E (1976) *Peasants into Frenchmen*, Stanford, USA: Stanford University Press.

Wolf, A (1992) *Mathematics for Vocational Students in France and England: Contrasting Provision and Consequences*, NIESR Discussion Paper 23, London: National Institute of Economic and Social Research.

Wolf, A (1995) 'Vocational Qualifications in Europe: The Emergence of Common Assessment Themes', in Bash, L and Green, A (eds) *Youth, Education and Work: World Yearbook on Education*, London: Kogan Page.

Young, M, Hodgson, A and Leney, T (1995) *Unifying the Post-Compulsory Curriculum: Lessons from France and Scotland*, Unified Curriculum at 16+ Series, Post-16 Education Centre, Institute of Education, University of London.

CHAPTER 7

Modularization and the 14–19 Qualifications System

Ann Hodgson and Ken Spours

Modularization – divisions and diversity in the English context

The relationship between modularization and 14–19 qualifications represents a paradox within the English education and training system. There is widespread enthusiasm for modularization as a tool, not only to respond to changing patterns of participation but as a means of developing a more flexible, unified and coherent qualifications system. At the same time, however, the development of, and even the debates on modularization are fragmented and reflect the major divisions within the qualifications system itself. What this chapter will argue is that two different strands of development and debate in relation to modularization have grown up on either side of the academic/vocational divide. If modularization is to be used as a tool in the design of a unified qualifications system, therefore, the developments and debates traditionally associated with either the academic or the vocational track will need to be brought together and reconciled in a more common way. In this chapter we will attempt to situate the English debates about modularization within the wider international picture in order to broaden the debate and to take it beyond the confines of the academic/vocational divide.

Not surprisingly the divisions within the English education and training system have given rise to debate and even confusion about the different forms of modularization and different uses of terminology. Throughout this chapter, the term 'modularization' will be used in a generic sense in order to recognize a range of approaches to curriculum delivery and qualifications reform. Within the broad term modularization, reference will then be made to three different approaches: 'modular qualifications', associated with the academic track, 'unitization of assessment outcomes', associated with the vocational track, and 'modular qualifications systems', associated with a future unified qualifications system. This threefold distinction recognizes the different roots of the debate about modularization and, at the same time, provides an analytical framework within which the development of a more coherent relationship between the three approaches can be discussed.

In this analysis, modular qualifications divide the curriculum into relatively short learning experiences; this encourages a gradual and staged approach to achievement by the student. This form of modularization has been developed in the academic track (eg, some GCSE and A-level syllabuses) and is also associated with modular delivery of the curriculum. Unitization of assessment outcomes, on the other hand, is mainly associated with vocational qualifications such as GNVQs, NVQs and, to a lesser extent, BTEC awards. In vocational awards and in the type of local unitization that has taken place in many further education colleges, there is a clear distinction made between units of assessment and modular delivery of the curriculum (FEU, 1995). Modular qualifications systems, for example the system already being developed in Scotland through *Higher Still* (SOED, 1994), attempt to relate and integrate academic and vocational qualifications into common and unified qualifications systems. These systems are characterized by modular design, modular assessment and modular delivery.

Throughout the 1980s and 1990s modularization has held a fascination for both practitioners and policy-makers because it has been seen as a practical way of responding to learner needs, as a valuable curriculum planning mechanism and also as a potential tool for reform of the qualifications system. The Learning for the Future Project has recently identified four major ways in which modularization operates in national education and training systems (Richardson *et al.*, 1995), which echo earlier work on European-wide projects (Raffe, 1992a).

According to both these sources, modularization can be an historical and established feature of the education system, as, for example, in the USA and, more recently, Scotland; it can be reactive to system weaknesses, such as low attainment, lack of flexibility and the effects of the academic/vocational divide; it can be responsive to system changes, such as rises in full-time participation and the need to change pedagogy; or, finally, it can be used as a proactive approach to future curriculum and qualifications needs. In this last case, modularization is seen as a tool for building more flexible but coherent national qualifications systems which underpin and contribute to the flexibility of the labour force, encourage higher levels of personal responsibility and support the concept of lifelong learning.

Unlike in Scotland, there is no national modular system in England and Wales. As a result, in this country modularization has been experienced in diverse forms and used by a variety of different agencies, but largely in the reactive and responsive ways indicated above. Prior to the introduction of the National Curriculum, for example, there was a great deal of local experimentation with modularization in secondary schools, often supported by the Technical and Vocational Education Initiative (TVEI) (Moon, 1988; Warwick, 1987). More recently there has been a rise in the development of modular syllabuses in GCSEs and A-levels, as well as the introduction of unitized vocational qualifications and local experiments in unitization and credit, largely undertaken by further education colleges (Fforwm, 1995; Post-16 Education Centre, 1991–1996).

These different approaches to modularization have arisen as the result of two forms of division: first, and most importantly, the division between academic and vocational qualifications, which have traditionally had different structures, assessment methods and philosophies; second, the development of a diversity of local experimentation in the absence of a national modular system. What we will return to in the final section of this chapter is the need for modularization to be used more extensively in a proactive way as a tool for shaping the unified qualifications system of the future.

International, national and local developments in modularization

International developments

The reform of education and training systems is taking place world-wide, though different approaches are being adopted in different countries. At present, a minority of education and training systems in Europe sees modularization as a central reform strategy (Lasonen, 1996). World-wide, those favouring modularization tend to be countries with more 'mixed' education and work-based systems, such as England, ones which emphasize individual student choice (eg, Sweden and Finland) or small systems such as Scotland or New Zealand (Lasonen, 1996). However, even if many systems do not see modularization as a central reform strategy, there is, nevertheless, growing interest in its development. Globalization of the economy and flexibility in relation to working practices are compelling an increasing number of education and training systems to look to the potential of modularization and credit accumulation and transfer as a future curriculum design tool, rather than simply as a means of responding to current problems.

A recent European-wide study of experiments in modularization highlighted a number of advantages of this strategy, which links individual learning, curriculum development, institutional flexibility, efficient uses of resources and the capacity to innovate. The project also saw that modularization could lead to four types of flexibility: individual (the ability of individuals to transfer skills); curricular (responsiveness to individual differences, to economic trends and technological change); of delivery; and of learning pathways (Raffe, 1992b).

While international projects have identified a broad agenda of interest in modularization, a brief comparative analysis of the US, various European systems and New Zealand suggests that there are three major types of development or stages. The first type – established but partial credit-based systems – can be seen in the USA, where this type of system covers a wide range of college and higher education provision, but not work-based training (Kazis, 1992; Robertson, 1993). The second type of development – partial modular vocational systems – is exemplified in the Netherlands and Luxembourg, where such systems have been introduced to respond to new types of participation or specific weaknesses in the system, such as progression barriers, low attainment or lack of flexibility (Raffe, 1992b). The third type, and a more ambitious stage of development, is the whole-system approach, which can be found, for example, in New Zealand, Scotland and, arguably, Sweden. In these countries, modularization and credit are seen as central features of the qualifications system.

This comparative analysis would suggest that the English system corresponds largely to the second type of development, with a plurality of approaches being taken to modularization at the local level. This clearly has implications for the development of a unified qualifications system in this country. We will return to this issue when we assess how modularization might be used as a tool for qualifications reform.

National developments

In the absence of a national modular system in England, those involved in national curriculum and qualification issues have seen modularization as one of the ways of responding to the perceived inadequacies of the qualifications system and national forms of accreditation. It has been seen both as a way of making the existing qualifications system more manageable and accessible to learners and, more radically, as a way of reforming the whole curriculum and structure of the qualifications system itself.

Modularization has been seen as a curriculum tool in four major ways at national level. First, it has been used as a way of dividing up full-time qualifications in both the academic and the vocational tracks – modular GCSEs and A-levels in the academic track and units of assessment outcomes in GNVQs in the vocational track. Second, modularization has provided a limited way of aligning units of both academic and vocational qualifications to create 'linkages' between the different qualifications tracks. In this way, it helps to encourage students to mix academic and vocational learning programmes (Dearing, 1996). Third, modularization has been seen as a way of creating a common core of learning across different courses, leading to the creation of 'Y-models' (Coates and Hamilton, 1996). Finally, in the longer term, modules of learning have been identified as the building blocks of a national and unified qualifications system (AfC et al., 1994; Finegold et al., 1990; Richardson et al., 1995; SOED, 1994).

Local developments

However, it is at the level of the individual school or college that many of the experiments in modularization have taken place over the last 15 years in this country. Throughout the 1980s, but prior to the introduction of the National Curriculum and GCSE, modularization was seen as a tool for redesigning the curriculum, particularly in secondary schools, in order to provide a structure, delivery model and accreditation for learning which fell outside the formal qualifications system. Modularization was thus used as a way of legitimating new forms of learning as well as motivating students by providing a greater element of choice, innovative approaches to pedagogy and broader opportunities for achievement (Macintosh, 1986; Moon, 1988; Warwick, 1987). For this reason, it also tended to be associated with programmes of study for lower attaining students. This has had an affect on the debates about modularization, particularly in relation to developments in the academic track.

This trend to use modularization as a tool for increasing student access to the curriculum has continued in the early 1990s, but schools and colleges have tended to work within the qualifications system as well as using it as a means of providing alternative forms of learning and accreditation. The development of modularization has also moved into the post-compulsory phase of education as a result of increases in post-16 participation, market-oriented reforms in institutional arrangements and the demand that schools and colleges raise attainment and promote progression (Richardson *et al.*, 1995).

The most noticeable trend in the late 1980s and early 1990s has been the take-up of modular GCSE and A-level syllabuses by schools and colleges, particularly in mathematics and science. In 1994, more than 50 per cent of new syllabuses were modular and by 1996 modular syllabuses accounted for as many as one-fifth of A-level entries and two-thirds of maths and science results (Pyke, 1996). Institutions see modular syllabuses as motivating students through shorter learning goals, clearer curriculum objectives and assessment criteria and higher pass rates (Richardson *et al.*, 1995).

Even where schools and colleges have not taken up modular syllabuses, there has been the spread of 'informal internal modularization'. This refers to a modular approach to schemes of work within linear GCSE and GCE syllabuses with the emphasis on more frequent and earlier formative assessment and feedback to students during their courses (Spours and Hodgson, 1996).

Further education colleges, in addition, have not only shown an interest in modular syllabuses but have also used unitization of learning outcomes as a tool for increasing curriculum flexibility. In response to changing patterns of participation, particularly among adults, and to FEFC funding methodology, there have been attempts to increase access to learning and accreditation by using unitization to provide more flexible entry and exit points, a wider range of courses and certification and more flexible delivery modes (Spours and Lucas, 1996; Young *et al.*, 1994b, 1995).

Most colleges involved in this type of experimentation have concentrated on partial unitization of foundation and adult provision, rather than unitization of courses for younger learners. Many of these colleges have developed some specific unit-related accreditation, often in conjunction with Open College Networks. On the other hand, some colleges such as Solihull, Wirral Metropolitan College and all the Welsh colleges, have undertaken full unitization of their curriculum offer and the development of internal Credit Accumulation and Transfer Systems

(CATs) (Fforwm, 1995; Hodgson, 1994). In these institutions, all provision is being unitized with the aim of establishing mass individualized learning programmes. However, the considerable problems in this type of development work have included a tendency to deconstruct the curriculum instead of using units to construct a new curriculum (Richardson *et al.*, 1995), organizational short-comings such as inadequate management information systems and approaches to timetabling (Young *et al.*, 1994a, 1994b) and uneven development of units (Atwell *et al.*, 1994).

On a broader front, there has been experimentation with regional cross-institutional CAT systems in Wales (Fforwm, 1995) and by the London Together/London TECs CAT Group (1994). Geoff Stanton's chapter in this volume will look at the significance of these developments in more detail.

What this section has attempted to show is that, unlike in Scotland, which has a recently established whole-system approach on which it is building, the English system is at a much earlier stage of development. While there is widespread support for the extension of modularization amongst education professionals (Leney and Spours, 1997), there are also fierce debates, both political and educational, about the role it should play and the form it should take (Spours and Young, 1996). These debates reflect the nature of the developments that have taken place to date in England and, more particularly, the divided system from which they have emerged. It is to these debates that we now turn.

The English debate on modularization – standards and access

Whereas in Scotland the recent debates about modularization have tended to focus on implementation issues, because of the stage of modular development in that country, in England the national debate is still very much at the political level, particularly in relation to modular developments in the academic track. In Scotland there is widespread acceptance that the qualifications system should be characterized by modular design, modular assessment and modular delivery: in England this is far from the case. As modular developments in the English system have begun to move from an institutional focus to a qualifications reform focus, so the debate at the political level has intensified (Pinnell, 1996).

The recent debates on modularization in the English 14–19 education system have been dominated by the two inter-related themes of 'standards and attainment' and 'flexibility and choice'. While these debates reflect a number of deep-rooted divisions within the system, they can be reduced to two main positions: a preoccupation with standards and attainment in the academic track and a concern about flexibility and choice in the vocational track, particularly in relation to further education and adults. These debates have taken place at both the national political level and at the local practitioner level. While the political arguments have largely been conducted around issues of standards and attainment, education professionals have stressed the importance of flexibility and choice in order to meet the needs of learners.

Modularization, standards and attainment

In the late 1980s there was a considerable growth of interest in modular syllabuses, associated with a parallel development of increased proportions of assessed coursework in GCSE and A-level syllabuses. A good example of this was the Wessex Modular A-level Project (Rainbow, 1993) in which the core modules (60 per cent of the award) were externally examined and the option modules (40 per cent of the award) were internally assessed. At this time, there were also rapid rises in student attainment (Spours, 1995).

However, since the 1991 White Paper (DfE/ED/WO, 1991) and the restriction of assessed coursework in GCSE and A-level syllabuses, SCAA has introduced a form of 'controlled modularization' in the academic track. GCSE and A-level modular syllabuses are only allowed a maximum of 20 per cent coursework assessment, in most subjects, and a minimum of 30 per cent of assessment through terminal examination. They are also subject to external end-of-module tests. It remains to be seen whether there will be any relaxation on this front as a result of the deliberations of the Joint SCAA/NCVQ Working Groups set up to implement the recommendations of the Dearing Report (Dearing, 1996).

This restriction reflects the Conservative government's concern that modular syllabuses are 'easier' than linear syllabuses. This is partly a reaction to the history of modularization and its association with lower attaining students. The other two major reasons that modular syllabuses are perceived as easier are first, that students are assessed on small chunks of learning, rather than having to show a synoptic grasp of the subject overall, and second, that they are allowed to retake modules and can then decide when to cash in their module test results for a full A-level. Both of these features of modular syllabuses are associated with arguments about a lowering of standards (Dearing, 1996; *The Guardian*, 1996; Pyke, 1996).

Those in education, on the other hand, argue that modular A-levels are no easier than linear A-levels, rather they demonstrate different abilities and skills (Pinnell, 1996; TES, 1996). Some even suggest that in some respects modular A-levels are more difficult, because students often have to demonstrate an A-level standard in specific areas of a subject early on in a course. In addition, it is argued, the step-by-step approach to A-levels allows students to receive more regular feedback and thus to build on their strengths over time. This is a strategy which rewards those who are prepared to work hard over a sustained period, rather than those who rely on a concentrated spurt at the end of a two-year course to pass a terminal examination.

A closer look at the two sides of this argument reveals three underlying themes. The first is ideological/political and revolves around the maintenance of standards and raising overall levels of achievement. The Conservatives place their emphasis on maintaining existing standards in the academic track by promoting the selective capability of A-levels that are supported by terminally examined and linear syllabuses. Increasing levels of achievement in the cohort is a role given to vocational qualifications not A-levels. Most educationalists and the opposition parties, on the other hand, place more emphasis on raising levels of attainment in the student cohort as a whole, both in the academic and the vocational tracks. Here the aim is to make standards more accessible, to be reached by dint of effort and hard work – this is the hallmark of modular syllabuses. The debate has been fuelled by the introduction of National Targets for Education and Training.

The maintenance of standards in the academic track argument is underpinned by a notion that only a minority of the population has an 'academic mind' (Dearing, 1996; MoE, 1959). This is seen as a peculiarly English approach to achievement (Spours and Young, 1996). Those who argue that academic standards should be more accessible are raising fundamental issues about the nature and future of the academic track. First, there is the assumption that the vast majority of the cohort is capable of attaining in general education beyond 16. Comparisons with other European systems, which have higher levels of participation, are cited in support of this (Green, 1995). Second is the view that the concept of 'academic education' should be broadened to 'general education', which would include both theoretical and applied approaches to learning.

The second and related theme of this debate focuses on the issue of whether building towards a qualifications standard step-by-step is as valid as demonstrating a synoptic grasp of the whole standard as measured by examination at the end of a course. Gradual knowledge- and skill-building is encouraged by modular syllabuses, whereas the 'final dash' to the terminal examination, which samples the grasp that a student has of the syllabus as a whole, is encouraged by linear syllabuses. As we will see in the final section of this chapter, these two positions are not as mutually exclusive as the political/ideological debate might suggest – a debate which is fuelled by the co-existence of both types of syllabus. One solution might be to arrive at a common form of design which combines the best features of modular syllabuses with the strengths of the linear syllabus.

The third theme surrounds the debate about skills for the future and the proportions of the population that can develop them. Modular and linear approaches to the curriculum are concerned with flexibility and transferability, but from very different points of view and for different proportions of the cohort. The linear approach assumes the need to preserve the integrity of the subject and the ability of a qualification to 'testify to achievements across a combination of knowledge, understanding and skills within a given subject or subject area' (Richardson et al., 1995, p.16). From this point of view, it is the achievements within a given subject area which provide the best guarantee that a student will be an effective and flexible learner. This concept of flexibility could be seen to be developed by specialized and examined syllabuses for a minority of the population who, at 18, would then have acquired the kind of mental processes needed for subsequent participation in a single-subject honours degree. On the other hand, modular approaches to learning stress other transferable skills and other types of flexibility and for a much broader section of the population. Here there is a recognition that step-by-step learning is a very effective method of learning for all students. In theory, at least, there is also a recognition that a more open model of the curriculum which encourages the learner to tackle that crucial process of arranging, combining and reinterpreting the elements of a modular programme (Wilson, 1993) is developing skills for the future, because the focus is not only on learning knowledge, but also on developing the skills to inter-relate different aspects of learning (see Chapter 3).

Unitization, credit and access

In response to the policy-led restrictions in the academic track, to the development and acceptance of the NCVQ outcomes model of curriculum design and to pressures for access from new participants in further education, the Further Education Unit developed the concept of a 'credit framework' (FEU, 1992). The focus of this development is not so much modular learning, but the use of 'credit' as a form of educational currency (FEU, 1993).

As we have seen in the previous section, since the beginning of the 1990s further education colleges have been experimenting with the idea of building a credit framework to embrace and accredit all forms of learning, including those outside the current qualifications structure. Credit frameworks are seen as a way of ensuring that all types of learning gain recognition by being assigned a credit value. They can work horizontally, so that students can access a range of provision and can carry credit to complete a whole qualification in one level, or vertically, where the aim is to encourage access and progression to higher courses. Credit is particularly important for adults and lower attainers who have not traditionally had access to the national qualifications system and have, therefore, found it difficult both to demonstrate what they have achieved and also to progress onto more formal or mainstream provision in further education, because they cannot satisfy the normal entry requirements.

As an 'open system' (Tait, 1993) consisting of units, credits and levels, a credit framework was intended to overarch the existing qualifications system. Its components could then be used by institutions to build their own systems which would eventually fit into a national credit framework. This multi-functional framework has proved to be attractive to practitioners, particularly in further education colleges. At one and the same time, the credit framework was seen as a pragmatic strategy for the present, because in the early 1990s significant national qualifications reform seemed to be off the political agenda (Wilson, 1993), and as a future vision of an open system which, in some senses, went beyond the confines of all qualifications (Robertson, 1993).

The state of the debate: polarization or potential for redesign?

If we return to look at the four major roles for modularization laid out at the beginning of this chapter, we can see that the reasons behind the development of unitization and credit appear to be a mixture of reactive, responsive and proactive. These developments have been reactive to the restrictions of the qualifications system and responsive to the needs of new constituencies of learners, while also attempting to find a proactive way of dealing with future curriculum and qualification needs. In this sense the restrictive national political approach to modularization in the academic track and to credit-based open systems in the further education and adult sector, can be seen as almost mirror-images of each other. But the two different debates have been polarized and have fragmented the argument for modularization, both in terms of what has been argued for on each side and in terms of each's solutions to changes within the system. On the other hand, both have suffered as a result of restrictions in the national policy on the qualifications system. Conservative government policy has been to restrict the development of modularization in 14–19 qualifications.

In response to the restrictions in the existing qualifications system, the unitization and credit strategy has been to circumvent rather than to seek serious structural change in the 14–19 qualifications system. First, it has placed its emphasis on local systems rather than on the 14–19 national qualifications system. Second, it has tended to focus on adults rather than on younger learners and has worked to bring marginal certification more into the mainstream. Debates on modularization in the academic track, on the other hand, have recently increasingly focused on bringing about changes in the national qualifications system.

However, the main interest of this chapter is to get beyond this polarization in development and debate. It is concerned with exploring to what extent the unitization and credit argument for 'open systems', together with the debate on modular, linear and synoptic syllabuses, can inform the debate for the use of modularization as a tool in designing a future qualifications system.

Modularization: a tool for qualifications reform?

A detailed debate on the role of modularization in the design of a unified national qualifications system has yet to take place. The design of such a system cannot emerge directly from what has been a largely polemical debate between 'restrictive' and 'open' systems. Nevertheless, there are valuable lessons to be learned from this debate, particularly in terms of looking for types of fusion between the different positions. In contrast to Scotland, where *Higher Still* is building on a decade of modular system development in vocational qualifications, the position south of the border is one of having to build a more unified qualifications system out of the elements of the divided debate and of diverse modular developments at a local and regional level.

At this stage of development in England, it is useful to evaluate the extent to which modularization can be used as a design tool for addressing the following four underlying aims of a future and more coherent 14–19 unified qualifications system (Richardson *et al.*, 1995): promoting participation, achievement and progression; encouraging breadth of learning; ensuring coherence of study; and promoting student self-management and skills for the future.

Promoting participation, achievement and progression

Promoting student access to education and training is one of the most important aims of the English qualifications system, particularly in the light of changing patterns of participation and the increasing involvement of adults. Tensions could arise, however, between the achievement and access arguments related to modularization. The access approach, promoted by the unitization and credit arguments, tends to emphasize accreditation of prior learning (APL) and the assessment of existing skills, both of which are seen as features of open systems (Wilson, 1993). The modular learning approach, on the other hand, tends towards advocating a tight and sequential system of learning and feedback. In designing a future 14–19 qualifications system, a balance needs to be struck between these two approaches.

In attempting to create this balance, it may be useful to draw a distinction between the needs of younger learners, who are likely to benefit more from structured learning programmes, and the needs of older learners, who may appreciate greater responsibility for designing their own learning to build on previous experience. Nevertheless, if we look at the relationship between modularization and achievement, there are benefits which both adults and younger learners can derive from modularization and which make the qualifications system more accessible to both types of learners. As we have seen earlier in this chapter, modularization does seem to have a positive impact on student achievement. Increases in achievement that can be attributed to modularization have been associated with at least three factors: first, the step-by-step learning approach, where students are assessed on relatively small and manageable sections of the curriculum, seems to increase levels of achievement. Second, modular approaches encourage a closer relationship between learning by the student, curriculum planning by teachers and formative assessment and feedback between the two. Third, the fact that students can retake modules (eg, in A-level) can lead to the improvement of final grades.

These features of modularization are all concerned with making qualifications standards more accessible to all types of learners. However, as recent press articles have shown (*The Guardian*, 1996; Pyke, 1996; *TES*, 1996), a shadow will continue to be cast over these achievements if modular syllabuses continue to co-exist with traditional linear and terminally examined courses in the academic track. Parity of esteem between the two types of syllabuses is clearly not a realistic aspiration, and co-existence will simply end up by producing new divisions within the academic track. The central issue for a more unified system, therefore, is to produce a common assessment design which will be attractive to the vast majority of students and will involve combining the strongest features of both modular and linear syllabuses.

Using modularization to address issues of both individual student progression and structural progression between different levels of qualifications is something which has not yet been tackled in any depth, certainly at a national level. However, it is clearly an issue that will need to be tackled if we wish to move from modular developments to a modular qualifications system in this country.

Facilitating student progression between different qualifications levels has, to date, often been addressed through institutional progression and guidance systems and the introduction of access courses and pre-vocational or vocational qualifications to bridge the gap between levels. There have been limited local experiments, where modules have been developed for certain groups of students to broaden learning programmes or to compensate for inadequate skills or knowledge in a particular area in order to facilitate progression (see, for example, Young *et al.*, 1994d). This type of modular development, however, has remained at the level of local experimentation and has not been evaluated in terms of its likely broader system-wide effects.

An evaluation of the Scottish Action Plan in the 1980s came to the conclusion that modular approaches were having some impact on progression, insofar as YTS trainees on modular programmes were more likely to complete their schemes than those on non-modular programmes, but beyond this there were few other signs of educational progression taking place (Raffe, 1988).

Currently it seems, therefore, that the greatest influence that modularization can have on progression is to increase achievement which, in turn, enables progression to take place. The relationship between modularization and achievement, as we have seen, however, is also the area where the ideological debate is at its most acute at the moment. Moreover, a 14–19 qualifications system that was 'progression-oriented' would have to do more than just promote progression by increasing achievement. It would have to facilitate individual movement, personal pacing and continuity of learning, as well as ensuring that progression was built into the structure of the system. This is again where the unitization and modularization debates need to be brought closer together in the discussion over the design of a unified qualifications system.

Encouraging breadth of learning

Modularization and unitization can be powerful tools for organizing opportunities for breadth of learning, but only if there are incentives for students and institutions to undertake broader learning programmes as part of the national qualifications structure (Young *et al.*, 1994d).

Modular approaches to the curriculum can be used to encourage breadth by breaking down long qualifications into short courses or even into individual units, which can then be studied alongside or instead of whole qualifications. For instance, the lateral AS-level described in the Dearing Report (Dearing, 1996) would allow more subjects to be studied by sixth form students and is an essential element in the design for the proposed National Diploma. Unitization, on the other hand, although sometimes used to encourage breadth of study (Young *et al.*, 1994d) is not often associated with breadth of learning. In fact, the opposite can be the case, with the emphasis on credit being used for APL (which tends to avoid additional learning) or by employers as a way of picking the bits and pieces of a qualification which are of immediate interest to them.

Modularization, therefore, encourages breadth only in conjunction with other strategies for broadening the curriculum. Complementary strategies include the demand of qualifications for particular combinations of study or a synoptic understanding of an area of study and assessment practices that encourage students to exercise broader skills. These strategies will be different for adults and for younger learners and any design for a unified qualifications system will need to ensure that it uses modularization to increase breadth in a way that satisfies both types of learner.

Ensuring coherence of study

At a high point of innovation and debate about modularization at the end of the 1980s, a leading specialist on modularization in Scotland suggested that the virtues of modularization should be combined with the virtues of long courses (Mack, 1989). What was being argued was the need for coherent combinations of modules. The concept of coherence can be understood in two ways – bottom-up and top-down. Those who advocate more open and student-centred systems see modularization as encouraging bottom-up coherence, that is encouraging students to put the pieces of the curriculum together themselves (see Chapter 10). In this sense, modularization is about individuals making sense of their own learning experience (MIN, 1993). On the other hand, coherence can also be externally determined and thus experienced top-down through the recommendation of modular combinations and recognized pathways. A future unified qualifications system, which will need to create a high skills and achievement environment for all learners, will have to strike a balance between top-down system-inspired and bottom-up individually derived coherence. The solution may well lie in building a relationship between a number of curricular features which go beyond modularization *per se*. These could include the construction of modular pathways, an element of modular free choice, and qualifications which demand integration of knowledge and skills and require the development of processes, such as action planning and recording of achievement, which encourage students to reflect on their patterns of study and paths of progression (Richardson *et al.*, 1995).

Promoting student self-management and skills for the future

Developing skills for the future in terms of the modularization debate has been very much informed by calls for open systems of credit and far-reaching student self-management (Robertson, 1994). However, there is the additional issue of whether the 14–19 curriculum, and hence the qualifications system, will require the development of new forms of intellectual skills and knowledge which are related to its content and not just to its structure. These might include, for example, the ability to apply analytical concepts to specialist knowledge, the process skills of personal organization, research and the creation of personal paths of lifelong learning or connective skills within areas of study and between theory and practice (Richardson *et al.*, 1995).

To date, modularization has encouraged learners to develop process skills to manage their own learning through a requirement to create coherent learning programmes from a fragmented offer. In this sense, institutions have tended to react to the effects of modularization rather than seeing it as a design tool for creating a new kind of curriculum content. What is required in the design of a unified qualifications system is that modularization is used proactively as a tool to design the content of a curriculum for the future. As international studies on modularization have shown, modules are ideal for this purpose because of their flexibility and responsiveness as a curriculum planning tool (Raffe, 1992b).

Conclusion

There is a clear role for modularization in the design of a more unified 14–19 qualifications system which aims to raise levels of achievement and to encourage breadth, coherence and student self-management. As we have argued in this chapter, modularization has a part to play in the structure and content of the system, as well as in the way that the curriculum is assessed and delivered. However, progress is likely to be gradual because modularization has not been an historical and established feature of the English education and training system. Moreover, as we have seen, the developments and debates related to modularization in this country have been at best fragmented and at worst deeply polarized. In addition, these debates have been beset by ideological concerns rather than focusing on practical implementation issues.

We have argued that a focus on future curriculum design and implementation issues would demand a re-evaluation and refocusing of the debate on modularization. It would need to move from a debate bounded by division and ideology to a debate on design and implementation strategies. It would also require a recognition of the limitations of modularization as a curriculum tool, particularly its tendency to lead to fragmentation and incoherence, so that a balance can be struck between the major strengths of integrated linear qualifications and courses (synoptic understanding and coherence) and the strengths of modular qualifications and courses (access, flexibility and choice).

References

Association for Colleges, The Girls' Schools Association, The Headmasters' Conference, The Secondary Heads' Association, The Sixth Form Colleges Association and the Society for Headmasters and Headmistresses in Independent Schools (1994) *Post-Compulsory Education and Training: A Joint Statement*, London: AfC.

Atwell, G, Davies, B and Carter, M (1994) 'From Modularisation to CATs: The Next Stage in Developing a Post-16 Framework for Wales', in Young, M, Morris, A and Hodgson, A (eds) *Unifying Strategies and Organisational Change in Post-16 Education Unified Curriculum at 16+*, Working Paper No 7, Post-16 Education Centre, Institute of Education, University of London.

Coates, P and Hamilton, J (1996) '16–19 Coherence Project', in Dearing, R, *Review of Qualifications for 16–19 Year Olds*, London: SCAA.

Dearing, Sir Ron (1996) *Review of Qualifications for 16–19 Year Olds*, London: SCAA.

Department for Education/Employment Department/Welsh Office (1991) *Education and Training for the 21st Century*, London: HMSO.

Fforwm (1995) *An Interim Report on the Wales FE Credit Framework*, Fforwm Wales Modularisation and Credit Based Development Project, Cardiff: Fforwm.

Finegold, D, Keep, E, Miliband, D, Raffe, D, Spours, K and Young, M (1990) *A British Baccalaureate: Ending the Division Between Education and Training*, London: IPPR.

Further Education Unit (1992) *A Basis for Credit? Developing a Post-16 Credit Accumulation and Transfer Framework: A Paper for Discussion*, London: FEU.

Further Education Unit (1993) *Discussing Credit: A Collection of Occasional Papers Relating to the FEU Proposal for a Post-16 Credit Accumulation and Transfer Framework*, London: FEU.

Further Education Unit (1995) *A Framework for Credit Framework Guidelines: Levels, Credit Value and the Award of Credit*, London: FEU.

Green, A (1995) 'Core Skills, Participation and Progression in Post-Compulsory Education and Training in England and France', *Comparative Education*, **31**, 1.

Guardian, The (1996) 'Exam Chiefs Attack Limit on Number of A Level Re-sits', 6 August.

Hodgson, A (1994) 'Key Credit Accumulation and Transfer (CAT) Developments at Gwent Tertiary College, Solihull College and Wirral Metropolitan College' in Young, M, Hodgson, A and Morris, A (1994) *Unifying Strategies and Organisational Change in Post-16 Education. Unified Curriculum at 16+*, Working Paper 7, Post-16 Education Centre, Institute of Education, University of London.

Kazis, R (1992) *Modular Training Systems and Strategies: An International Meeting*, Jobs for the Future, Washington DC.

Lasonen, J (1996) *Reforming Upper Secondary Education in Europe: Surveys of Strategies for Post-16 Education to Improve the Parity of Esteem for Initial Vocational Education in Eight European Educational Systems*, Finland: University of Jyväskylä Press.

Leney, T and Spours, K (1997, forthcoming) *A Comparative Analysis of Submissions and Responses of Educational Professional Associations to the Dearing Review of 16–19 Qualifications Draft Discussion Paper*, Post-16 Education Centre, Institute of Education, University of London.

London Together/London TECs CAT Group (1994) *Establishing the Credit System for London*, London Together/London TECs CAT Group.

Macintosh, H (1986) 'Modular and Unit Credit Systems', in Nuttall, D (ed.) *Assessing Educational Achievement*, London: Falmer Press.

Mack, D (1989) 'The Scottish Action Plan', in Spours, K, Mack, D, Jones, J, Sauve, E and Holifield, J (1989) *Modularisation and Progression: Issues in the 14–19 Curriculum*, Working Paper No 6, Post-16 Education Centre, Institute of Education, University of London.

Modular Information Network (1993) *Modularity and Effective Learning: Case Study No 4*, Modular Information Network, Addlestone: MIN.

Ministry of Education (1959) *15 to 18: Report of the Central Advisory Council for Education – England (Vol. 1)*, London: HMSO.

Moon, B (ed.) (1988) *Modular Curriculum*, London: Paul Chapman.

Pinnell, H (1996) 'Testing for Fool's Gold', *The Guardian*, 6 August.

Post-16 Education Centre (1991–1996) *Unified Curriculum at 16+*, Working Papers 1–12, Post-16 Education Centre, Institute of Education, University of London.

Pyke, N (1996) 'Modules Could Boost Exam Passes', *TES*, 9 August.

Raffe, D (1988) 'Modules and the Strategy of Institutional Versatility: The First Two Years of the 16-Plus Action Plan in Scotland', in Raffe, D (ed.) *Education and the Youth Labour Market*, London: Falmer Press.

Raffe, D (ed.) (1992a) *Modularisation in Initial Vocational Training: Recent Developments in Six European Countries*, Edinburgh: Centre for Educational Sociology, University of Edinburgh.

Raffe, D (1992b) *Innovations in Training: The Potential of Modular Courses. Report of a Conference held in Lisbon, June 1992 in the Framework of the EC PETRA Programme*, Brussels: European Commission.

Raffe, D (1994) 'Modular Strategies for Overcoming Academic/Vocational Divisions: Issues Arising from the Scottish Experience', *Journal of Education Policy*, **9**, 2.

Rainbow, R (1993) 'Modular A and AS levels: The Wessex Project', in Richardson, W, Woolhouse, J and Finegold, D (eds) *The Reform of Post-16 Education and Training in England and Wales*, Harlow: Longman.

Richardson, W, Spours, K, Woolhouse, J and Young, M (1995) *Current Developments in Modularity and Credit*, Working Paper No 5, Learning for the Future Project, Institute of Education and University of Warwick.

Robertson, D (1993) 'Credit Frameworks: an International Comparison' in FEU, *Discussing Credit: A Collection of Occasional Papers Relating to the FEU Proposal for a Post-16 Credit Accumulation and Transfer Framework*, London: FEU.

Robertson, D (1994) *Choosing to Change: Extending Access, Choice and Mobility in Higher Education*, London: Higher Education Quality Council.

Scottish Office Education Department (1994) *Higher Still: Opportunity for All*, London: HMSO.

Spours, K (1995) *Post-16 Participation, Attainment and Progression*, Working Paper No 17, Post-16 Education Centre, Institute of Education, University of London.

Spours, K and Hodgson, A (1996) *Value-added and Raising Attainment: A Formative Approach. A Resource Pack for Practitioners*, Poole: Institute of Education and British Petroleum Education Service.

Spours, K and Lucas, N (1996) *The Formation of a National Sector of Incorporated Colleges: Beyond the FEFC Model*, Working Paper No 19, Post-16 Education Centre, Institute of Education, University of London.

Spours, K and Young, M (1996) 'Dearing and Beyond: Steps and Stages to a Unified System', *British Journal of Education and Work*, December.

Tait, T (1993) 'Introduction', in FEU, *Discussing Credit: A Collection of Occasional Papers Relating to the FEU Proposal for a Post-16 Credit Accumulation and Transfer Framework*, London: FEU.

TES (1996) 'Rituals On-line', 9 August.

Warwick, D (1987) *The Modular Curriculum*, Oxford: Blackwell.

Wilson, P (1993) 'Developing a Post-16 CAT Framework: the Technical Specifications', in FEU, *Discussing Credit: A Collection of Occasional Papers Relating to the FEU Proposal for a Post-16 Credit Accumulation and Transfer Framework*, London: FEU.

Young, M, Hodgson, A and Morris, A (1994a) *Unifying Strategies and Organisational Change in Post-16 Education*, Unified Curriculum at 16+ Working Paper No 7, Post-16 Education Centre, Institute of Education, University of London.

Young, M, Wilson, P, Oates, T and Hodgson, A (1994b) *Building a Credit Framework: Opportunities and Problems – Report of Hamlyn Seminar 2*, Unified Curriculum at 16+ Working Paper No 4, Post-16 Education Centre, Institute of Education, University of London.

Young, M, Hodgson, A, Hayton, A, Bell, R and Melliss, N (1994c) *Modular Strategies and the Hamlyn/CILNTEC Post-16 Unified Curriculum Project*, Unified Curriculum at 16+ Working Paper No 6, Post-16 Education Centre, Institute of Education, University of London.

Young, M, Hodgson, A, King, C, *et al.* (1994d) *Progression and Core Skill Issues in the Hamlyn/CILNTEC Post-16 Unified Curriculum Project*, Unified Curriculum at 16+ Working Paper No 8, Post-16 Education Centre, Institute of Education, University of London.

Young, M, Hodgson, A, Jamieson, J, *et al.* (1995) *Putting Credit Into Practice: A Hamlyn/CILNTEC Unified Curriculum Project Perspective*, Unified Curriculum at 16+ Working Paper No 10, Post-16 Education Centre, Institute of Education, University of London.

CHAPTER 8

Unitization: Developing a Common Language for Describing Achievement

Geoff Stanton

Introduction

This chapter is based on two related propositions: first, that there should be a common approach to the definition of achievement to be used for all qualifications routes and all kinds of achievement; second, that discussion of the content and characteristics of qualifications is much more fruitful if it is related to the units of achievement of which they are comprised. This will produce a simpler, more flexible and comprehensible system in the medium term. In the short term, it may be difficult to convey what is proposed to all concerned, because for some people the 'language' they currently use will interfere with their understanding. It may, therefore, be helpful to begin with an overview of the argument being made before providing the details.

I suggest that there are four major reasons why the English education and training system would benefit from an agreed protocol for defining achievement: first, in order to facilitate the implementation of Sir Ron Dearing's recommendations for 16–19 qualifications (Dearing, 1996); second, to make the guidance, progression and transfer process more effective for students; third, to provide curriculum managers with more efficient and coherent curriculum management tools at an institutional level; and finally, to support the eventual creation of a more coherent or unified system.

This protocol, or 'common language', would not change the essential nature of the achievements represented by different qualifications. There is a danger of such distortion at present, arising from attempts to make comparisons or establish equivalencies by defining the achievements accredited by one qualification in terms of another.

The most promising approach to the development of such a common protocol is to use it in order to define those outcomes which have to be demonstrated by a candidate if they are to be awarded a pass or a grade, and to form units comprising coherent groups of such outcomes. This does not require that all outcomes have to be in the form of behavioural objectives, or NVQ-type competences; nor does it mean that each unit needs to be taught or assessed separately, though this remains an option for use when appropriate.

The identification of such units of achievement and the development of a common language in which to express them would also increase the practicality and value of a credit accumulation and transfer (CAT) system. However, a CAT system also requires there to be agreement on the extent and purposes for which a credit awarded by one body will be recognized by another. The complex problems arising from this, which are to do with educational politics as much as educational technicalities, should not cause us to delay the development of a common language. Its existence would be of immense value in enhancing our ability to analyse the choices which policy-makers, providers and participants have to make and to identify the strengths and weaknesses of the present system. The improved quality of the resultant debate would extend to that surrounding the feasibility of a post-14 CAT system.

Other countries have already come to similar conclusions and have therefore redesigned their systems from scratch along these lines. This would be difficult in England, given the current state of play and the size and complexity of our provision. However, it would be possible to cause our system to evolve in the right direction, towards provision which was not only more manageable and fit for current purposes but was also capable of continual improvement without disruption. This evolution would be through a series of stages, each of which had value in its own right.

The first such stage is unitization, that is the analysis of existing qualifications into units of achievement. This needs to be distinguished from modularization, which is sub-dividing courses into modules of delivery.

The context for unitization

It is no coincidence that many of the relevant developments in the area of unitization have taken place in and around the further education (FE) sector. FE colleges have always offered a very wide range of qualifications. In the early 1980s these would have included vocational qualifications at operative, craft and technician level, offered by a wide range of awarding bodies, together with higher level qualifications for junior managers and advanced technicians which were at the equivalent of degree level. As the role of the colleges expanded, because of the demands from adults for a 'second chance' and from 16-year-olds for an alternative to school, O-levels, A-levels and adult Access courses were added to their portfolio.

At one time the organizational disadvantages of this multiplicity were limited by the fact that each department (or even section) operated relatively independently, even down to having its own admissions procedure and timetable grid. However, by the mid-1980s many colleges were attempting to develop and apply college-wide policies and procedures, because of the improvements in quality and efficiency this produced. At the same time, as we have seen from Chapter 1, parallel moves were taking place at a national level, for reform at the level of the system.

By the late 1980s government policy was that within a few years all qualifications taken in the post-16 (FE) phase would either have been accredited by SCAA (and before that SEAC), or by NCVQ. As late as 1991, the then junior minister was saying 'In a very short space of time, NVQs will dominate the vocational provision offered by FE Colleges' (Eggar, 1991).

Even if this had happened it would still have produced problems for FE colleges attempting to manage in a coherent fashion a curriculum that was made up of academic and vocational qualifications which were defined in such different ways. Of course the problem was not nearly so acute for other providers, whether they were schools or industrial trainers, because these tended to offer qualifications from only one of the tracks. On the other hand, students attempting to progress from one track to another, or even to combine them, certainly shared the colleges' problem.

Despite the introduction of the NVQ framework, many of the traditional vocational qualifications were still showing signs not only of life but of popularity in the market. This was partly because NCVQ had defined their accreditation criteria so tightly that NVQs became, in effect, new (and competing) qualifications rather than part of the inclusive framework advocated by the White Paper which created NCVQ (DES/DE, 1986).

At this time there were also a growing number of modular courses, usually designed for adults wishing to gain access to university without doing A-levels, which were accredited by Open College Networks and which lay outside the aegis of both SCAA and NCVQ.

With the introduction of GNVQs, complexity was increased because it became apparent that GNVQ units were crucially different from NVQ units, and even more different from both the modules which made up Open College Courses and those which made up the (increasingly popular) modular A-levels.

A comparison with the National Curriculum is salutary. The National Curriculum had been difficult enough for schools to manage, but at least the same approach was adopted to the definition of achievement within it, whatever the nature of the subject matter. By contrast, colleges found themselves managing a range of qualifications and their associated courses, each of which had its own way of specifying even the same subject matter (mathematics, for instance). This was making it difficult to give good initial student guidance, to facilitate transfer between courses, to ensure equitable funding across courses and to promote transfer of good practice.

Colleges were very much in the market for a framework which could contain all that they did. Preferably, this should be a national framework but if this was not feasible, then at least they wanted one which could be used for local curriculum management.

Even if at first this was seen as a problem only for the colleges, the equivalent difficulties for students and the effect on their ability to choose well, to progress and to achieve their full potential, eventually made the matter one of national concern, and to some extent the focus of the Dearing Review of 16–19 qualifications (Dearing, 1996).

Dearing stopped short of recommending the kind of unitization developments being designed and implemented in some colleges and some regions. This may have been because he overestimated their complexity and the level of political risk. I would argue, however, that if the technical power of simple unitization had been realized, then the Dearing recommendations would have made existing curriculum management more efficient and effective, facilitated the implementation of his own proposals and enabled the longer-term and incremental building of a more unified system.

What is required?

At one level what is required is very simple. Whether the person trying to interpret a qualification is a candidate, provider, or someone wishing to recruit for a course or a job, they will certainly wish to know both what the qualification certifies that the holder knows, understands and can do and how challenging the required learning was, in terms of the level and amount of achievement that the award represents. Although this is not always made clear, some employers and admission tutors are also looking for evidence of additional factors, such as the ability to integrate, select and deploy what has been learned, either in a further course of study or in a workplace task, and how far the applicants have learned to learn and can discipline themselves to complete tasks and assignments even under pressure.

This is simply put, and appears reasonably obvious, but the way in which qualifications or the requirements of recruiters are currently described rarely does equal justice to all these elements. There are two main reasons why qualifications, as currently described, fail to provide all the required information. First, there is a tendency to emphasize some of the features described above while leaving the rest implicit, or a matter for reputation rather than definition. Thus A-levels clearly specify the topics covered while often being vaguer about the skills which are or must be demonstrated through them. The reverse is true of GNVQs. Here the skill and required outcomes are clear, but the syllabus content is less so.

A second cause of difficulty is that attempting to communicate at the level of subjects – as opposed to at the level of the units of which they are composed – is not usually productive. For instance, if you ask employers what they require in terms of mathematics as a subject, they are likely to feel inadequate and guilty that they do not know more about modern education, and/or to ask for 'a good O-level pass', since that used to provide them with people who had what they needed.

This, in turn, produces questions about how far any new qualification is equivalent to the old, without it being possible for either side to be clear about what kind of equivalence is meant or needed. On the other hand, the conversation becomes much more fruitful if it focuses on what units of mathematics are required. We may then find that, for instance, the job or course does not have any great requirement for a high level of generic mathematical ability, but does need someone who is competent and comfortable with the concepts and techniques of statistics. This could even mean that some people who have passed A-level mathematics (while being weak on that particular part of their exam paper) are unsuitable for a given post, while others who have no desire to take the whole subject, but who are perfectly capable of gaining the relevant unit, are well fitted.

In summary, the argument is that we not only need a 'language' which enables us to compare and contrast outcomes, levels and volume of learning, but that we need to apply it at the level of units rather than at the level of whole subjects.

The technical proposals

The following is based largely on the FEU's proposals (FEU, 1995), with less emphasis on the award of credit (for reasons which I shall explain) and more on the respective role of practitioners, awarding bodies and what Dearing (1996) labels the 'regulatory bodies'.

A unitized system of qualifications should have the following characteristics:

- The nation's post-14 curriculum offer would be made up of an array of units which could be arranged into a number of frameworks for different purposes.
- Most units would be derived from analysis of existing academic and vocational qualifications. Others could be proposed by practitioners (usually acting as part of a local consortium) or by awarding bodies. New units would be required for updating purposes, in order to meet market demand, or in order to take advantage of local facilities or expertise.
- Responsibility for the validation of a unit would lie with the national regulatory body,[1] though the approval process would be delegated to regionally based panels of practitioners acting under its supervision. Not only would this make the task more manageable, it would also spread good practice amongst the assessment community and back to the centre from them.
- In order to be validated, a unit should have:
    - a unique title/number
    - learning outcome statements, clearly expressed
    - assessment criteria
    - a designated level
    - a designated size.
- The learning outcomes should be specified in a manner similar in principle to that already adopted for NVQs and GNVQs, using a common convention

for describing what the learner has to be able to know, understand and do. These and the assessment criteria should be supported by the use of exemplars and by meetings of assessors, so that the written definitions can be kept more succinct than is currently the case with (G)NVQs, while reliability of interpretation is maintained or increased. By the same means, A-level subjects would become more transparent and easier to monitor.

- The validation panels would also determine the unit's level and size, working to nationally agreed definitions, once again supported by exemplars. There would be a total of eight levels, from what Dearing called 'Entry' level through to postgraduate. Although each unit would be allocated to only one level, the assessment criteria would make it possible to achieve that unit at one of a number of grades, corresponding to those currently in use at, for instance, GNVQ Level 3.

- The size of a unit would be defined in terms of the amount of learning (not teaching) time required by the average student to achieve it under typical conditions. The standard unit size would be 30 hours, though units could have sizes which were multiples of this if the need for coherence of subject matter made this necessary.

- Awarding bodies would define which combinations of (mandatory or optional) units would make up given qualifications and which assessment methods they considered to be appropriate to these units, singly or in groups, working to criteria defined and monitored by the regulatory body.

It is important to note that this technical specification is neutral with regard to such issues as whether the teaching programme is modular or integrated, or the extent to which assessment is via assignments, observation of performance or conventional examinations. Unitization makes it easier to debate which of these options is most appropriate in given circumstances and easier to implement that decision once made, but it does not, in itself, require or even promote any particular course of action.

The FEU specification of units adds determination of 'credit value' to the list of requirements I have given above. I prefer to regard this as one of the many uses to which unitization can be put, rather than as a compulsory feature of a unit. As the FEU says:

> It is possible for a group of institutions to agree about the size of a unit without all of them agreeing to recognise its credit value, or without agreeing it for all purposes. It is for this reason that we recommend that the context and purpose for which the value is recognised should be stated. (FEU, 1995, p.13)

This illustrates well that the issue of credit value is both complex and negotiable. This variability is amplified if applied nation-wide. Therefore, to insist on its inclusion may create serious obstacles, causing the more straightforwardly technical issue of unitization to be seriously delayed, along with the many benefits it could bring.

The issue of complexity

There is often an assumption that an array of units might be too complex for most people to understand or use. However, as we have seen, the present qualifications system is neither user-friendly nor simple in practice and, in any case, the fear of increased complexity may be unfounded.

Let us examine the question of numbers of units as opposed to numbers of whole qualifications. The Dearing Report states that there are 'at least 16,000' qualifications available to 16–19-year-olds (Dearing, 1996, p.11). Since both academic and vocational qualifications continue to evolve, this number will not decrease and even though some become redundant each year, will probably continue to grow. Economic and technological factors will create more and different types of occupations and the development of academic knowledge is never ending. These factors, allied to a culture in which increased customer (ie, student) choice is encouraged, make the pressure for new qualifications irresistible.

In a non-unitized system, even a minor modification to an existing qualification creates a brand new one. By the same token, potential users have a problem learning about the new product and in understanding whether the changes make it more or less fitted to their purposes. However, all that may have happened, in effect, is that, for instance, 10 per cent of units which make up a qualification have been replaced by others. This may be in order to prepare people for a different but related job/subject, or for updating purposes. At the same time, a limited number of key units will not only occur in both old and new versions of the qualification, but also in other qualifications. This leads us to a crucial point of logic – the number of component parts is less than the number of qualifications which can be formed from them.

In addition, it is possible to categorize and group units so as serve various purposes. One grouping might form a series of 'learning pathways', putting together those units which make sensible combinations for specified purposes and showing where the pathways overlap. Even if, in the first instance, this process simply reassembled the units into conventional schemes and subject combinations, these schemes and combinations would become more transparent and would gain the potential for more flexible delivery and development.

Alternatively, the same array of units could be grouped by subject matter and level, so that an employer, for instance, could choose what kind and level of mathematics best suited their purposes and a student could see both what was currently expected of them and what other units they could then progress to.

It is easier and more productive to arrange units (rather than subjects) into frameworks, because the characteristics of units are easier to identify than can ever be the case with larger and more diverse subjects or vocational areas. This fact has important implications for some of the Dearing proposals for the mixing of qualifications from different tracks.

Lessons from elsewhere

An awareness of the potential advantages of unitization has led many higher education institutions (HEIs) in this country to devise modular degrees. This type of structure enables them to produce a 'catalogue' of modules from which students can construct (in theory) an almost infinite number of courses to suit their individual requirements. In practice, HEIs impose 'rules of combination' to ensure that a degree is awarded only when an appropriate number, range and balance of modules has been taken, and there will also be timetabling constraints which restrict choice. But the logical point remains: the number of potential courses is greater than the number of modules.

Not only does a modular system make it easier to understand what a degree represents, it also allows employers and others to identify which modules are particularly relevant to their needs. They can therefore specify both an overall degree performance (if they think this represents important general qualities) and also, within that, which elements are crucial or optional.

HEIs devise their own courses and choose the assessment regime which they think will best test how well the students have succeeded on them. This means that they tend to think in terms of teaching/learning 'modules' which are then assessed. It also means that each catalogue of modules is unique to that institution (or even department) and that if a student wishes to transfer from one to another, some kind of system has to be devised whereby it can be determined how much 'credit' their previous learning is worth.

The potential of a country-wide CAT system in and between universities has been exhaustively explored in the Higher Education Quality Council's Project coordinated by Professor David Robertson. Robertson recommended that a common system should extend across both further and higher education (Robertson, 1994). Although this proposal has tremendous potential, it may in fact have been counterproductive. The complexities which Robertson highlights may have deterred policy-makers from considering simpler but very fruitful developments in the FE phase.

Looking beyond the English education and training system, there are also lessons to learn from Scotland, New Zealand and Wales, which have experimented with unitization.

The Scots, as Chapter 12 points out, are in the process of reorganizing their fifth and sixth years of secondary education along these lines. Their scheme does not include Scottish Vocational Qualifications (SVQs), but otherwise it is intended to provide both general vocational and more academic qualifications for all abilities. The Scots judge that something like 3,000 units, over five levels and requiring an average of 40 hours study per unit, will give this coverage. In English terms, this would allow for all existing GCSEs and A-levels to be provided from this 'bank' of units, plus all three levels of GNVQs.

New Zealand is being even more ambitious. There, an Education Act in 1990 set in motion a scheme which is planned to bring all secondary, further and higher education and training qualifications within an eight-level framework. The New Zealand Qualifications Authority estimates that some 6,000 units[2] will be required for the post-compulsory qualifications.

In many ways, Wales provides the most interesting case study, because it demonstrates the potential power of linking bottom-up developments to national standards and quality frameworks. Over the last few years, the colleges and Open College Networks (OCNs) of Wales, together with FEU (now FEDA) and the Welsh Access Unit, have unitized the majority of the FE programmes in Wales. The work was funded by the Welsh Office through FFORWM, the network of Welsh FE colleges. Unitization was undertaken by practitioners whose work was validated using OCN procedures, involving peer-group panels (Pierce, 1996). This was referred to as the 'writing and approval' of units, which has led to fears that this system is in competition with, for instance, NVQ frameworks. This is a real danger but – in theory at least – units should only be created for learning not as yet recognized nationally, or where non-unitized qualifications (such as many A-levels) are being analysed into their component parts for local purposes, such as planning progression routes or managing programmes containing different types of qualification. Existing units, such as those within NVQs, still need to be processed locally in order to identify their individual level and size, and it is the value given to these parameters which needs to be 'approved'.

Two lessons arise from this. First, there needs to be collaboration between local and national initiatives in order to avoid confusion and overlap. Second, national agencies can capitalize on a range of local expertise and enthusiasm, which can save them work, provide tried and tested units for the national 'bank', and make practitioners feel involved and influential rather than mere recipients of prescriptions. This frees the agencies to focus on quality criteria, including reliable national standards, which only they can supervise.

Barriers to change

Although the developments in other phases, such as higher education, and in other countries, such as Scotland, New Zealand and Wales, provide very helpful insights into what could be done in the FE phase in England, they can also create barriers.

The university model tends to cause people to confuse unitization of assessment, which is what I am advocating, with modularization of delivery and the use of credit points. As I shall explain, both of these are made easier after unitization, but they are not essential and certainly not prerequisites. Both also bring difficulties and it is often anxiety about overcoming these that deters policy-makers from espousing unitization.

The examples of the other countries can give the impression that such developments can only occur in a place where size and recent history makes it possible to create a new qualifications system from scratch. The size and complexity of the English scene has not, in recent times, prevented government from instituting large-scale and radical changes to vocational qualifications and the school curriculum, but the fact that these have not yet bedded down makes the suggestion of yet more change unwelcome.

The irony is that had the National Curriculum and NVQs/GNVQs been conceived on a unitized basis, this could have made their introduction both more productive and more manageable, and the Dearing Review of Qualifications for 16–19-year-olds might have been unnecessary. In fact, it remains the case that without unitization it is difficult to see how many of Dearing's recommendations can be implemented.

This is why the proposition, put forward by the FEU in 1993 and developed further since then, is so important. The FEU argued that it was possible to start from the present situation in England and Wales and, through systematically analysing the array of new and traditional qualifications currently in use post-14, to enable a unit-based system to evolve. In other words, existing qualifications could be analysed into the units of which they are (usually implicitly) composed, rather than being assembled from a newly created bank of units.

This need not change the current qualifications at all. However, as has already been indicated, there are a number of benefits which can flow from this analysis, since it makes it much clearer to all concerned what is currently going on.

Since forms of unitization – albeit different ones – are already in use with regard to NVQs and GNVQs, it may be the fear of the effect on A-levels which produces the greatest obstacle. In fact, unitization would helpfully clarify what candidates have to know, understand and be able to do in order to be awarded an A-level, thus underpinning public confidence in them as they necessarily evolve and as more people are enabled to achieve them. This greater transparency would also help students in making choices and in creating subject combinations and would show others where there is a risk of 'double counting' because the same learning is assessed within different subjects. Unitization need not produce incoherent programmes because rules of combination could be specified. The need to assess candidates' ability to integrate learning could be met by a unit specifically designed for this purpose.

A common but mistaken assumption is that the more unified system that would result from these proposals would also be too uniform. In fact, it does not follow at all that using a common protocol to define achievement makes that achievement more homogeneous. The National Curriculum is an obvious example which disproves this argument. On the contrary, using a common terminology makes it possible to define some crucial differences better than we now can, which will help to ensure that they are preserved. It will doubtless also reveal that some other differences are more due to reputation than to reality, and that will be all to the good, particularly if this contributes to enhancing parity of esteem on an objective basis.

A further set of objections comes from those who see such an exercise as 'undermining the rationalisation of qualifications with which both NCVQ and SCAA are charged' (NCVQ, 1996, p.155). In part, this belief arises from the fact that NVQs and GNVQs are already made up of units. Therefore, it can seem that re-analysing them into a new set, as some colleges have done, is to 'develop their own qualifications and units of qualifications; often representations of national qualifications but in altered form' (NCVQ, 1996, p.155).

However, the rationale for undertaking the re-analysis is that NVQ units do not, as they stand, give the simple information that many users need. For instance, within a given NVQ, one unit of which it is composed may be considerably bigger (in that it represents considerably more learning time) than another, and may be at differing levels (in terms of the practical or intellectual skills required). Different NVQs at the same level contain different numbers of units, whereas GNVQs are composed of similar numbers of units, all of which have the same size and level.

Therefore, how far a GNVQ and an NVQ programme overlap, are complementary, or are equivalent is not immediately apparent. If a student wishes to take a programme which contains both NVQ and GNVQ units, there is no simple way of indicating the total value of the whole programme – unless all components are translated into a *lingua franca*. But if the translation is properly done, the original meaning – that is, the achievement to which the qualification attests – should not be changed.

It may seem remarkable to an outside observer that it can be so difficult to relate NVQs to GNVQs, and that although, say, NVQs in catering and business studies may both contain economics, that component is defined in ways which are unique to each NVQ. Nevertheless, that is the case. It largely derives from the fact that in order to encourage employers voluntarily to take up NVQs, each industry was given the freedom to define their needs independently. This is healthy as far as it goes: the real problem arises when the related qualifications are required to use these definitions as they stand, rather than translating them into units of assessment, which are demonstrably part of the same overall framework and are therefore common to different qualifications.

Less remarkable, perhaps, is the lack of links between (G)NVQs and GCSE/A-level. At least they were the responsibility of different quangos. Nevertheless, the extent of the academic/vocational divide, and the failure of the government to see or to manage the education and training system as a whole, is well evidenced by the fact that at the same time as SEAC was developing a set of ten levels to cover the curriculum for 5- to 16-year-olds, NCVQ was starting to implement a different system of five levels for vocational qualifications post-16. This led, for instance, to a situation in which Level 3 referred both to vocational qualifications of national diploma standard[3] and to what the average primary school child would achieve at the age of 8.

Now that the government has confirmed the intention to create a single Qualifications and National Curriculum Authority, there is an excellent opportunity to correct these anomalies, and – more positively – to transfer best practice from one regime to another. The proposals being made here would facilitate this and would reduce the risk of existing barriers and stereotypes being recreated within the new organization.

The potential benefits of unitization

Not only is talking in terms of units simpler and easier to relate to everyday requirements, but in adopting this approach we can gain useful insights into existing qualifications. It therefore brings new benefits, as well as dealing with current problems.

For students, unitization has the potential to:

- improve the quality of guidance, since it makes it easier to compare and contrast programmes and to show the level and type of achievement required for success;[4]
- make more transparent the overlap and gaps produced when a particular combination of qualifications is chosen to form a programme;
- facilitate transfer between programmes by showing what units have already been covered and which will have been missed;
- promote parity of esteem between qualifications by showing their similarities and distinctive differences.

For schools and colleges unitization has the potential to:

- enhance recruitment procedures by making it easier to identify prerequisite units and possible progression routes;
- improve resourcing and timetabling, by allowing resources to be linked to the number and nature of units in a programme and by showing where units on different programmes could be taught together (Coates and Hamilton, 1996);
- promote the development and transfer of good practice by showing the effect of different methods of teaching towards the same units (for instance, statistics in both psychology and business studies);
- enable achievement audits to be introduced, showing the relationship between the deployment of different types and amounts of teaching resources and the achievement of units by students at given points during a programme.

In his report on 16–19 qualifications, Dearing flirted with the idea of an entirely unitized system on the lines of that being developed in Scotland, but in the end fought shy of it, probably because he (or others) fell foul of the very confusion about terminology which he identifies, and mistakenly linked the idea of unitization with unresolved anxieties about modularization (as experienced in the A-level context) and credit (as used by HEIs).

Nevertheless, it remains the case that unitization would make many of Dearing's policy recommendations much easier to implement. I have already discussed the contribution which unitization could make to the possibility of combined programmes which cross present divides, to transfer between programmes, and to quality assurance in the form of achievement auditing. I would go further and say that without unitization some of Dearing's recommendations cannot be undertaken effectively. For example, it would only be feasible to include the four broad domains required for a Diploma programme if planning, timetabling and assessment took place at the level of units, particularly if the key skills are also to be covered. It is also self-evident that the achievement represented by the units needs to be defined according to a common protocol, if the required breadth and depth is to be recognizable. Similarly, if students are genuinely to use the National Record of Achievement throughout 'lifetime' learning, as Dearing recommends, then there is a requirement that achievement of all types should be recorded in a common language which reflects the nature, level and volume of that achievement.

Dearing also recommends that 'subject areas' should be allocated to one of the three 'pathways' – academic, applied and vocational. If this recommendation is to be taken up, such characteristics would be much easier to attribute to units rather than at the level of whole subjects.

Conclusion

In his foreword to the 1991 White Paper, John Major said that it was the government's aim to 'end the artificial divide between academic and vocational qualifications' (Major, 1991). There are, of course, important differences between qualifications and learning programmes, some of which need to be recognized and even protected if we are also to provide the necessary diversity and choice for a post-compulsory phase of education and training. It is the argument of this chapter, however, that the divide which is most artificial and now needs most attention is the fact that achievement on different routes is defined in such different terms. This has implications at three levels. First, at the level of learners, it makes it more difficult for them to understand their choices and to transfer or progress. Second, at the institutional level, it inhibits the development of integrated, flexible and cost-effective provision. Finally, at national level, it works against such policies as the establishment of parity of esteem, the publication of examination results in an understandable and equitable form, the enhancement of breadth and key skills in all areas and the creation of a coherent framework of qualifications.

The need for a coherent framework has been voiced by virtually every significant report or policy statement over the last decade. Failure to make progress has often been attributed to problems of educational or national politics. The argument of this chapter has been that it has also been because of two comparatively simple technical problems: the lack of an agreed approach to the definition of achievement and a debate which has taken place at the level of whole subjects or qualifications, instead of at the level of their component units. This has prevented some crucial conclusions being reached and has inhibited action in those areas where there is agreement.

There is a strong analogy between what is being proposed here and the development in the earlier part of this millennium of an agreed language in which to discuss and to describe the physical world. Before that, progress was stultified by such things as the inability to distinguish differences of terminology from disagreements about facts, to define hypotheses and the evidence which would test them or to record progress made so that those following could build on it. As a result, medical treatments, for instance, were a matter of fashion and fervent assertion, rather than anything else. They came, they went and then they reappeared. Is this not characteristic of current educational developments?

The protocol or common language which I am proposing is not itself a reform of qualifications or of the learning programmes which lead to them. It would, however, make appropriate reform more feasible and more effective. Work on it is not, therefore, an alternative to other developments, it is a prerequisite of them.

There are already many local initiatives, not least in Wales and Scotland, from which we can learn. The technical issues are not as complex as their unfamiliarity may lead some to believe. There certainly remains more work to be done and this will doubtless produce some unforeseen problems, but in view of the prize to be won, the sooner we make a start on the necessary investigations the better!

Notes

1. Now NCVQ or SCAA; from September 1997, the Qualifications and National Curriculum Authority.
2. Each slightly smaller that those in the Scottish model, requiring the equivalent of 30 hours of learning.
3. Usually requiring the equivalent of two years study after a good school-leaving performance at 16.
4. For instance, at present only teachers with experience of both can explain the difference between a GNVQ in Business and three A-levels in subjects such as economics, business studies and law. Even they do not always agree.

References

Coates, P and Hamilton, J (1996) *16–19 Coherence Project*, London: SCAA.

Dearing, Sir Ron (1996) *Review of Qualifications for 16–19 Year Olds: Full Report*, London: SCAA.

Department of Education and Science/Employment Department (1986) *Working Together: Education and Training*, London: HMSO.

Eggar, T (1991) DES Press Release, DES 21March.

Further Education Unit (1995) *A Framework for Credit*, London: FEU.

Major, J (1991) 'Introduction', *Education and Training for the 21st Century*, London: HMSO.

National Council for Vocational Qualifications (1996) Written evidence to the Education Committee of the House of Commons, London: *Hansard*, 17 January.

Pierce, J (1996) *Inform*, London: FEDA.

Robertson, D (1994) *Choosing to Change*, London: HEQC.

CHAPTER 9

Assessment and Achievement

Tim Oates

Introduction

This chapter will make two key points about assessment. First, it will postulate the existence within education and training systems of the 'unintended outcome' effect. Second, it will argue that assessment is never value-neutral (Gipps and Murphy, 1994; Wood, 1991). The first point can be explained by analysis of successive innovations and by analogy. I will start with analogy.

In the late 19th century, the Pacific islands saw the first attempts at biological control of pests. The indigenous bird-life was being decimated by rats which had colonized various islands after leaving European trade ships. Wishing to protect the colourful and unique bird-life, concerned European botanists deliberately introduced cats, who would kill the rats, and thus the diverse fauna would be preserved. A cunning plan, apart from the fact that the birds had never set eyes on a cat before and thus each sat there meekly until a cat pounced. A friendly tropical bird is after all greatly more attractive to a cat as a meal than an angry rat, its cunning well-honed by a difficult life in the hold of a Dutch Trader. Rats and cats duly flourished, while the bird population plummeted.

Changes in assessment are often like that. You can switch to a new assessment regime in order to secure a specific change, greater access to assessment, increased rigour and so on, only to find that a wide range of unintended effects occur. This chapter will look at changes to 14+ assessment in order to examine this effect, including the introduction and unfolding changes to General National Vocational Qualifications (GNVQs). The intention is to make clearer the impact on the education and training system, and particularly on student achievement, of particular approaches to assessment.

Turning to the second key point, I want to highlight that assessment is never value-neutral. Values particularly are expressed through a desire to assess some things rather than others and, increasingly, in assumptions that standards are only maintained by certain forms of assessment. In addition, assessment has become increasingly politicized as assessment-led change has come to dominate change strategy in education and training (Oates, 1995). This chapter takes as its main theme the idea that we are beginning to understand with more sophistication the impact of assessment on student achievement, but that we are not yet at a level of understanding which allows us to manage that relationship in order to maximize student achievement. Hence the opening analogy. In each policy move around assessment there are unintended effects – sometimes beneficial, sometimes not. The close association of active learning styles with GNVQs; the strategies of schools in the face of performance tables; the strategies students use to improve their final grade in modular schemes – all of these contain an unintended element.

Unintended outcomes

One of the most powerful explanations for the increasing level of political and public controversy over the summer examination results is that perhaps too many functions have been combined together. GCSE and A/AS results are now used for: recording students' achievements; communicating students' achievements to a number of audiences – students themselves, their parents, prospective employers, prospective further and higher education institutions; measurement of institutional performance, particularly through 'league' tables; and monitoring increases or decreases in 'national standards'. Increasingly, qualifications results are also being used to control funding, for example outcome-related funding regimes in further education and government training programmes.

While it may make superficial economic sense to use the same information for a variety of purposes, I would suggest that these purposes are often in conflict or strong tension, distorting policy intentions. They almost certainly turn assessment into a very high-stakes affair, not only for the student or candidate, but also for teachers, trainers and providers. For example, outcome-related funding puts pressure on trainers and assessors in the NVQ system to pass candidates even when they have failed to reach the required standard (Beaumont, 1995), thus stimulating a move to external assessment and much tighter, more expensive quality assurance mechanisms.

The use of exam grades for such a wide variety of functions was not always in vogue. A very different approach was present in the late 1970s and early 1980s, with the establishment of the Assessment of Performance Unit (APU). Set up to monitor national standards, the APU developed validated test instruments within a survey method of increasing sophistication (Gipps and Goldstein, 1983). One feature of the APU approach was that results were only valid to the level of individual local education authorities. It was not possible to detect individual schools which fell below or above national norms or expected levels of achievement. Ironically, this lack of measurement of individual school performance meant that participation in APU surveys was not difficult to secure (Gipps and Goldstein, 1983) and the government was presented with high-quality, well-validated information on student performance. Though not without technical difficulties and political tussles, APU surveys gave a well-grounded view of national standards (Murphy and Broadfoot, 1995). However, in the late 1980s the government became interested in increasing the accountability of individual institutions by producing public records of school performance. The policy choice was either to change the basis of the APU surveys or simply to close the APU and to rely on National Curriculum tests (Standard Assessment Tests/Tasks) and GCSE results. Why keep the APU when using qualifications results would give information on the performance of individual schools? With the advent of National Curriculum testing and the assumption that GCSE grades could be tied closely to National Curriculum levels – an assumption which proved to be ill-founded – the demise of the APU was clearly on the cards.

But as usual with matters of assessment, the unexpected outcome effect has come into play. By using GCSE scores for KS4 tables measuring school performance, the spotlight has been very firmly fixed on the rigour of awarding processes, particularly whether it is easier to gain higher grades with certain examination boards.

Performance tables based on qualifications would be more robust and meet their avowed policy intentions were qualifications first, to be criterion-referenced – allowing schools to demonstrate absolute rather than relative performance while at the same time measuring over time any national upward or downward drift in standards – and second, assessed with complete precision and rigour. I will not here go into the issues of value-added approaches and the fact that all subjects are not equal. At the moment, GCSEs are not fully criterion-referenced; they contain substantial compensation in grade determination (Stobart and Gipps, 1991) and, where examination boards have to review their grade distribution, in a political climate sensitive to upward or downward movement in standards and in a market climate where there is pressure from performance tables, schools may act on ideas of 'easy' and 'tough' boards.

The answer to the question, 'Why the apparent increase in attainment in GCSE and A/AS in recent years?' is complex. Within this, modular A-level has emerged as a villain associated with 'slipping standards' and the proliferation of 'soft' subjects. Statistics in this area have to be approached with caution. In implicating modular A-level as 'easier', with the qualifications yielding a higher than expected attainment profile, the statistics omit the proportion of students who have embarked on the course but do not enter the final examination. We simply do not currently have adequate national statistics to make these strong claims. What is known about modular programmes is that students have early feedback on performance by taking the end of module tests, often switching to a more suitable course. In addition, they therefore do not sit the final examination if they know, on the basis of this early feedback, that they are not ready. These factors tend to tilt the profile of grades in modular programmes towards higher grades. Standards may therefore not be slipping, it's just that the students who are actually taking the exam are meeting higher standards.

The controversy over the 'rigour' of modular A-levels in the press coverage of the 1996 results is an example of the way ideological and technical issues can become unhelpfully entangled. Modular A-levels also provide an important illustration of the relationship between assessment patterns, learning approaches and student achievement.

The intention behind the modular innovation in A-levels was essentially the elevation of attainment by making both learning and assessment more student-centred. However, the increasing focus on using examination outcomes for measuring student performance, institutional performance and national standards has put the spotlight firmly on the effects of modular programmes. There are high stakes for everyone in such a situation – schools (performance table position); examining boards (market share and income); and government (slipping or improving national standards).

A superficial reaction to the idea of upping the role of examination results in measuring the performance of students, schools and the education system might be that, 'It's a sensible idea... if all this information on student performance is being created by exams, why not use it for a variety of purposes?' Indeed, this was the assumption in initial policy work on performance tables. But the unintended outcomes effect came straight into play: schools and staff have changed their behaviour and adopted tactics closely related to the performance tables. Three 'tricks' have emerged:

Trick 1: pull out candidates who look unlikely to score five A–C grades.
Effect: none. DfEE percentages are based on the numbers of students enrolled at the beginning of the year, not the number of candidates.

Trick 2: concentrate school resources on D grade students.
Effect: considerable. This has a proven track record of boosting league positions, but studies show a direct correlation between improving A–C scores and neglect of other students.

Trick 3: scratch poor students from the register.
Effect: may boost league table position but highly risky, because the money a school receives is based on its number of students. However, as younger students are more lucrative than children of GCSE age, some schools risk losing money in the short term to attract new pupils on the basis of apparently good results.
(*The Observer*, 1996)

'Playing the indicators' is not a new game (Theodossin and Thompson, 1987). But it is clear that substantial distortions are creeping into schools' and colleges' curriculum decisions, distortions quite at odds with the original policy intentions of civil servants responsible for designing and implementing performance tables, and of those in examination boards responsible for designing motivating, modern and robust qualifications.

Coherence and convergence

The idea of coherence permeates the Dearing revisions. But what kind of coherence? As outlined at the outset of this chapter, structural change in England and Wales has been assessment-led, using revisions to qualifications in particular as a principal mechanism. So often coherence in the education and training system has been discussed solely in terms of qualifications: duplication, proliferation, progression, cost, rigour and so on. Seldom discussed are students' direct experience of the differences in assessment approaches within individual learning programmes.

There are two distinct sources of variation in assessment approaches: first, decisions by teachers and tutors to use assessment approaches in the course of learning programmes which are different to those used to gain the qualification; second, different models used within different qualifications. An example of the first would be a teacher marking non-coursework A-level English literature essays using a very different set of criteria to that used by markers of the examination. Students are shown past papers but are not shown the assessment objectives from the syllabus or any model answers supplied by the examining board. An example of the second would be a student in a further education college studying one A-level in maths (non-coursework, graded A–E, non-modular) and a GNVQ in Engineering (predominantly coursework-assessed, graded pass, merit and distinction, unit-based).

A glance at different grading systems gives us an interesting insight into the variations which exist across and within the education and training system:

B
GCSE English MEG, 1994

784/1000
military selection interview

B++?
university term paper

80+50+120+70+47+81=B
mark scheme for modular A/AS

merit
GNVQ Science, 1994

W
working towards level 1 in the National Curriculum

78%
mark on term paper – new university

v. good work
it made me feel like I was there
teacher's summary comment on
GCSE English work – diary *c.* 1900

Remember that the diversity I highlight here relates only to the notation for grades, not to how they are arrived at (the assessment processes and grade determination processes), nor the assessment and grading strategy adopted by teachers/trainers within a programme in relation to the formal assessments demanded by a qualification. These are all sources of further variation. Some of this variation is readily understandable – the function of a military selection system is different to that of a general education qualification. The differences in function are detectable in different systems, but participants often are unaware that grading carries multiple functions:

1. providing feedback on attainment
2. differentiating individuals
3. generating a culture of aspiration and achievement
4. communicating achievement – to parents, to higher education institutions, to employers
5. assessing performance of teachers
6. assessing performance of departments
7. assessing performance of institution
8. assessing performance of the education/training system.

Note in particular the use of student grades as a measure for 5 to 8 above. There are fundamental tensions here to which I will return. Some of these differences in grade and assessment systems mark fundamental tensions between both the philosophical and technical assumptions underpinning different qualifications in different parts of the education and training system – for example, the status and role of coursework in its contribution to final grades, and the adherence to principles of 'mastery' rather than 'compensation'. In different qualifications there are different positions on the extent to which assessment is dedicated to maximizing learning; the extent to which feedback during programmes focuses on effort and not ability; and the links between assessment and instructional strategy. In particular, we see with the overall assessment-led change strategy and the prominence of assessment in the discussions about the purposes of different qualifications, the emergence of a high-stakes assessment system. Dearing confirmed the importance of the distinctiveness of the 'pathways', with key aspects of this distinctiveness being defined by differences in assessment and learning (Dearing, 1996). These differences will remain in the post-Dearing world.

Assessment and learning styles

How does this impact on learning? A fundamental assumption behind the Dearing Review is a careful balancing of coherence and distinctiveness – removing unnecessary duplication within pathways and ensuring that pathways carry defining, distinctive characteristics. Indeed, this balancing act was one which enabled Sir Ron Dearing to calm competing constituencies into a widespread subdued welcome of the Review rather than to gain enthusiastic support from some and white-hot adverse reaction from others. The contrasts in learning and assessment styles in the different pathways seem set to continue.

While it is clear that learners are highly adaptive, coping with different assessment and grading systems within different qualifications, sub-optimal performance is stimulated under two conditions. First, where expectations are unclear; this can be remedied by more open processes within learning programmes, making more clear to students the assessment objectives and grade determination procedures, thus enabling them to focus on appropriate learning behaviours and outcomes. Second, and perhaps more significantly, we are beginning to understand that certain types of assessment stimulate different forms of learning:

> Many students succeed on 'objective' tests without necessarily understanding the material they are learning. But real learning involves constructing one's own interpretations and relating this to existing knowledge and understandings.... gradually, however, the teachers committed to these initiatives (e.g. records of achievement and the accompanying action-planning and reviewing) came to realise that what was really making a difference in students' motivation and in the quality of their learning were the changes they were introducing actually in the classroom. These changes included sharing and discussing curriculum goals with students; encouraging students to set their own learning targets and to draw up more general action plans; involving students in assessing their own work so that they were both more willing and more able to monitor their own learning; and teacher and student reviewing progress together. The opportunity for one to one discussion in particular made an enormous impact on many students who had never before had the chance of an individual conversation with a teacher about their learning on a regular basis. An important element of all these processes is their impact on the students' view of themselves and their learning. (Gipps, 1995)

This assessment-learning relation has been thrown into sharp relief within GNVQs. Evaluations have indicated that GNVQs are linked with certain learning styles – principally activity-based learning styles where learners perceive a greater degree of control over their own learning (OFSTED, 1994; Solomon, undated; Stern et al., 1996). These studies indicate that learners otherwise disaffected by previous experiences of qualifications had been re-motivated by the styles of learning and assessment in GNVQs and that GNVQs were not solely attracting low-ability students. Indeed, the programmes were considered to be demanding by students and by teachers but also highly motivating when delivered in competent centres (FEFC, 1994; OFSTED, 1994). These evaluations have repeatedly shown that GNVQ programmes are not treated as an 'easy option' by either students or teachers. While the Dearing Review recommended that NCVQ attend to urgent streamlining of the assessment process, the distinctiveness of the qualification was recognized and supported.

Preliminary research undertaken for NCVQ by the A-level Information Service (ALIS) research team has examined the extent of the contrast between A-levels and GNVQs (Fitz-Gibbon and Wright, 1995). Using the ALIS learning activity observation methods to examine both A-levels and selected GNVQs, on a consistent basis, the team compared the incidence of different classes of learning activities.

On the question, 'Do these learning styles enhance achievement?', the precise measures of improvement or enhancement are problematic. Studies of matched groups have yet to be completed, but the size of the GNVQ cohort now permits sophisticated comparison of learner groups within different pathways. Research completed to date (Solomon undated) does not deal directly with this question, but includes two important insights related to it. First, learners are attracted to the learning styles and assessment regime in GNVQs and thus continue to participate in education where they might previously have felt less motivated to continue to participate. Second, learners within GNVQs have an increased awareness of the way in which they learn; in contrast to learners within GCSE programmes, developing a vocabulary for describing the way in which they tackle activities and the quality of the outcomes which they attain.

Across the education and training system, assessment is being seen less and less as a question of simple measurement of achievement. However, protagonists propose markedly different models but claim equally strongly that 'their' model will maximize achievement (Gipps, 1995, Marks, 1996). There are interesting contrasts between 'criterion-referenced mastery' and 'mark-based compensation-sampling' models, but I will go on to argue that while there are differences in principle and practice, these are often over-stated.

Before contrasting the commitments of the assessment models underpinning the different pathways in the Dearing system of 16–19 qualifications, some myths need to be laid to rest. First, the assessment techniques in A-levels are more varied and more innovative than is often claimed. For example, few realize that some A-level assessment includes the provision of pre-seen materials (such as case studies, bodies of data) which allow students to prepare for an examination which follows later. Second, GNVQs ask students to produce very substantial quantities of written information as evidence of achievement for a qualification which is reputedly about 'demonstrating by doing'; the evidence indicators require pro-duction of a very large volume of reports, case studies and summaries. Third, coursework and peer assessment have levels of reliability which are higher than popular opinion suggests (Brown and Dove, 1991) and traditional systems have lower degrees of precision than is popularly assumed (Wood, 1991).

If students on qualification often lack detailed knowledge of the intricacies of awarding procedures in public examinations, the awareness of the general public is even less developed. Certainly, there is little general understanding that differ-ent qualifications take quite different approaches to crucial matters such as the extent to which the assessment processes aim to cover the content specifications.

There are two major approaches currently in operation: 'compensation-sampling-based assessment' (eg, GCSE, A/AS) and 'mastery-based assessment'. The first is the sampling of outcomes of the syllabus in the final assessment (eg, three essay-style questions on a selection of the topics in the syllabus rather than on all of them). It is claimed that this approach motivates students and teachers to cover and revise all topics in the syllabus since they cannot predict which ones will come up in the assessment. The second – mastery-based assessment (eg, as used in GNVQs/NVQs) – demands full coverage of the outcomes listed in the qualification specifications. Here it is claimed that selectors in education and employment seek to know with precision what a candidate can do and the mastery model guarantees coverage of the outcomes.

In reality, within the compensation-sampling model, teachers and students do make studied guesses on 'what will come up this year' and work on some topics in more depth than others. In the face of these problems, mastery-based assessment seems to offer a clear remedy: all of the required outcomes are assessed. However, GNVQs and NVQs increasingly include very general outcomes, such as skills of critical analysis and an understanding of the role of legislation. Such generalized outcomes can be met by a wide variety of student responses, undermining the idea of absolute precision in the final certification.

In addition, in GNVQs, the trend has been towards including more and more content in the unit specifications (Wolf, 1995). Meanwhile, in A/AS the subject core development has led to more sharply focused content in these qualifications; with a closer relationship being demanded between assessment criteria and syllabus content. Moreover, the drive to increased clarity and fairness in assessment in GCSE and A/AS has led to decreased radical sampling, more alerting of students to assessment topics (through, for example, increased proportions of coursework, pre-seen material leading into the exams, increased numbers of optional questions/topics within papers). This, in conjunction with profile reporting (eg, of module scores, of performance in specific topic areas or on specific papers) has pushed GCSE, A and AS closer to the precision of the mastery model, just as the mastery model moves closer to them.

It has also been increasingly recognized that all assessment, including competence-based mastery assessment, involves sampling of performance (Wood, 1991). The degree and type of sampling has very material consequences, but it is certainly a matter of degree, rather than a difference in principle, between A/AS and GCSE on the one hand and GNVQs and NVQs on the other.

Another area where convergence is taking place in term of assessment regimes is in 'compensation'. Compensation is a crucial component of GCSE and A/AS and involves the facility for one student to gain a grade by collecting marks from certain parts of the assessments and a second student to gain the same grade by collecting marks from different parts of the assessments. Compensation is not antithetical to criterion-referencing. The award of individual marks or groups of marks to coursework and examination question responses can be based on stated criteria. However, compensation can be introduced into the way those marks are aggregated to give a final grade and to determine a pass or fail in the qualification.

Compensation has two major functions. First, in examinations for those under 19 it is recognized that students are still maturing; their conceptual development may be unpredictably uneven, and it is not possible to predict in what areas individual students may be weak or strong. Therefore, it is argued, it is essential to have different routes to the same overall level of attainment. Second, it is recognized that in the 'snapshot' of a limited assessment such as a single terminal examination, many factors (eg, stress, confusion over the precise meaning of questions, mis-read rubrics) may interfere with a student's performance in one part of an examination on the day. Compensation means that the effects of this are not catastrophic for students; they will still gain the qualification, although perhaps at a lower grade.

While GNVQs originally imported the mastery model at the heart of NVQs, the rapid evolution of the assessment model has brought aspects of compensation into GNVQs, albeit in a different form to that within GCSE and A/AS. In GNVQs, compensation makes an appearance in four main ways. First, the external tests, while all need to be passed, have a pass mark of 70 per cent, thus giving the facility for different students successfully to pass the test on the basis of performance in different parts of the tests. Second, while all the grade criteria (planning, information seeking and handling, evaluation and quality of outcomes) have to be met at a particular level (eg, all at distinction to gain a distinction, if you fail to attain distinction in one of these themes then you drop to a merit overall), the judgement is made on one third of the evidence. In other words, a minimum of one third of the evidence (from any part of the qualification) must point to a specific level in the grade criteria. For different students, this can be drawn from different parts of the qualification. Third, GNVQ units list very general outcomes: for example, 'investigate the effect of the natural environment on the built environment' (Advanced GNVQ Construction and the Built Environment). Unlike many NVQ outcomes, these are general enough to allow a wide variety of outcomes to meet the requirements of the units. Finally, the evidence indicators in the units are exactly that: indicators. They are not absolute requirements. Teachers and students can negotiate with external verifiers alternative evidence to that stated in the unit. The evidence can be different in kind but must be equivalent to the original evidence indicator. For example, if the indicator states that two case studies should be produced, then the student may be able to produce a single report which covers the same ground and meets the performance criteria for the unit. Again, different routes can be used by different students.

So, compensation plays a role in GNVQs, in GCSEs and in A/AS qualifications, albeit in different forms. As qualifications in the different pathways have evolved, different compromises between cost, utility, purpose and consistency have been generated: different ratios of external and internal assessment, different types of compensation, different approaches to sampling performance. Different views of learning and of desirable outcomes have driven these different models, and alongside these, quite different ideas of what motivates students – with the strongest contrast being that between tough examinations at the end of programmes and phased coursework and tests which provide early feedback on performance. This contrast is best expressed as a strong opposition of views about whether student achievement is more effectively attained by extrinsic or intrinsic motivation.

Conclusion

This chapter has argued that assessment and achievement are profoundly inter-twined. Assessment theory and practice is impoverished if it is viewed as being concerned only with effective measurement. The education and training system is exactly that: a system, with the various parts acting on each other in subtle and often unpredictable ways. Who would have predicted the effect of A-level modu-lar mark schemes on the overall distribution of grades (Quinlan and Ellwood, 1993), or the extent to which the outcomes-driven model in GNVQs would become associated with distinctive styles of learning? In its recommendations about assessment does the Dearing era auger the end of ideology in thinking about assessment and achievement? Of course not – values are always embedded in the compromises and messy solutions of practical assessment systems. Once we acknowledge the interaction of learning and assessment (Gipps, 1995) and the fact that assessment models are value-laden, we come closer to understanding the relationship and thus closer to managing it deliberately. It is naive to argue that values should be detached from thinking about assessment (Gipps, 1994). Rather, it is essential that we acknowledge the relationship and thus expose the assump-tions and values to more open scrutiny and critique.

The Dearing Review recognizes the distinctive learning and assessment styles in GNVQs and thus reinforces a strong relationship between assessment, moti-vation and achievement. Assessment theory has undergone a significant trans-formation in the last decade. It has moved from an introspective, measurement-oriented paradigm towards a more outward-looking explanation of the role of assessment within socio-political systems (Murphy and Broadfoot, 1995; Wood, 1991). In other words, a wider explanation of the role, function and effect of assessment has been developed in order to explain more fully why particular things are assessed rather than others and to explain the effects of assessment systems which use particular approaches rather than others for assessment, recording, certification and quality assurance. But it is important to recognize that the Review did not deal with funding (a key factor in the characteristics of the education and training system and those within it) nor did it look in any direct way at delivery strategies. It was set firmly in the mould of previous 'top-down' system revisions.

Throughout this chapter I have examined how we are moving slowly towards a more detailed understanding of how assessment processes affect learning. While gaining a clearer understanding of causal relationships in this area, I would argue that we are, however, a long way from managing these relationships effectively. By 'effectively' I mean the process of choosing and implementing assessment processes which maximize learning, principally through clarity of expectation and creation of learner motivation. If one causal relationship should be encouraged by our management of assessment within the system, I believe that it should be this one:

assessment mode—▶ motivation—▶ learning—▶ achievement

But it is a set of other interests which drive the combatants in the battles about proportions of coursework and exams, about profile reporting and grades, about compensation and mastery – battles which still rage post-Dearing and will continue to do so. Dearing may have introduced a greater measure of coherence in the system by introducing national levels, by encouraging easier combination of qualifications from different pathways and by enhancing parity of esteem. However, Dearing is lodged firmly in the tradition of recent educational change: it is at system level, it deals principally with qualifications and the coherence it introduces is thus strictly limited. Perhaps most significantly of all, from an assessment perspective, Dearing confirmed the distinctiveness of the different pathways and thus confirmed within the system the co-existence of qualifications with quite different views of the motivation-learning-achievement relationship. How uneasy are the tensions between GNVQs, NVQs, GCSEs and A/AS? How distinctive will A/AS and GNVQs remain? What aspects of the Dearing Review will mutate in the messy flux of implementation?

There is a simple reason why predictions on these matters are very difficult. Dearing suggested a framework but included the requirement for diversity in different tracks. The Dearing system looks like a stable solution, with recommendations about the type of coherence which should be pursued. But the apparatus of regulatory bodies and awarding bodies is not yet stable: the NCVQ and SCAA will be merged; academic and vocational awarding bodies are undergoing a series of mergers. These are not simple transformations. These organizations have different cultures and curriculum principles: it is in this process of transformation of apparatus that particular views about assessment and learning, coherence and diversity will be in strong competition. In matters of assessment, the details count. The details will emerge from the mergers, the discussions on the characteristics of A/AS, GNVQs and NVQs and the outcomes of pilots of new approaches. That is why precise predictions are extremely hard to make. One new form of consensus is arising in the discussions on assessment across the system and that is that three factors are dominant: rigour, cost and manageability. One feature shines through – increased central control through qualifications.

A final analogy perhaps best characterizes the situation post-Dearing – it is probably like the Balkans: every so often an outsider draws some neat but totally artificial lines on the map and peace breaks out for a while. Then the underlying tensions get the better of those that actually inhabit that space and the sound of shooting starts once again to echo round the hills.

References

Beaumont, G (1995) *Review of 100 NVQs and SVQs*, A Report submitted to the DfEE, London: DfEE.

Brown, S and Dove, P (1991) *Self and Peer Assessment Paper No 63*, Standing Conference on Educational Development, Newcastle Polytechnic.

Dearing, Sir Ron (1996) *Review of Qualifications 16–19 Year Olds*, London: SCAA.

Fitz-Gibbon, C and Wright, M W (1995) *Advanced GNVQs and A-levels – evidence from the A-level Information System*, London: NCVQ.

Further Education Funding Council (1994) *GNVQs in the Further Education Sector*, Coventry: FEFC.

Gipps, C (1994) *Beyond Testing*, London: Falmer Press.

Gipps, C (1995) 'The Influence of Assessment on Learning', British Educational Research Association for Regional Seminars, Bristol, 12 May.

Gipps, C and Goldstein, H (1983) *Monitoring Children – An Evaluation of the Assessment of Performance Unit*, Oxford: Heinemann.

Gipps, C and Murphy, P (1994) *A Fair Test? Assessment, Achievement and Equity*, Buckingham: Open University Press.

Marks, J (1996) 'Foreword', in Chew, J, *Spelling Standards – How to Correct the Decline*, London: Centre for Policy Studies.

Murphy, R and Broadfoot, P (1995) *A Tribute to Desmond Nuttall*, London: Falmer Press.

Oates, T (1984) *Modular Approaches*, London: Manpower Services Commission.

Oates, T (1995) *A Converging System? Explaining Difference in the Academic and Vocational Tracks in England and Wales in Occupational Standards – International Perspectives*, Ohio State University, USA.

Observer, The (1996) 'Comprehensives Win in the Fight for GCSEs – Tricks in the Trade in Numbers Game', 25 August.

OFSTED (1994) *GNVQs in Schools 1993/4*, London: OFSTED.

Quinlan, M and Ellwood, V (1993) 'Paper to AEB Seminar', London: University of London Examinations Council.

Solomon, J (undated) *Student Case Studies in the Pilot Year of GNVQ Science at Advanced Level*, Sheffield: Employment Department.

Stern, L et al. (1996) *Evaluation of GNVQs*, London: NCVQ.

Stobart, G and Gipps, C (1991) *Assessment – A Teacher's Guide*, London: Routledge.

Theodossin, E and Thompson, C (1987) *Performance Indicators: Theory and Practice*, Coombe Lodge Report Vol. 20, No 1. Bristol: FESC.

Wolf, A (1995) *Competence-based Assessment*, Buckingham: Open University Press.

Wood, R (1991) *Assessment and Testing – A Survey of Research*, Cambridge: Cambridge University Press.

CHAPTER 10

Models of Student Guidance in a Changing 14–19 Education and Training System

A G Watts and Michael Young

Introduction

The role of guidance is receiving ever-greater attention, in relation both to educational change and to lifelong career development. The notion of more individually driven 'careers for all', linked to continuous learning throughout life, is being viewed as the means of achieving the 'skills revolution' Britain requires if it is to achieve competitive advantage in the global economy (CBI, 1989), as well as sustaining social cohesion within flexible labour markets (Watts, 1996). Effective guidance within compulsory education is seen as critical to laying effective foundations for lifelong career development; continuing access to guidance is viewed as essential for supporting the process of such development.

The role of guidance in relation to the curriculum and qualifications structures for the 14–19 age-group is central to these debates. Such structures lie at the transition point between compulsory schooling, based on a standard curriculum entitlement and diverse individualized routes through specialized learning and work structures. The ways in which they reconcile the competing 'forward' pressure for continued entitlement and the 'backward' pressure for diversification will affect the kind of guidance that is offered and how its provision is structured.

This chapter will start by clarifying the nature of guidance and its relationship to the curriculum. It will then explore the current structures of guidance provision, its relationship to the present three-track qualifications structure at 16–19, and the impact of 'learning markets'. Finally, it will explore the role of guidance in relation to the three possible models for the future outlined in Chapter 1: rigid qualification tracks, a flexible common framework, and a unified system.

The nature of guidance and its relationship to the curriculum

Guidance can be defined as a range of processes designed to enable individuals to make informed choices and transitions related to their personal, educational and career development. Different commentators and different guidance systems attach varying weight to the three adjectives 'personal', 'educational' and 'career'. Some see career as subsuming educational; some view personal as embracing both educational and career; some are very concerned to maintain the boundaries between the three. At the level of the individual student, the boundaries become difficult or impossible to maintain. But they are useful in conceptual terms, and they are often important in defining the terms of reference of particular guidance services. The main focus of this chapter is on educational and career guidance but it also recognizes that these need to be viewed as part of a broader guidance process that includes wider aspects of personal development.

The 'range of processes' which guidance encompasses was influentially defined by the Unit for the Development of Adult Continuing Education (1986) as comprising seven activities: informing, advising, counselling, assessing, enabling, advocating, and feeding back. Because this definition comes from an adult guidance background, it tends to view guidance as lying outside the curriculum. When the Standing Conference of Associations for Guidance in Educational Settings (SCAGES, 1993) sought to broaden the definition to embrace the role of guidance within schools and colleges, it extended this definition to include the institutional role of guidance and also what Marland (1980) termed the 'pastoral curriculum', which is based on a concern 'to help all the individuals without always giving individual help' (p.153): in other words, 'to transpose the aims of guidance into the aims of a curriculum' (Law, 1996, p.214). SCAGES (1993) accordingly added 'teaching', 'managing' and 'innovating/systems change' to the list. 'Teaching' here is defined as 'providing a planned and systematic progression of learner-centred experiences to enable learners to acquire knowledge, skills and competences related to making personal, educational and career decisions and transitions' (p.37).

The difficulties which SCAGES experienced in extending the definition in this way underline the problems of reconciling the individual-centred concept of guidance with organizational structures in general and the curriculum in particular. It is useful in this respect to distinguish three possible models of the relationship between guidance and the curriculum: the 'boundary' model, the 'enclosed' model, and the 'systemic' model (Watts, 1990).

Under the boundary model, guidance is viewed as being separate from the central learning functions of educational institutions, but as enabling these functions to operate effectively. Thus guidance might be seen as dealing with personal problems which impede learning, or as responding to individual problems that stem from the learning process – like the need for career redirection. In effect, guidance patrols the boundaries between the curriculum and the personal

149

life of the learner, so permitting the design of the curriculum to be based on other criteria and other organizing principles – in particular, the nature of knowledge and the perceived needs of society. From this boundary position, those entrusted with guidance can seek to feed back issues related to the personal experience of learners, so that these can be taken into account in the curriculum-development process: this role is much more strongly developed in adult continuing education (Oakeshott, 1990) than in initial education.

Under the enclosed model, guidance is seen as being a distinctive part of the learning functions of the institution. This can be seen in schools, for instance, in the development of programmes of personal and social education (PSE) which have a clearly bounded place within the curriculum. Usually such programmes are given a limited amount of time and do not deal in the hard currency used by the rest of the curriculum – notably, examination passes. They accordingly tend to attract lower status and perceived legitimacy from staff and students alike (Whitty *et al.*, 1994).

Under the systemic model, guidance is viewed as a concept which permeates the curriculum and makes it subject to negotiation with the individual learner. Within this model, guidance can become so closely interwoven with the learning process that it may lose its boundaries altogether. It may for example be viewed not as a specialist function, but as an integral part of the role of the teacher. This is shown diagrammatically in Figure 10.1(c), which also attempts to show how such a concept breaks open the walls of the curriculum, making it all continuously subject to adaptation to the learner's needs.

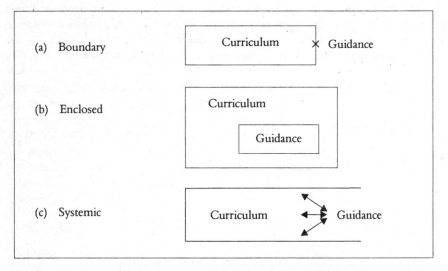

Figure 10.1 *Three models of guidance in relation to the curriculum*

Guidance, however, is arguably not concerned with meeting the individual's needs in some kind of social vacuum. Many would agree with the view advanced

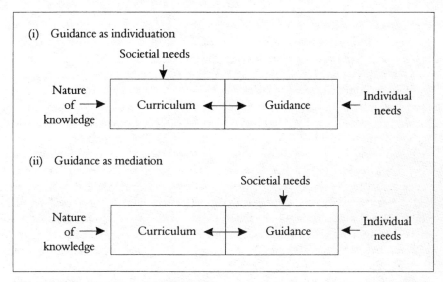

(i) Guidance as individuation

(ii) Guidance as mediation

Figure 10.2 *Guidance and societal needs*

by Morris (1955) in his seminal paper on guidance as a concept in educational philosophy: that its essence is as a process of mediation between individual needs and societal needs. We will conveniently ignore for present purposes the problematic nature of the concept of 'needs', its relationship to 'wants', and the issue of who is to define such needs and on what basis. In these simple terms, however, the concept of mediation poses an important issue. It has been suggested above that the design of the curriculum itself tends to be based upon the perceived needs of society as well as upon the nature of knowledge: such a view leaves guidance as serving what tends to be seen as a second-order role of 'individuation' – in other words, relating it to individuals' needs. In principle, however, the mediation model (Figure 10.2) opens up the possibility that societal needs could be infused into the curriculum through the role of guidance. There are strong hints of this, as we shall see later, in the concept of 'learning credits': the underlying notion here is that societal needs will be met in significant measure through the learning choices of individuals, supported by guidance provision which ensures that these choices are informed by labour-market demand. Such a notion places guidance in a position of much greater significance in terms of public policy.

Current structures of guidance provision

The nature of guidance provision in schools and colleges is varied and its limits are not easy to define with precision. In schools pre-16, for example, careers education and guidance is conventionally described as comprising five components: a planned programme of careers education within the curriculum; continuing access to individual guidance as part of the pastoral-care system and from the Careers Service; access to information resources on educational and vocational opportunities; active experiences of the working world through work-experience programmes and the like and the processes of recording achievement and action planning (NCC, 1990; SCAA, 1995). Some of these – notably access to individual guidance and to information – are compatible with the boundary model as outlined above. Careers education within the curriculum, on the other hand, can encompass specific programmes in careers education *per se* (narrow enclosed model), inclusion of careers education in PSE programmes (broader enclosed model), and infusion of elements of careers education across the curriculum (systemic model). Similarly, work-experience programmes can be separated from the rest of the curriculum (narrow enclosed model), attached to the careers or PSE programme (broader enclosed model), or linked to the curriculum as a whole (systemic model) (Miller *et al.*, 1991). Again, the processes of recording achievement and action planning can be viewed as part of the pastoral-care structure (boundary model) or as integrated into the curriculum itself (systemic model) (Watts, 1992).

In schools with sixth-forms, and in sixth-form colleges developed from a school tradition, many of these practices are sustained or adapted post-16. In colleges of further education and tertiary colleges they tend to assume a different shape, linked to the vocational tradition of the colleges, their complex structures, and the mixing of school-leavers and adult students (Hawthorn, 1996). Traditionally, further education was the educational sector in which guidance was least well established. It was assumed that students were on set courses leading towards predetermined vocational targets, and therefore had no further need of guidance. Now, however, the growth of modularization and of more broadly based course structures has meant that guidance is required on a continuing basis to help students to build up and review their learning programmes. As a result, further education is the sector in which guidance has become most strongly institutionalized. The funding procedures, inspection guidelines and audit requirements developed by the Further Education Funding Council attach considerable importance to guidance on entry to, during and on exit from learning programmes. The reification of guidance for accountability purposes, together with the heavy emphasis on guidance on entry to learning programmes, has tended to lean provision towards the boundary model; on the other hand, the potential for application of the systemic model would seem greater than in schools.

Organizationally, current structures of guidance provision within schools and colleges fall into three categories. The first is specialist services based outside the institution. The Careers Service has a statutory remit to provide a neutral guidance service, free of charge, for individuals in full-time education and on part-time courses concerned with preparation for employment (other than in higher education), and also for young people who have left education or full-time training up to two years earlier. It thus covers virtually all individuals in the 14–19 age-group. The process of competitive tendering introduced following the Trade

Union Reform and Employment Rights Act 1993 removed the service from the mandatory control of Local Education Authorities. In most cases the contracts have been awarded to companies formed through partnerships between LEAs and Training and Enterprise Councils, though the creation of a quasi-market has also resulted in some elements of 'expansionism' (such companies winning contracts in areas other than their own) and of 'new entrants' (contracts being won by private companies). The position of careers services, and their present subjection to rigid activity targets imposed by central government, means that they are largely confined to the boundary model. On the other hand, research by Morris *et al.* (1995) has demonstrated that the most effective practice is based on a 'community guidance' model in which careers services are able to play flexible roles in relation to guidance structures within the institution, including contributions to programmes based on the enclosed and systemic models.

The second category is specialist services based inside the institution. This includes, in schools, the role of careers coordinator. In almost all cases, however, careers coordinators are only weakly professionalized: their career guidance role takes up only part of their time, alongside subject-teaching responsibilities and few of them have received accredited training for their guidance responsibilities (Andrews *et al.*, 1995). In colleges there is more likely to be a central student services unit which coordinates and manages the whole guidance process from admission to exit from the institution: this may include an admissions tutor, a careers officer, a careers coordinator and a welfare officer (FEFC/OFSTED, 1994). Such services tend also to operate a boundary model, but have stronger opportunities than the Careers Service for making specialist contributions to the curriculum (enclosed model) or for supporting teachers and lecturers in their guidance roles (potentially, systemic model).

The third category is guidance as part of the role of teachers and lecturers, integrated into the teaching and learning process. Most teachers and lecturers combine their teaching roles with roles as tutors. Particularly post-16, guidance provision tends to centre on tutorial systems, where tutors meet groups of students on a regular basis (FEFC/OFSTED, 1994): such provision is based on the enclosed model. The doubling of roles should in principle make it easier for guidance to influence their teaching roles, so leading towards the systemic model. As we shall shortly see, however, some curricular structures lend themselves more readily to such influence than do others.

The role of guidance within the triple-track structure

As outlined in Chapter 1, the current system of qualifications post-16 is a triple-track system based on academic qualifications (A/AS-levels), broad vocational qualifications (GNVQs), and occupationally specific qualifications (NVQs plus others). The tracks tend to be distinct and are based on different principles of curriculum and assessment. They are also strongly insulated: combining elements of different tracks or moving between tracks is difficult and tends to be discouraged. The extension of Part 1 GNVQs to the 14–16 curriculum is producing some element of differentiation at this level too, though in this case students normally combine the GNVQ elements with GCSEs, so the tracking is less rigid.

Within a strongly tracked structure, a key role of guidance is to help students in making the critical choices between the tracks. As a result of the National Curriculum, curricular differentiation at 14–16 is more limited than it used to be. Accordingly – prior to the advent of Part 1 GNVQs – most schools have not considered such differentiation sufficient to require formal careers education and guidance provision in Year 9 (Morris, 1996). The choices made at 16, however, are critical ones, and tend to dominate 14–16 guidance programmes.

The effectiveness of current guidance programmes in relation to choices at 16 is open to question. A survey by OFSTED (1996) found that students were generally well aware of the range of longer-established A- and AS-levels available to them; their knowledge of GNVQs was, however, generally poor. Moreover, in about a quarter of schools with sixth forms there were unresolved tensions as to how far students should be encouraged to see for themselves what was on offer in other local institutions. This evidence reinforced long-standing criticisms of the tendency of some schools with sixth forms to bias guidance at 16 in order to encourage students to stay on (with the financial advantages this brings to the school) rather than to move on to learning opportunities elsewhere (HMI, 1992).

Guidance in relation to choices between tracks is based on the boundary model. In relation to ongoing guidance post-16, the role of guidance tends to differ strongly from track to track, because each track's different curriculum structures vary in their capacity to accommodate guidance elements.

Within the academic A/AS-level track, guidance tends to be largely based on the enclosed model. While all schools and colleges provide opportunities for students to transfer from one subject to another during the first half-term of such courses, it is much more difficult to do so thereafter (FEFC/OFSTED, 1994). The introduction of modular A/AS-levels could produce some degree of greater flexibility, though even here the rules of combination are usually very restrictive. The content of syllabuses tends to be strongly theoretical and knowledge-based, and to pay limited attention to vocational relevance: few A/AS-level courses, for example, include examination requirements for work experience or work-related assignments (FEFC/OFSTED, 1994). Accordingly, attention to guidance tends to be concentrated in group tutorial periods.

In the broad vocational track the more integrated curriculum design of GNVQs, together with the vocational focus and the emphasis on negotiated learning, lean strongly toward the systemic model. Careers education is likely to be embedded within the mainstream curriculum (FEDA, 1996). Separate careers education and guidance units are being developed, but based on the same model of performance criteria, range statements and evidence indicators as are used for other units. Work experience is common and fully integrated into the curriculum structure, as are recording of progress and action planning. In the occupationally specific track, the diversity of learning programmes, and the separation of learning from assessment within NVQs in particular, makes it more difficult to generalize about the role of guidance. The specificity of the occupational destinations tends to exclude guidance from the curriculum and confine it to a boundary role. Many individuals working towards such qualifications are work-based rather than college-based; for those who are college-based, work experience is designed for 'preparatory' rather than 'exploratory' purposes (Miller *et al.*, 1991). There is nonetheless evidence that many young people within this track tend to sample various types of work-based learning and to follow varied pathways before 'settling down' (Payne, 1995).

An important role of guidance 16–19, however it is structured, is to help young people to the next stage of their progression in learning and work. This includes, for some, progression into higher education. With the erosion of student grants, such guidance increasingly needs to take account of financial issues. It seems likely that the roles of career guidance and financial guidance will become ever more closely intertwined (Collin and Watts, 1996) – with important implications for the skills and knowledge required of guidance practitioners.

The impact of 'learning markets'

The current position of guidance in relation to education and training provision 14–19 has been elevated – and complicated – by the government's policy of introducing market competition in learning provision, with the student viewed as 'customer'. This is relevant in three respects: current market competition between institutions; emergent internal markets within institutions; and the concept of learning credits.

One effect of market competition between institutions at 16 has already been mentioned: the pressures exerted by some schools to encourage students to stay on rather than to explore learning opportunities elsewhere. This has been in tension with other aspects of government policy, notably the promotion of new work-based options including Modern Apprenticeships. The way government has sought to resolve the dilemma is by looking to the Careers Service to provide the impartial guidance which it cannot depend upon from schools themselves. This has been the rationale for enhanced funding for the Careers Service's work within schools, plus proposals for legislation to secure students' access to its services (DTI, 1994; 1995).

The other effect of competition at 16+ has been on the guidance offered within colleges. The pressure of financial incentives on colleges to recruit students has meant that some colleges regard guidance provision on entry as a form of marketing. This is exacerbated by the fact that, under FEFC regulations, such provision is only funded if it leads to enrolment. The FEFC's hope is that funding penalties for non-completion of courses will outweigh the inducement to enrol, so encouraging colleges to protect the impartiality of the guidance they offer – the government is now proposing to apply a similar model of output-related funding to school sixth forms (Cabinet Office, 1996).

In both of these cases, there is an important distinction between two levels of impartiality. 'Reactive impartiality' is passive and minimalist: it may involve, for example, schools making available information on colleges only to those who seek it, and colleges providing information on courses in other institutions only in fields which they do not cover themselves. 'Proactive impartiality', on the other hand, involves making positive efforts to provide information and advice about the full range of opportunities, outside as well as inside the host institution. In the case of schools this might include an active programme of visits to local colleges or, in the case of colleges, information and advice about the pros and cons of all local courses in fields of interest to the individual. In general, the survey by FEFC/OFSTED (1994) found that:

> students had a better knowledge of the full range of provision available for 16 to 19 year olds in local institutions in areas where partnerships or consortia, involving local schools and further education colleges, had been established; where cooperative arrangements existed between the different providers; or where local careers services provided material describing the provision. (p.6)

The market-driven nature of recent government policy seems to have been designed to obstruct rather than support the development of such cooperative arrangements.

The second aspect of learning markets relevant to our concerns here is the emergent development of internal markets within institutions. As noted in Chapter 1, modularization is not necessarily designed to increase student choice: it is frequently more concerned with breaking down qualifications into smaller units of learning which can be assessed in a more immediate and transparent way, and the rules of combination often severely limit the range of choices which is permitted. Insofar as such choice is extended, however, and insofar as the allocation of funding within the institution is linked to recruitment of students on to particular modules, the result is the development of an internal market in which teaching units are competing with one another for student recruits. The role of impartiality accordingly arises here too. It is unrealistic to expect teacher/lecturers or tutors to provide fully impartial guidance in such situations, since they have an interest in the outcome of the students' decisions. If such guidance is to be available, therefore, internal markets of this kind tend to strengthen the case for specialist guidance services, whether based inside or outside the institution.

This suggests a further important distinction in relation to impartiality, based on its range: the distinction between 'comprehensive impartiality' relating to the full range of options open to individuals, and 'intra-institutional impartiality' relating more narrowly to the full range of options within the institution in question. In these terms, a possible three-level structure of provision might involve the Careers Service offering comprehensive impartiality, particularly on entry and on exit; central guidance services within the institution offering at least intra-institutional impartiality, both on entry and when a student wishes to transfer between learning programmes; and teachers/lecturers and tutors making no claim to impartiality but offering guidance and support on-programme. Some central guidance services within institutions might seek to offer comprehensive impartiality, particularly where this is based on a *concordat* with other local institutions.

The third aspect of learning markets is the concept of learning credits. The basic notion here is to direct public funding for learning at 16+ to the 'customers', ie, the young people themselves, rather than to education and training providers. Young people are accordingly provided with a publicly-funded voucher which enables them to 'buy' their learning programme. Strongly promoted by the CBI (1989), the application of the concept has so far been limited to work-based learning through a system of youth credits. The government has however confirmed its intention to extend the scheme to cover the full range of education and training post-16 (Cabinet Office, 1996).

Such a scheme is likely greatly to enhance the role of guidance. It in principle leaves individuals responsible for the decisions about what they are to learn, and expects providers to adapt their provision in response to such consumer demand. As noted earlier, the synchronization of learning provision with societal needs – including, in particular, the needs of the labour market – is accordingly mediated through the choices of individuals. This makes it essential to ensure that such choices are informed in relation to labour-market demand. Access to high-quality guidance is therefore widely recognized as critical to the success of any learning credits scheme (CBI, 1989; Coopers & Lybrand, 1995). Whether even this is likely to be adequate is open to question: Hodkinson and Sparkes (1993) found that the 'pragmatically rational' way in which young people reported making career decisions was very different from the 'technically rational' system of guidance built into the design of the original training credits scheme. But the onus to resolve such tensions falls on the guidance services themselves. In effect, guidance becomes, in policy terms, a 'market-maker': a way of making the labour market and the learning market work effectively, by ensuring that the supply-side actors within these markets have access to market information and are able to read market signals (Watts, 1995).

Some pressure groups have argued that the application of market principles should be extended still further, to the delivery of guidance itself. In particular, the CBI (1993) suggested that 'creating an effective and informed market in careers guidance provision is the best way to guarantee that the range of individuals' needs can be satisfied, that individual choices are maximised and that customers remain the focus' (p.22). The government has accepted this argument in relation to adults, but not young people. For the latter, application of market principles to guidance delivery has been limited to competitive tendering for

Careers Service contracts, as outlined earlier, to deliver what is still in effect a local public-service monopoly. The notion of moving toward a multi-provider, market-led approach, based on guidance vouchers, was rejected by Coopers and Lybrand (1995) on the grounds that 'the potential for confusing young people through overlaying one market (for guidance) on top of another (for education and training) would be substantial and might run the risk of jeopardising the success of learning credits entirely' (p.55) (see also Watts, 1995).

Role of guidance in possible future structures

For the future, the role of guidance at 14–19 depends a great deal on what structure of qualifications and curriculum emerges as the dominant model (see Chapter 1). If rigid tracking continues, then the role is likely to remain much as at present. If, on the other hand, the notion of learning markets breaks down the rigidity of this model, moving towards a flexible common framework in which modularization is extended in response to individual choices, then guidance is likely to be cast largely in a boundary role, detached from the curriculum, in order to assure its impartiality. Cooper & Lybrand (1995) emphasized the importance of ensuring that guidance is delivered 'by agencies with no actual or even perceived interest in the outcome' (p.53). This does not negate possible additional roles for guidance, based on the enclosed or systemic models, but it tends to downplay their significance.

The third option is a unified system based on a series of alternative 'pathways' through a common framework of units and assessment strategies, with a common core. The argument for such a system is based on the concept of 'connective specialization', enabling specialists to share an overall sense of the relationship between their specialization and the curriculum as a whole (Young, 1993). Guidance can support such 'connectivity' by linking the curriculum as a whole to its value for career development (Law, 1996). Within such a structure, guidance based on the systemic model could accordingly form an integral element of the core. Thus, in the proposals for a British Baccalaureat (Finegold et al., 1990), all students would do work/community-based modules: these could be extended to include guidance elements. Also the emphasis on core skills could provide a mechanism for infusing guidance elements into other modules, particularly if career management skills were added to the list of core skills. Alongside this, guidance based on the boundary model would be needed to support the choice of individual pathways. Guidance and counselling are accordingly included in the list of 'core processes' which it would be mandatory for institutions to provide in order to enhance personal progression and student learning.

As noted in Chapter 1, the report by Sir Ron Dearing (1996) does not move significantly away from the current triple-track system. It does, however, emphasize that 'central to maximising achievement and reducing wastage is the provision of expert independent careers education and guidance to young people in their choice of pathways and goals' (p.127). It also stresses the importance of core skills, including 'self-management of learning programmes', which could readily be extended to cover career management skills more broadly. Moreover, its proposals for a relaunch of the National Record of Achievement emphasize the relevance of the requisite underlying processes to the development of such skills, including 'setting personal objectives, monitoring performance, reviewing work plans in the light of achievement, and reviewing both short-term objectives and long-term aspirations' (p.42). The radical implications of these proposals do not seem fully recognized in the Dearing Report as a whole. If, however, they are seriously followed through, they provide a base on which development towards a strong role for guidance within a unified system could be built.

Conclusion

The functions of guidance in relation to education and training systems can be seen in three ways. One is 'remedial', helping to make good the confused nature of the system itself by enabling individuals to find their way through it. There are strong elements of this within the current system which, despite the rigidity of the three tracks, is in many respects a complex and confusing structure. The second is 'operational', enabling a coherent system to run effectively. Within a cohesive framework system based on modularization, for example, guidance would be the essential means of enabling students to build learning programmes linked to their career aspirations. The third is 'augmentative', enhancing the learning which the system is designed to foster. Where guidance is viewed in these latter terms, enabling learners to develop the skills and competences to manage their lifelong career development, it is most likely to be seen not just as a desirable support to the curriculum, but as an integral part of the curriculum itself. A unified system would seem to provide the best prospect of making guidance based on such a view available to all young people up to the age of 19.

References

Andrews, D, Barnes, A and Law, B (1995) *Staff Development for Careers Work*, NICEC Project Report, Cambridge: CRAC/Hobsons.

Cabinet Office (1996) *Competitiveness: Creating the Enterprise Centre of Europe*, Cmnd. 3300, London: HMSO.

Collin, A and Watts, A G (1996) 'The Death and Transfiguration of Career – and of Career Guidance?', *British Journal of Guidance and Counselling*, **24**, 3, 385–98.

Confederation of British Industry (1989) *Towards a Skills Revolution*, London: CBI.

Confederation of British Industry (1993) *A Credit to Your Career*, London: CBI.

Coopers & Lybrand (1995) *Learning Credits Consultancy Study: Final Report*, London: Coopers & Lybrand (mimeo).

Dearing, Sir Ron (1996) *Review of Qualifications for 16–19 Year Olds*, London: SCAA.

Department of Trade and Industry (1994) *Competitiveness: Helping Business to Win*, Cmnd. 2563, London: HMSO.

Department of Trade and Industry (1995) *Competitiveness: Forging Ahead*, Cmnd. 2867, London: HMSO.

Finegold, D, Keep, E, Miliband, D, Raffe, D, Spours, K and Young, M (1990) *A British Baccalaureate: Ending the Division Between Education and Training*, London: IPPR.

Further Education Development Agency (1996) *Careers Education and Guidance for Students in Transition from Further Education*, London: FEDA.

Further Education Funding Council/OFSTED (1994) *Guidance 16–19*, Coventry: FEFC/OFSTED.

Hawthorn, R (1996) 'Careers Work in Further and Adult Education', in Watts, A G, Law, B, Killeen, J, Kidd, J M and Hawthorn, R, *Rethinking Careers Education and Guidance: Theory, Policy and Practice*, London: Routledge.

Her Majesty's Inspectorate (1992) *Survey of Guidance 13–19 in Schools and Sixth Form Colleges*, London: Department of Education and Science.

Hodkinson, P and Sparkes, A C (1993) 'Young People's Career Choices and Careers Guidance Action Planning: a Case-Study of Training Credits in Action', *British Journal of Guidance and Counselling*, **21**, 3, 246–61.

Law, B (1996) 'Careers Education in a Curriculum', in Watts, A G, Law, B, Killeen, J, Kidd, J M and Hawthorn, R, *Rethinking Careers Education and Guidance: Theory, Policy and Practice*, London: Routledge.

Marland, M (1980) 'The Pastoral Curriculum', in Best, R, Jarvis, C and Ribbins, P (eds) *Perspectives in Pastoral Care*, Oxford: Heinemann.

Miller, A, Watts, A G and Jamieson, I (1991) *Rethinking Work Experience*, London: Falmer Press.

Morris, B (1955) 'Guidance as a Concept in Educational Philosophy', in *The Yearbook of Education 1955*, London: Evans.

Morris, M (1996) *Careers Education and Guidance Provision for 13 and 14 Year Olds*, QADU/RD10, London: Department for Education and Employment.

Morris, M, Simkin, C and Stoney, S (1995) *The Role of the Careers Service in Careers Education and Guidance in Schools*, QADU/RD7a, Sheffield: Employment Department.

National Curriculum Council (1990) *Curriculum Guidance 6: Careers Education and Guidance*, York: Longman for the NCC.

Oakeshott, M (1990) *Educational Change and Curriculum Change*, London: Further Education Unit/Unit for the Development of Adult Continuing Education.

OFSTED (1996) *A Survey of Careers Education and Guidance in Schools*, London: HMSO.

Payne, J (1995) *Routes Beyond Compulsory Schooling*, Youth Cohort Report No 31, Sheffield: Employment Department.

School Curriculum and Assessment Authority (1995) *Looking Forward: Careers Education and Guidance in the Curriculum*, London: SCAA.

Standing Conference of Associations for Guidance in Educational Settings (1993) 'Statement of Principles and Definitions', in Ball, C (ed.) *Guidance Matters*, London: RSA.

Unit for the Development of Adult Continuing Education (1986) *The Challenge of Change*, Leicester: UDACE

Watts, A G (1990) 'The Role of Guidance in Educational Change', in Watts, A G (ed.) *Guidance and Educational Change*, Cambridge: CRAC/Hobsons.

Watts, A G (1992) 'Individual Action Planning: Issues and Strategies', *British Journal of Education and Work*, **5**, 1, 47–63.

Watts, A G (1995) 'Applying Market Principles to the Delivery of Careers Guidance Services: a Critical Review', *British Journal of Guidance and Counselling*, **23**, 1, 69–81.

Watts, A G (1996) *Careerquake*, London: Demos.

Whitty, G, Rowe, G and Aggleton, P (1994) 'Subjects and Themes in the Secondary-School Curriculum', *Research Papers in Education*, **9**, 2, 159–81.

Young, M (1993) 'A Curriculum for the 21st Century? Towards a New Basis for Overcoming Academic/Vocational Divisions', *British Journal of Educational Studies*, **40**, 3.

CHAPTER 11

Building Institutional Capability for National Education Reform: The Case of the 'Formative Value-Added System'

Ann Hodgson

Introduction

In common with some of the earlier chapters in the book, this chapter highlights the important role that 'bottom-up' process-based initiatives have played and continue to play in reform of the English education and training system. By process-based initiatives I mean those such as 'unitization' or 'records of achievement' that are designed to bring about improvements in specific elements of the education system, but which do not set out to and cannot make structural changes to the whole national qualifications system. Here, I will take the case of the 'formative value-added system' (Spours and Hodgson, 1996)[1] as an example of such a 'process-based' initiative. I will also build on the argument, laid out in Chapter 1, that this type of process-based initiative, which has the potential to develop schools' and colleges' capacity to change and respond in a proactive way to qualifications reform, is a necessary and powerful tool in bringing about fundamental change to the system.

As Chapter 1 suggests, 'top-down' proposals for a unified qualifications system will only succeed if they build on, and are responsive to, some of the institutional and regional bottom-up initiatives that have evolved as a pragmatic reaction to the divided qualifications system in this country. What is also certain is that in our devolved education and training system, unless schools and colleges fully understand and support future proposals for reform, these proposals will founder. It is important first to recognize the strength of the tradition and support for process-based bottom-up initiatives in English education reform and second, to harness this in order to build a consensus both on the vision of a unified qualifications system and the practical steps required to achieve this vision.

The formative value-added system, as this chapter will demonstrate, is a typically English response to an education system in which there is a history of individual student underachievement, autonomous but responsive education institutions, a voluntaristic approach to the post-16 curriculum and a complex and divided national qualifications system. In such a context, it is the school or college which acts as the articulator or mediator between the individual student and the national education system. English schools and colleges enjoy a much greater degree of autonomy than their European counterparts in the way that they operate and respond to national education legislation (Green, 1993). As Chapter 1 pointed out, it has, therefore, been at the institutional level that much of the reform of the English education and training system has traditionally taken place, at least in its preliminary phases.

The formative value-added system can be seen as typical of this strong process-based reform tradition in that it works at the individual student and institutional level and within the constraints of the national qualifications system. The particular contribution of the formative value-added system is that it focuses on assessment – one of the most powerful drivers in the English education and training system – is designed to raise levels of student achievement and has the potential to strengthen and unify the way that schools and colleges work.

What this chapter will also argue is that this type of system, like many other process-based reforms (eg, records of achievement, modularization and unitization), can be seen as a tool for supporting more fundamental reform of the qualifications system. In developing formative value-added systems, this chapter suggests, institutions are building their capacity to respond to the introduction of a future unified qualifications system and, equally importantly, their ability to tackle the type of changes which will be required in the period leading up to such fundamental reform.

The concept of 'value-added'

To understand how the formative value-added system developed, it is necessary first to explore how the general concept of value-added came to be used in the education context.

The educational concept of value-added entered the public domain in the early 1990s when, on the surface, it was seen as a response by the education profession to examination league tables. At this time, value-added seemed to provide a possible 'fairer' way than 'raw scores' of reporting student achievement in national qualifications, because it took the starting point of the student into account when measuring performance. A closer examination of the reasons for this upsurge of interest in value-added, however, reveals a much wider and more complex set of issues which relate to concerns about underachievement in the English education and training system, the role of qualifications within this system and the specific contribution of schools and colleges to raising levels of achievement.

Value-added, used in an educational context, has aroused considerable interest since it has the potential to create direct links between individual student progress, measured in terms of national qualifications achievement, and school/college performance. Value-added methodology has thus been seen to date as having three distinct but interrelated possibilities as an educational tool. First, it has been recognized as a way of making institutions become more accountable for their performance by comparing the amount of student progress in one institution against that made by similar types of students in another institution. Second, it has been viewed as a tool which institutions can use to evaluate their own performance with different types of students and in different areas of the curriculum, in order to make targeted improvements. Third, there are those who argue that value-added methodology, as part of a student-centred assessment, tutoring and guidance system, has the potential to raise student and teacher expectations and to focus institutions on the central task of raising levels of achievement.

The first two of these educational dimensions of value-added, although still relatively new, have become the subject of widespread discussion both at the level of academic study (for example, Fitzgibbon, 1996; Fitzgibbon and Tymms, 1993; Goldstein *et al.*, 1993; Gray *et al.*, 1990; Sammons *et al.*, 1994) and, more recently, at local education authority and school/college level (Farnsworth *et al.*, 1994; Thomas and Mortimore, 1995). The third use of value-added data as part of a coherent formative value-added system for monitoring student performance within a single institution is much newer and still very much in the early stages of development (Conway, 1993; FEDA, 1995; Spours and Hodgson, 1996).

The fact, however, that recent work on value-added has largely used student performance in national qualifications as its major measure, brings a fourth and little explored dimension to the debate on value-added: the relationship between value-added and the national qualifications structure and, more particularly, the role of value-added in qualifications reform.

This chapter will touch on all four of these dimensions of value-added, but will focus mainly on the last three, since it is these which relate to the debate on the role of institutions in educational reform.

'Formative' value-added

The previous section has tried to lay out some of the different dimensions of value-added by looking at the different purposes for which it has been and is being used within the education context. These dimensions of value-added can broadly be divided into two main types – 'comparative' and 'formative' (Spours and Hodgson, 1996) – each of which has its own distinctiveness in terms of methodology and, more importantly, purpose. What we will see from the description of the formative value-added system outlined briefly in this section, however, is that in practice, at institutional level, there is a close interrelationship and interdependency between the two. It is the combination of the two types of value-added approaches within the formative value-added system that constitutes the power of the model.

The underlying theme behind comparative value-added work, which is described extensively elsewhere (for example, Fitzgibbon, 1996; Fitzgibbon *et al.*, 1993; Goldstein *et al.*, 1993; Gray *et al.*, 1990; Sammons *et al.*, 1994) can be seen as the development of a methodology for creating a level playing field between education institutions before comparing their performance in terms of student achievements. It thus provides a valuable common measure for retrospectively comparing the differences between individual institutions with different students in different areas of the country.

Formative value-added work, on the other hand, uses comparative value-added data as a predictor and as a spur to future action, as well as a means of retrospectively reflecting on past performance. In this sense it can be criticized for being statistically less rigorous but, arguably, of more immediate practical use to schools and colleges in tackling the problem of student underachievement. Moreover, it could also be argued that formative value-added work has an additional dimension that is not seen in comparative value-added work: it has the potential to make a contribution to institutional reform and, by building institutional capacity for change, to reform of the national qualifications system. This dimension will be discussed more fully in the final section of this chapter.

Here, I am using the term formative value-added in connection with a set of practices which uses the data derived from comparative value-added work, in both a reflective and a predictive way, as a means of bringing about changes in the behaviour of teachers and students within an institution, rather than as a source of information that can be used to distinguish performance between institutions. Formative value-added work, therefore, tends to be associated with school or college self-evaluation and improvement strategies, particularly in relation to assessment and curriculum planning.

A more significantly new aspect of this work, however, is the development of the 'formative value-added system' (Spours and Hodgson, 1996). In such a system, value-added data are used retrospectively as a tool for evaluating and improving institutional performance, but also in a predictive way with students as part of a rigorous assessment, tutoring and guidance system which sharpens students' own awareness of their strengths and weaknesses. In this way, the formative value-added system has the potential to work both at an institutional level and at a student level. It provides a mechanism for unifying and strengthening assessment and curriculum planning practices within schools and colleges, while also addressing the important issue of student self-management of learning and the development of the skills of lifelong learning. It is this use of value-added data, in both a reflective and a predictive way as part of a whole-institutional system to tackle the underlying issue of student underachievement, that constitutes the novelty and power of the formative value-added system. Earlier formative value-added developments have tended to concentrate either on institutional improvement or, in fewer cases, on student learning, but have not fully exploited the use of value-added data to address both issues in one strategy.

The most well-known examples of formative value-added development work which operates at an institutional rather than at a student level, are the National Foundation for Educational Research's QUASE Project (Quantitative Analysis for Self-Evaluation) and ERIC Project (Examination Results in Context) and the ALIS (A-level Information Service) and YELLIS Projects (Year 11 Information Service) based at Durham University. In all cases, the purpose of these projects is to provide external value-added data for use in institutional internal evaluation. In addition, many individual local education authorities are also now providing their schools with value-added data which are intended to stimulate discussion about improvement. The problem with this kind of activity, however, is that unless institutions are given sustained guidance and support, data are often not fully understood nor actively used as a tool for improvement.

The use of value-added data at student level as part of a formative student monitoring and assessment system began in a very small-scale way at the end of the 1980s. One of the best known examples of these early systems was created by the principal at Greenhead College in Huddersfield, who was able to demonstrate significant increases in student attainment over the years that the system has been in operation (Conway, 1992, 1993). However, these early systems were few in number – despite the Further Education Unit's attempts to promote this kind of work – relied on locally produced value-added data and, in the vast majority of cases, were restricted to use with students on A-level courses and thus to post-16 institutions.

Over the last few years, interest in this area of work has increased dramatically as a result of the Further Education and Development Agency's work with further education colleges (FEDA, 1995; FEU, 1993, 1994) and the work of the Value-added and Attainment Research and Development Project at the Post-16 Education Centre at London University's Institute of Education with schools, colleges and whole local education authority areas. This work has also been spurred on by the availability, since 1995, of national value-added data on the correlation between GCSEs and A-levels (DfE, 1995). However, the fact that schools and colleges are wanting to develop formative value-added systems for students other than those taking A-levels suggests that it is the power of the system rather than the existence of robust national data which is encouraging change.

The formative value-added system

The central focus of the Value-added and Attainment Research and Development Project at the Post-16 Education Centre at London University's Institute of Education is the development and evaluation of the formative value-added system (see Figure 11.1). As can be seen from the figure, there are eight major components to this system and it is their connectiveness – that is, how one part makes demands on the other parts – which constitutes the power of the model. Many of the components of the system may already be taking place in schools and colleges, but our initial research and development work suggests that it is the process of creating the whole system, which all teachers and students understand and to which they all adhere, that is most likely to bring about changes in assessment, curriculum planning, student achievement and skill development.

The formative value-added system basically involves the use of value-added data in two ways; first for the evaluation of institutional performance (see points 1 and 8 of Figure 11.1), and second, to calculate a 'target minimum grade'(TMG)[2] for each student. Individual student progress is then monitored regularly against this TMG. It is important here to stress that the TMG represents a minimum prediction of student performance at the end of a course or stage of education. The formative value-added system relies on subject teachers generating 'estimated grades/levels'[3] for each student on a half-termly or termly basis throughout a course/stage of education. These are then shared with each student and compared with her or his TMG in order to generate a discussion about strengths and weaknesses in performance. In addition, the subject teacher will be asked to provide feedback on other 'underpinning performance data' such as participation, meeting work deadlines, attendance, punctuality and effort. She or he will also be expected to suggest a specific subject-based strategy or target for improvement, which will be reviewed at the next 'subject teacher review' (see Point 3 of Figure 11.1).

Data from the subject teacher review are then fed to the student's tutor for discussion in a one-to-one 'tutor review' (see Point 5 of Figure 11.1). At this interview, the student's overall progress is reviewed, patterns of uneven performance are discussed and learning targets and strategies for improving the student's ability to manage her or his own learning are negotiated and agreed for review at the next session.

At the end of the academic year a 'management review'(see Point 8 of Figure 11.1) is held where teachers and managers in the institution discuss the working of the system as a whole, with a particular focus on the consistency of assessment information generated within the institution, how curriculum planning is responding to issues raised by the system and the effects of the system on teaching, learning and student achievement.

The distinctiveness of this formative approach to value-added, as part of a whole-institutional system, is that it focuses on individual student progress and, at the same time, stimulates a coordinated institutional response to assessment, attainment and curriculum planning. What this type of value-added work demands is the development of a consistent and rigorous whole-institutional approach to assessment, tutoring and guidance within which comparative value-added data are used to provide an additional but vital external perspective on student and institutional performance. This need for regular feedback to students also often leads to a more modular delivery of the curriculum where assessments

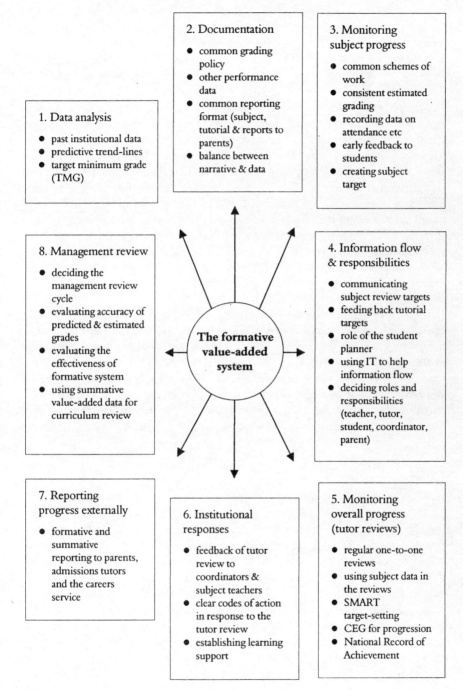

Figure 11.1 *Components of the formative value-added system*

for use in the student monitoring system are made at the end of each module. Moreover, the requirement for subject teachers and tutors to negotiate clear and measurable learning targets with students as part of the review system, demands that they be more explicit about both learning objectives and assessment criteria for modules of study.

Schools and colleges developing formative value-added systems, I would argue, are not only developing effective curriculum and assessment systems, but are also developing capability as learning organizations responsive to what is happening both inside and outside their organization. In this type of system, data are used as a way of understanding what is going on at all levels of the organization – at individual student level, at departmental/programme area level, at whole-institutional level and, to some degree, at national level. In addition, all parts of the organization are in communication, in a formal way, with all other parts – students with teachers, teachers with teachers, teachers with parents, teachers with managers – on a regular and cyclical basis. Finally, and most importantly, mechanisms are built in so that the institution can be responsive at all levels – the capacity to change as a result of information received is thus inherent to the system.

It could be argued that the development of this type of unified approach to assessment, modularization, curriculum planning and student learning constitutes a move, albeit at the institutional level, towards the Framework Stage of qualifications reform described in Chapters 1 and 13. Schools and colleges developing formative value-added systems are thus not only developing practices and structures which help them to succeed within the current qualifications structure, but are also building the capability to tackle future reform of the education and training system.

Assessing the impact of the formative value-added system

It is too early to assess whether the potential theoretical benefits of the formative value-added system will be borne out in practice, since there are currently few institutions which have fully operational formative value-added systems up and running. In the absence of any significant national evaluation of formative value-added work, it is perhaps useful here to establish a framework within which to judge the likely effects of this work on building institutional capability for change and on supporting student learning. I will therefore start the next two parts of this section with two definitions of institutional improvement – one of the measures of an institution's capacity to change – and one of the major findings of some international comparative work on high-performing education and training systems. Using these as my baseline, I hope to be able to demonstrate that many of the features of the formative value-added system have the potential to improve institutional performance and capability and to support student learning in order to raise levels of achievement and to develop the skills of lifelong learning.

Institutional capability for change

In their book on school improvement, van Velzen *et al.* (1985) define school improvement as: 'a systematic sustained effort aimed at change in learning conditions and other related internal conditions in one or more schools, with the ultimate aim of accomplishing education goals more effectively' (p.48). Hopkins *et al.* (1994), in a later book on the same subject, stress more explicitly the importance of making changes which affect students directly, when they define school improvement as: 'a distinct approach to educational change that enhances student outcomes as well as strengthening the school's capacity for managing change' (p.3).

In both cases, however, there is a strong suggestion that school improvement strategies should develop institutional capability, in a generic way, so that the institution can take on and use any new initiatives or challenges it faces in the future. It is the development of institutional capability as a means of addressing future reform to which I will return in later parts of this chapter.

What the burgeoning school effectiveness and school improvement literature also provides is some analysis of the features of effective schools and some preliminary indications of which school improvement strategies are likely to make a difference to institutional performance. Brown and Riddell (1991, p.68), for example, note that:

> Effective schools are *demanding* places, where teachers expect and ensure high
> standards of work and behaviour; at the same time they are responsive to pupils,
> for the teachers are approachable and, since they value pupils, seek to involve
> them in the life and work of the school. It is this combination of pressure and
> support which characterises the effective school.

If one looks at the way that the formative value-added system makes demands on teachers in terms of regular and public assessment of individual student performance, as well as curriculum planning, explicitness about learning objectives and clarity about future strategies for improvement, one can see that the system encourages many of the features of effective schools as outlined in the quotation above. An institution which develops all the components of the value-added formative system cannot be anything but 'a demanding place' which combines 'pressure and support'.

Although, as has already been stated, there are few institutions that have, as yet, developed fully-fledged formative value-added systems, our research and development work shows that those which have developed such systems have noted a change in the culture of the institution which affects both staff and pupils. As a result of the introduction of the system, institutions claim that there is a more widespread focus on achievement, there is a more consistent approach to grading and assessment, there is more open and precise discussion about student performance and progress and there is a greater understanding of learning strategies and student support (Spours, 1995; Spours and Hodgson, 1996; Spours and Young, 1994). As Stoll (1991, p.53) points out:

Ultimately. the key to success of any school improvement or change effort lies in the involvement of and respect for the opinions of those who have the final responsibility to make it work, namely the teachers. If this is achieved, school self-evaluation can be a meaningful process that can lead to the growth and development of adults and pupils in schools. A further benefit will be a shared desire on the part of the teachers, to be professionally accountable for their efforts.

Unlike many of the recent reforms in the English education system that have been centrally directed and consequently resented by teachers because they have brought with them an additional workload and a sense of loss of control, formative value-added work has been essentially institutionally led. The formative value-added system requires and promotes professional accountability. Although within this system external data are used to give a harder edge to the assessments teachers make about individual student progress and their own performance in terms of examination success, the drivers within the system are all internally controlled by the teachers and their students. The external value-added data that are used within the institutional assessment, tutoring and guidance system are not intended to replace teacher generated assessments, rather, they make additional demands on teachers to be more explicit and open about how they exercise professional judgement. In a very real sense, therefore, the formative value-added system can make a contribution to raising the status of teacher professionalism. This has been recognized as a strength in institutions where formative value-added systems have been developed and have been used as a powerful lever in bringing about whole-institutional change and improvement.

The contribution of value-added to the support of student learning and achievement

As other chapters of this book have already pointed out, underachievement is still, in international comparative terms, a feature of the English education and training system. It is also a feature which has stimulated much of the process-based reform within our system, as well as impacting on post-16 participation rates (Raffe and Rumberger, 1992).

The formative value-added system could be seen as one further example of this type of process-based reform, which tackles the problem of underachievement in a practical way at institutional level, but does little to change the qualifications system that is one of the root causes of this underachievement.

While recognizing this viewpoint, this chapter has argued that certain process-based reforms, such as the formative value-added system, not only have the potential to address problems at the institutional level – and this is clearly important – but also to transform the nature of the school or college in this process and thus make it more capable of tackling future whole-system reform. The two major issues which the formative value-added system is designed to address – raising student aspirations and expectations and developing students' capacity for managing their own learning and for building the skills for lifelong learning – are both, I would argue, issues which any future qualifications structure would also need to tackle.

Green and Steedman's work on international comparisons between education and training systems suggests that increasing teacher and student expectations of these systems is one of the keys to raising levels of achievement (Green and Steedman, 1993). From the limited evidence that has emerged so far about formative value-added systems (OFSTED, 1996; Spours, 1995; Spours and Hodgson, 1996; Spours and Young, 1994) it appears that these systems have the power to increase student and teacher expectations and, according to some institutional reports, to raise levels of achievement. The provision of clear target minimum grades for students, far from capping expectations as some teachers were initially concerned they would, appear to have engendered a spirit of 'target busting' (James, 1996). While it is self-evident that this type of increase in expectations and aspirations at an individual institutional level in no way equates with the kind of national cultural differences to which Green and Steedman refer, nevertheless, it is a powerful tool for incremental reform.

It could also be argued that a modular or staged approach to assessment and feedback required by the formative value-added system encourages students to pace their learning better and thus to work to build more systematically towards the achievement of qualifications and awards. In this sense, the formative value-added system is replicating the patterns that are used within modular qualifications and is likely therefore to benefit from the same rises in levels of achievement that these courses have brought about (Spours, 1995). Because students are made aware of their progress much earlier in a course, often by the end of the first term, they have more time to put into practice strategies for improving their performance. This, together with teacher explicitness about course objectives and external assessment criteria demands, has led, in many institutions, to a more challenging but also more supportive culture for student learning and achievement.

An important further dimension to this system is the provision of clearer guidance on the connection between achievement in external qualifications and specific progression possibilities in relation to further or higher education. This type of guidance can help students to gain a more concrete idea about the relationship between their academic performance and future education and training possibilities. A recent TVEI study has shown that this type of academic self-referencing can have a strong motivational effect on students (TVEI/NFER, 1993).

In terms of developing students' capacity for managing their own learning and for building the skills for lifelong learning, Murphy and Broadfoot (1995) suggest that central to this goal is the need 'to equip individuals with the skills and resources they need to become self-reliant and self-motivated learners' (p.249).

If this is the case, then again there are clear indications that the formative value-added system is able to make a significant contribution in this direction. In both subject teacher reviews and tutor reviews, students are given detailed feedback on their performance and are encouraged to use this to focus on their own strengths and weaknesses and to negotiate learning targets for future improvement. Although this type of target-setting is likely to be teacher-led, particularly in subject teacher reviews, there is an opportunity for the student to engage in an active dialogue about her or his own learning based on specific evidence of previous performance. It is this sharing of precise data on students with students, as well as the detailed discussion on what is required in order to succeed in a particular subject area, that provides them with the information they need to achieve. It also encourages students to take greater responsibility for their learning by helping them to discover their own learning styles and to identify strategies for success.

In conclusion, although the formative value-added system has not yet been evaluated extensively, there are some initial indications that this type of work contributes both to the building of schools' and colleges' capability for reform and to the development of students' skills in the management of their own learning.

Current limitations to the formative value-added system

Despite the promise of value-added as an educational tool for change, there is a danger of over-expectation. In order to assess the significance of the formative value-added system it is important to understand both its potential and its limitations. There are currently three major ways in which this system is limited: in relation to the methodology involved, in terms of resourcing and, most significantly, as a result of the nature of the present education and training system itself.

An immediate and very real limitation of all types of value-added work is the nature of its methodology. Despite its associations with progressive philosophies of learning gain, current value-added methodology, based on correlations between qualifications, depends on a narrow form of measurement by seeking to define value-added solely in terms of examination grade points. Used in this way, the concept of measuring value-added as learning gain is only as good as the qualifications being used. If the qualification is specialized and narrow, like A-levels, then the definition of learning gain is also narrow. Broader forms of learning gain, not recorded by qualifications, are ignored.

Moreover, at present, the only nationally available value-added data relate to GCSE and A-level. In order to use a formative value-added system with students other than those on A-level programmes, it is necessary to use much less rigorous data. The crudeness of the data currently being used in such systems, while not proving an insurmountable problem, is undoubtedly a limitation.

Second, the funding formula for further education colleges and the constant pressure on resources within schools and colleges means that the type of student-intensive work demanded by the formative value-added system is difficult to resource. This difficulty is increased by over-congested timetables in Key Stage 4 and significantly reduced student contact hours in full-time post-16 courses.

Finally, there are features of the English education and training system – particularly the qualifications structure and the lack of articulation between the secondary and post-16 phases – which make value-added difficult to measure even within one stage of education and certainly across stages of education. There are real difficulties, for example, in measuring value-added gain between GCSE and vocational qualifications because of their different internal structures and assessment regimes. There are also some problems in attempting to measure learning gain between Key Stage 3 and Key Stage 4, where there is a move from assessment by National Curriculum level (and broad levels at that) to assessment by grading in GCSE.[4] Until a common system of measurement is developed, these difficulties will remain and will limit both the statistical rigour of comparative value-added work and the credibility of data used within the formative value-added system.

In summary, the formative value-added system has considerable potential as a strategy for improving institutional capability for reform and raising levels of student achievement but, in the national education policy context of the 1990s, it has to operate within a restrictive qualifications and curriculum framework, with resourcing constraints and in a climate which encourages institutional competition rather than cooperation.

Conclusions

The formative value-added system is, I have argued, a typical example of the English approach to reform. Like many of the other process-based initiatives that have grown up since the 1980s (eg, recording of achievement, modularization, unitization and credit), the formative value-added system has all the strengths of bottom-up reform: teacher commitment, local relevance and immediate practical application. It also, to some extent, suffers from the same weakness: an inability on its own to overcome the impact of external education system factors (Post-16 Education Centre Unified Curriculum at 16+ Series, 1991–1996; Young et al., 1994), such as the divided qualifications structure, funding mechanisms and the lack of articulation between the different phases of education.

The formative value-added system has thus essentially developed as a pragmatic but potentially progressive institutional response to the wider education and training context of the 1990s. It demands a unified and consistent approach to assessment and curriculum planning, common student support structures regardless of the qualification route, as well as good communication between subject teachers, tutors and senior managers within the school or college. It thus emphasizes the need for a collective understanding of institutional purpose, sets up mechanisms for internal improvement of the organization and encourages collegiate ways of working rather than isolationism and individualism. Moreover, in its common approach to student learning, the formative value-added system has the potential to lessen the divisions between different forms of study and to challenge the concept of a triple-track qualifications structure.

In terms of the tracks, frameworks and systems debate, therefore, the formative value-added system, like many of the other process-based initiatives, can be seen as a tool which has grown up as a response to the track-based system, belongs within the Framework Stage and has the potential to work towards and within a unified system.

In this sense, I would argue, process-based initiatives such as the formative value-added system can be seen as important tools for future qualifications reform. This particular initiative can be seen as a step towards a unified qualifications system, since it promotes in schools and colleges the kind of features required by learning organizations equipped to respond to the changes demanded by a unified qualifications system. In addition, there is a strong indication that the formative value-added model would in fact work more effectively in a unified system, where there was a common measurement methodology for all qualifications, where there was more modularity, more common core learning and where progression pathways were more clearly interlinked. The whole-institutional connective approach that is demanded by the formative value-added system can therefore be seen as helping to bring in a reform process that will, in the end, make that system itself easier to operate.

Local and institutionally based process reforms have been one of the strongest features of the English reform tradition. Formative value-added work is, arguably, a powerful example of this tradition because of its emphasis on connecting different process-based practices and developing whole-institutional approaches to change. Moreover, any new reform process, such as the introduction of a unified qualifications system, requires a judicious balance between a national top-down lead and a professional bottom-up response to that reform by teachers and managers in schools and colleges. The formative value-added system, which works within such a balance, can thus play a significant role both in supporting the implementation of a new unified qualifications system and in making it operate more effectively once in place.

Notes

1. This type of system will be described in more detail later in the chapter, but basically it is a whole-institutional approach to assessment, tutoring and guidance, curriculum planning and delivery. It involves institutions using value-added data to reflect on their own performance as well as that of the individual student as part of an assessment, guidance and monitoring system.
2. Currently there are no national value-added data available except for the charts published by the DfEE which show correlations between average GCSE scores and either average A-level scores or total A-level point scores. However, individual institutions and groups of institutions working with higher education institutions or local authorities have been developing other types of value-added data. Some of these data, for example, show correlations between student attainment in Year 7 (eg, NFER Cognitive Abilities Tests or reading tests) and their subsequent attainment in GCSE, others look at the correlations between GCSE scores and

attainment in vocational qualifications and there are also some early attempts to look at correlations between end of National Curriculum Key Stage tests and their relationship with GCSEs (Jesson, 1996). All of this work is, however, still localized and at the experimental stage. Where institutions do not have adequate value-added data, other institutionally based measures of prior student performance, such as results in internal examinations, are used in combination with external tests such as National Curriculum End of Key Stage Assessments, to give teachers a baseline for setting a predictive target minimum grade for each student.

3. An 'estimated grade/level', as defined in the formative value-added system, is a teacher generated grade which denotes the grade/level that the student is likely to attain at the end of a course or stage in education if she or he continues to work in the manner in which she or he is currently working.

4. Recent research by Jesson for the DfEE, however, claims that 'GCSE performance appears highly correlated with the assessments made of pupils two years earlier, and to that extent, use of the Key Stage 3 Assessments represents a considerable opportunity for comparative evaluation of institutional performance using a common "starting point"' (Jesson 1996, p.12).

References

Brown, S and Riddell, S (1991) 'Promoting School Effectiveness: Key Issues', in Riddell, S and Brown, S (eds) *School Effectiveness Research: Its Messages for School Improvement*, Management of Educational Resources Unit, the Scottish Office Education Department, London: HMSO.

Conway, K (1992) *A Level Analysis for Added Value: Good Value for Students*, Huddersfield: Greenhead College.

Conway, K (1993) *Measuring Quality at A Level Using Added Value Systems*, Huddersfield: Greenhead College.

Department for Education (1995) *GCSE to GCE A/AS, Value Added Briefing for Schools and Colleges*, London: DfE.

Department for Education/OFSTED (1996) *Setting Targets to Raise Standards: A Survey of Good Practice*, London: DfEE

Farnsworth, S, Everett, S and Jesson, D (1994) *Beyond League Tables: A Value-added Analysis of GCSE and A Level Results in Nottinghamshire in 1993*, Nottinghamshire County Council Education.

Fitzgibbon, C T (1996) *Monitoring Education: Indicators, Quality and Effectiveness*, London: Cassell.

Fitzgibbon, C T and Tymms, P (1993) *Value-added: A Perspective on the Contribution of Examination Results*, Discussion Paper 1, Leicester: Centre for the Study of Comprehensive Schools.

Further Education Development Agency (1995) *Current Developments in Value-added*, London: FEDA.

Further Education Unit (1993) *Value-added in Further Education*, London: FEU.

Further Education Unit (1994) *Value-added: An Update*, London: FEU.

Goldstein, H, Rasbash, J, Yang, M, Woodhouse, G, Nuttall, D and Thomas, S (1993) 'A Multi-Level Analysis of Examination Results', *Oxford Review of Education*, **19**, 4, 425–33.

Gray, J, Jesson, D and Sime, N (1990) 'Estimating differences in the examination performances of secondary schools in six LEAs: a multi-level approach to school effectiveness', *Oxford Review of Education*, **16**, 2, 137–58.

Green, A (1993) *Educational Achievement in Britain, France, Germany and Japan: A Comparative Analysis*, Working Paper No. 14, London: Post-16 Education Centre, Institute of Education, University of London.

Green, A and Steedman, H (1993) *Education Provision, Education Attainment and the Needs of Industry: A review of the Research for Germany, France, Japan, the USA and Britain*, National Institute of Economic Research, Report No 5, London: NIESR.

Hopkins, D, Ainscow, M and West, M (1994) *School Improvement in an Era of Change*, London: Cassell.

James, J (1996) 'Case Study 2: Implementing a Value-added Monitoring System in a Sixth Form', in Spours, K and Hodgson, A (eds) *Value-added and Raising Attainment: A Formative Approach. A Resource Pack for Practitioners*, Poole: BP Educational Service.

Jesson, D (1996) *Value-added Measures of School GCSE Performance*, London: DfEE.

Murphy, R and Broadfoot, P (1995) *Effective Assessment: The Improvement of Education*, London: Falmer Press.

OFSTED (1996) *Effective Sixth Forms*, London: HMSO.

Post-16 Education Centre (1996) *Value-added and Raising Achievement in the 14–19 Curriculum*, Report from the National Conference, 24 January, London: Post-16 Education Centre, Institute of Education, University of London.

Post-16 Education Centre Unified Curriculum at 16+ Series (1991–1996) Working Papers 1–12, London: Post-16 Education Centre, Institute of Education, University of London.

Raffe, D and Rumberger, P (1992) 'Education and Training for 16–18 Year Olds', in Mcfarland, L and Richardson, W (eds) *Something Borrowed, Something Blue? A Study of the Thatcher Government's Appropriation of American Education and Training Policy: Part I, Volume 2*, Oxford Studies in Comparative Education, Yatton: Triangle Publishing.

Sammons, P, Thomas, S, Mortimore, P, Owen, C and Pennell, H (1994) *Assessing School Effectiveness: Developing Measures to Put School Performance in Context*, London: OFSTED.

Spours, K (1995) *Value-added Strategies for Raising Attainment and Achievement*, A Report by the Post-16 Education Centre/Essex TVEI.

Spours, K and Hodgson, A (1996) *Value-added and Raising Attainment: A Formative Approach. A Resource Pack for Practitioners*, Poole: BP Educational Service.

Spours, K and Young, M (1994) *Enhancing the Post-16 Curriculum: Value-added Perspectives*, Post-16 Education Centre Report, Institute of Education, University of London.

Stoll, L (1991) 'School Self-Evaluation: Another Boring Exercise or an Opportunity for Growth', in Riddell, S and Brown, S (eds) *School Effectiveness Research: Its Messages for School Improvement*, Management of Educational Resources Unit, the Scottish Office Education Department, London: HMSO.

Thomas, S and Mortimore, P (1995) 'Report on Value-added Analysis of 1993 GCSE Examination Results in Lancashire', *Research Papers in Education*.

TVEI/NFER (1993) *Experiencing TVEI Extension 14–16: Overview Report 1991 Survey*, Slough: TVEI/NFER.

Van Velzen, W, Miles, M, Ekholm, M, Hameyer, U and Robin, D (1985) *Making School Improvement Work: A Conceptual Guide to Practice*, Belgium: Acco.

Young, M, Hayton, A, Hodgson, A and Morris, A (1994) 'An Interim Approach to Unifying the Post-16 Curriculum', in Tomlinson, S (ed.) *Educational Reform and its Consequences*, London: IPPR/Rivers Oram Press.

CHAPTER 12

The Scottish Experience of Reform: From 'Action Plan' to 'Higher Still'

David Raffe

Introduction

Education and training debates have acquired an international frame of reference. Other countries are trawled for benchmarks for the UK's relative performance or for ideas on how this performance might be improved (DfEE and Cabinet Office, 1996; Keep, 1991). But other countries are at best a source of lessons to be drawn than policies to be borrowed (Finegold *et al.*, 1992, 1993) and even when we keep to lesson-drawing, we find that the lessons from different countries are not equally transferable to our own situation (Rose, 1993). It is not surprising, therefore, that some commentators have advocated the greater use of comparisons within the UK, and particularly with Scotland, as a source of policy lessons (eg, NCE, 1993, Richardson *et al.*, 1995). Such 'home-international' comparisons are more likely than those with overseas countries to yield valid lessons for policy and practice (Raffe, 1991). But they need to be based on knowledge and understanding of the different education and training systems of the UK. In this chapter, I describe the Scottish system for 16–19-year-olds and developments in this system over the last two decades, in order to inform current debates in England and Wales.

Home-international comparisons have become even more attractive since the Scottish Office published *Higher Still*, its new policy for post-16 education (Scottish Office, 1994a). From 1998 Scotland will have a 'unified curriculum and assessment system' covering all post-16 education below higher education. As such it has been a source of inspiration for many 'frameworkers' and 'unifiers' south of the border, to borrow the terms used by Hodgson and Spours in Chapter 1 of this book. This chapter describes the reform and the issues raised in its implementation, and identifies lessons for policy south of the border. However *Higher Still* is still in the process of development; there is not yet any empirical evidence of the reform in practice. This chapter argues, however, that current debates in England and Wales have as much to learn from the recent past of Scottish education and training as from current developments.

Two earlier episodes are particularly important. The first was the *Action Plan* reform of 1984, which introduced a national modular system to cover all non-advanced vocational education in colleges, schools and training schemes. The *Action Plan* pre-dated English proposals for credit frameworks, module banks and qualifications frameworks, all of which may learn from its experience. It also extended vocational provision within schools and facilitated more flexible combinations of academic and vocational courses – another source of valuable experience.

The second episode was the series of debates surrounding the appointment of the Howie Committee in 1990 to review the post-compulsory stages in Scottish secondary schools, and the publication of its report in 1992 (SOED, 1992). The Committee's own proposal for a two-track system was rejected, but its analysis of existing problems was influential and led to the government's own proposals published in *Higher Still* in 1994. Equally important, it inspired a rare level of debate and critical analysis of Scottish education – a collective learning experience from which other countries may also learn.

In the next section of the chapter, I briefly describe the Scottish system at the end of the 1970s, when my account begins. In the following sections, I outline the three episodes described above – the *Action Plan*, the Howie debate and *Higher Still* – and I describe other significant events as the narrative unfolds. In the final section, I relate the Scottish experience to the conceptual framework presented by Hodgson and Spours, and I draw lessons for current debates in England and Wales.

Prelude: Education and training for 16–19-year-olds in Scotland at the end of the 1970s

At the end of the 1970s most young Scots attended schools which were comprehensive and co-educational. Pupils transferred to secondary school at 12 and attended for at least four years, until the minimum leaving age of 16. At the end of fourth year (S4) many took O-grade examinations. O-grades had originally been designed for the able minority of school pupils but they were now taken by a majority. In 1977, two government reports had proposed that O-grades be replaced by new 14–16 courses and qualifications, to be designed for all pupils. The new courses, known as Standard grade (roughly analogous to GCSEs), were phased in from 1984.

Compared to England, full-time participation was higher at 16-plus but lower at 17-plus: in the late 1970s about a third of 16-year-olds stayed on at school to S5 and one in six stayed on to S6 (Burnhill, 1984; SED/SEB, 1982). Participation was rising slowly but steadily. As in England, the post-compulsory curriculum consisted of subject-based courses which students could choose relatively freely. The main post-compulsory course, and the main qualification for entrance to university, was the Higher grade of the Scottish Certificate of Education. Unlike the A-level, the Higher was a one-year course. High-flying students took five Highers in S5; a significant minority of young people left school after S5 to enter university, having already gained the necessary qualifications (Robertson, 1990). Most S5 students took fewer than five Highers and combined them with new or repeated O-grades (McPherson, 1984a). S6 students took combinations of O-grades, Highers and the Certificate of Sixth Year Studies (CSYS) – a post-Higher course to prepare for university study (McPherson, 1984b). The Scottish curriculum was not as broad as some of its supporters claimed, but it was broader than that of England (Gray *et al.*, 1983).

Further Education (FE) played a smaller and more specific role than in England. Only about 7 per cent of school leavers entered full-time FE courses, although nearly one in five (predominantly males) attended part-time (Croxford *et al.*, 1991a). FE provision for 16–18-year-olds was almost entirely vocational – colleges were not allowed to offer academic courses to young people.

Youth unemployment was a growing problem. The proportion of school leavers in full-time jobs fell from nearly two-thirds (64 per cent) in 1979 to 38 per cent in 1983 and 30 per cent in 1987 (Raffe, 1988a). The decline in school-leaver employment was matched by a growth in work experience and training schemes run by the Manpower Services Commission (MSC). At their peak, these schemes attracted more than 40 per cent of Scottish youngsters (Raffe, 1988b), but they were British-wide measures; the MSC's remit covered the whole of Great Britain.

The Scottish system is usually portrayed as more centralized than that of England. At the head of this system was the Scottish Education Department (SED), subsequently reincarnated as the Scottish Office Education Department (SOED) and later as the Scottish Office Education and Industry Department (SOEID). The SED played a more active role in policy formation than the DES; it tended to perform this role through skilful consensus management and by relying on the system's tradition of 'looking to the centre for a lead' (McPherson and Raab, 1988). However, the SED's control was only partial; it did not assume control over the Scottish universities until 1992–93, or over training until 1994.

Episode 1: The reform of vocational education and training (1979–1989)

By the end of the 1970s there was growing pressure for reform. In 1979, a government Consultative Paper argued that education had to raise participation, increase the employability of young people, and cater for a broader range of students (SED, 1979). However, neither the Paper nor the responses settled on the specific policy measures to achieve these goals. In 1981 the MSC launched its

New Training Initiative, covering the whole of Britain. This heralded the introduction, in 1983, of the Youth Training Scheme (YTS) to replace the existing measures for unemployed young people. The Technical and Vocational Education Initiative (TVEI) was announced in 1982 (but its introduction in Scotland was deferred until 1984, a year later than in England). These developments helped to precipitate the publication of the SED's (1983) *16–18s in Scotland: An Action Plan* in January 1983 and its implementation the following year.

The *Action Plan* replaced existing non-advanced vocational courses by a national system of modules. These were accredited by a single National Certificate (NC), awarded by the Scottish Vocational Education Council (SCOTVEC) which was created by the merger of two existing bodies in 1985. Each module was typically of 40 hours' duration, defined primarily in terms of outcomes and internally assessed on the basis of specified criteria. In principle, students could construct a wide variety of possible programmes of modules, although in practice colleges tended to offer ready-made programmes, often with little scope for choice. Schools tended to offer modules on more of a pick-and-mix basis.

The *Action Plan* aimed to rationalize provision, to encourage participation and to extend choice and opportunity, especially for the 'less academic' stayers-on. In the process of converting courses to modules, it also modernized the vocational curriculum, encouraged a more student-centred pedagogy and introduced internal assessment. The *Plan* referred approvingly to other measures to rationalize provision, including greater collaboration among neighbouring schools and colleges. It expressed a liberal philosophy of education which rejected any 'abandonment of broadly based education' at this age, and which argued that 'in young people's development the separation of education and training is a false one, and that more is to be gained from a planned interaction of the two' (SED, 1983, pp.6–17).

It also had a further aim: to win back control and initiative from the MSC. Through the *Action Plan*, the SED was able to reassert its authority over vocational education in Scotland, to pre-empt further incursions from the south and, through its control of the modular curriculum, to maintain its influence over developments such as YTS and TVEI (Raffe, 1985).

The *Action Plan* had a longer-term vision:

> It will also be for consideration, but at a later stage when experience of the proposals here has been gained, whether there should be an extension of this process to include in one certificate all forms of academic and vocational awards for the 16–18 age group. (SED, 1983, p.46)

Long before these ideas surfaced in England, the government in Scotland was voicing not only the possibility of a unified system at 16-plus, but also the notion of incremental progress towards one.

The *Action Plan* was implemented with exceptional speed: a catalogue of more than 2,000 modules was constructed and the system was substantially in place by the start of the 1984–1985 session. NC modules soon accounted for most FE provision, including most certificated provision for YTS trainees (Croxford *et al.*, 1991a). The modules found a large demand among adults, attracted by short-course provision that was nationally certificated and flexible. The '16–18s Action Plan' soon became the '16-plus Action Plan'.

FE colleges had been the main targets for the *Action Plan* reforms, but before long there were more NC students based in schools than in colleges, even if they were studying fewer modules. NC modules were used to cater for the growing number of 'winter leavers' – students who were not eligible to leave school until the December of S5. Modules were used extensively in the TVEI curriculum, and 14–16-year-olds on TVEI were given special dispensation to take the '16-plus' modules. This was subsequently extended to all 14–16 students. NC participation also grew among post-compulsory school students, especially at the end of the decade when O-grades were phased out. Standard grade courses were less suitable for study in S5 and NC modules filled the gap. By 1994–1995, 87 per cent of S5 students and 68 per cent of S6 students were registered for NC modules (Scottish Office, 1996).

NC modules were variously used in schools as an alternative to Highers for lower-attaining students, in conjunction with Highers (as a bridge or safety-net), to extend the Highers curriculum (adding vocational enhancements, interest courses or filling small gaps in the timetable), or to deliver areas of the curriculum where Highers certification was unavailable or inappropriate (Croxford *et al.*, 1991b; Weir and Kydd, 1991). But very few S5 or S6 students studied programmes mainly composed of NC modules. The role of modules in the post-compulsory curriculum was largely complementary or interstitial in relation to Highers.

The growth in post-16 participation in schools had three important consequences. First, it enabled schools to develop expertise in the delivery of vocational or pre-vocational education and to maintain their position as the main providers of full-time education at 16-plus. Second, in many areas schools and colleges gained experience of collaboration in the delivery of modules. Third, the *Action Plan* helped to prevent the emergence of clearly defined tracks, and especially of a 'general vocational' middle track, in Scottish education. It prevented a clear boundary from emerging between (general) vocational and academic education, since most school students combined the two; and it linked general vocational education with occupational provision in a single framework.

The Advanced Courses Development Programme, launched by SCOTVEC in 1988, extended the modular approach to Higher National Certificates and Diplomas, while retaining the grouped awards.

The NC had considerable success in updating the curriculum, increasing flexibility, reforming pedagogy and enhancing the coherence of the system. It met with generally favourable reactions from students and employers. But there were criticisms of fragmentation of the curriculum, and concerns about the reliability of internal assessment and the time that it required. These concerns were expressed most frequently by college lecturers, who tended to view the NC less favourably than either students or employers (Black *et al.*, 1991; Howieson, 1992; SOED, 1992). NC modules also tended to have low status and an uncertain market value in the labour market and higher education. Their low status was most evident in schools, where students studied modules alongside academic courses and were particularly aware of the differences in content, pedagogy and assessment, as well as in the attitudes of teachers (Croxford *et al.*, 1991b; Howieson *et al.*, 1990).

The NC increased the education system's capacity for progressive evolutionary change and its ability to accommodate innovations such as TVEI and YTS. It also increased the flexibility of 'pathways' for students within the system. But flexibility was still restricted by institutional rigidities and barriers to progression (Croxford *et al.*, 1991a). Moreover, even when the NC reduced rigidities and increased opportunities for participation and progression, it did not itself supply strong incentives for students to take advantage of these opportunities, particularly given its uncertain market value. It did not have a major impact on aggregate patterns of participation and progression among young people (Croxford *et al.*, 1991a; Raffe *et al.*, 1993).

The *Action Plan* embraced full-time and work-based qualifications and revealed some of the issues involved in combining the two in a single framework. Full-time qualifications were typically used for occupational selection and emphasized the 'vertical' differentiation of students; work-based qualifications were used for occupational preparation and enhancement and emphasized 'horizontal' differentiation (Raffe, 1992). A unified framework has to reconcile these different functions and pressures. However, the main factor dividing full-time from work-based provision was the pressure from south of the border for an analogue to NVQs. Scottish Vocational Qualifications (SVQs) were introduced in 1990. They were grouped awards, specified at the same levels as NVQs, and as such responded to employers who had found modular certification hard to deal with. However, SVQs also had to conform to other aspects of the NCVQ approach, such as workplace assessment, for which there had been little demand within Scotland. Rather than change the character of NC modules, SCOTVEC introduced 'workplace-assessed' modules, which serve as the basis of most SVQs, although some are based on NC modules. As a result, the boundary between full-time and work-based vocational provision was partly re-established. Although the *Action Plan* was initially intended to unify vocational provision, its most lasting effect may have been to weaken the boundary between academic and vocational education within schools.

Episode 2: The Howie debate over upper-secondary education (1990–1993)

The 1980s saw the emergence of a critique of upper-secondary school courses in Scotland, which gathered momentum towards the end of the decade. This identified several weaknesses of the current system: that it lacked breadth and especially depth and set lower standards of attainment either than A-levels or than continental systems; that it failed to cater adequately for the wider range of young people entering S5, especially the 'less academic'; and that its short courses (notably the 'two-term dash' to Highers) and frequent examinations increased stress and fostered a teacher-centred pedagogy, which prevented students from acquiring independent study skills.

In 1990 the government appointed a committee, chaired by Professor John Howie, to review courses, assessment and certification in S5 and S6. Many people expected it to recommend an extension of Highers courses from one to two years, an idea which had been floated in the recent debates. However, the prospect of a 'two-year Higher' aroused fears among many educationists. Would it threaten the relatively high rate of staying-on in Scottish schools, believed to be due to the one-plus-one-year course structure? Would it strengthen academic/vocational divisions, by making it harder to mix Highers and NC modules? Would it discourage less advantaged students, especially in the west, for whom the opportunity to progress to higher education at 17 had been an incentive to study? Would it further Anglicize Scottish education? The universities were particularly concerned, since the one-year Higher (and the consequent possibility of entry to higher education at 17) was symbolically important in defending the Scottish four-year Honours degree and the higher level of public spending that it required.

As a result, many submissions to the Howie Committee took a relatively conservative position. They accepted the need for some change, but argued that this should be evolutionary and should preserve and enhance the strengths of the present system (McPherson, 1992). Any changes should build on the flexibility of the existing system and allow flexible pacing (with the same certificates achievable in S5 or S6), variable combinations of academic and vocational courses and incremental decision-making, with an exit point at the end of S5. Some submissions proposed an extension of modularization and greater compatibility between Highers and NC modules.

In April 1991, with the Howie Committee in the middle of its deliberations, the government announced that General Scottish Vocational Qualifications (GSVQs) would be introduced in Scotland (SOED, 1992). The timing of this announcement, with the Howie Committee still deliberating, underlined that GSVQs were a response, not to internal Scottish debates, but to the political requirement for a Scottish counterpart for GNVQs. GSVQ pilots were introduced in 1992 in five broad occupational areas at Levels 2 and 3, with a non-specialized award at Level 1. Further subjects were added, but GSVQs remained in pilot mode until 1996. Uncertainties over the national policy context restricted their development, especially in schools, and student numbers remained small (Murray, 1996). Scotland had no middle or 'broad vocational' track, and GSVQs lacked the ready-made constituency that GNVQs found south of the border.

The Howie Committee published its report in 1992. It 'wholeheartedly endorse[d] Scotland's broad educational traditions' and re-stated the aims of 16–18 education, emphasizing breadth and drawing on the *Action Plan* and the Munn Report of 1977 which proposed the Standard-grade curriculum (SOED, 1992). It agreed with the criticisms of the current system, summarized above, and identified further weaknesses: the low attainments of many S5 students; the incoherence of modular choices; and an 'uneven gradient of difficulty' over the stages of secondary schooling. It proposed that Standard-grade courses be brought forward (from 14–16 years to 13–15 years), to leave space for a three-year upper-secondary stage. At 15 years students would enter one of two tracks leading to a grouped award. The upper track would be a three-year course with two principal lines (arts and science), and would cater for 35 to 40 per cent of each cohort. The lower track would be a two-year modular programme, with a certificated exit point after one year. It would have occupational and general variants and be offered in colleges as well as schools. It would 'incorporate' GSVQs but have a stronger emphasis on breadth and general education. 'Bridges and ladders' would link the two tracks.

More than 4,500 responses to the Howie Report were received. They varied widely but tended to agree on two key points: that the *status quo* was no longer an option (Howie had established a case for change), and that his proposal to introduce tracking was unacceptable. Tracking was condemned for its divisiveness, for its conflict with the Scottish comprehensive tradition, for problems of timetabling and delivery, and for the likely difficulty of switching between tracks.

Even judged as a 'multi-track system', the proposed model was flawed by the weakness of its lower track (Raffe, 1993). Howie's lower track lacked a clear vision, purpose or institutional base. The Report insisted that both tracks would include both academic and vocational elements and they would be distinguished solely by the 'level of demand' they would place upon students. In other words, parity of esteem would be ruled out from the start and the lower track would have no basis on which to develop its own identity or ethos. In addition, the Committee's remit, restricted to schools, made it impossible to design an effective lower track; in effect it could only design a one-and-a-half-track system.

The Scottish debates on education focused mainly on schools and were conducted in relative isolation from the British-wide debates on vocational training. They had not yet acquired a 'whole-system' focus (see Hodgson and Spours, Chapter 1). Scottish developments in training paralleled those in England, but with important differences. In 1990, Scottish Enterprise and Highlands and Islands Enterprise were set up to replace the former Development Agencies and to oversee the activities of the newly created local enterprise companies (LECs). The new structures have been more effective than the TEC network south of the border (Bennett *et al.*, 1994), but they have tended to see training largely in operational terms, giving more priority in their strategic thinking to economic development (Fairley, 1996). This may have partly reflected a strategic vacuum at the centre: only in 1994 did the Scottish Office gain control of training policy. The LECs' main measure for the 16-plus age group is Skillseekers, the Scottish version of Youth Credits, introduced from 1991 onwards, and which now incorporate Modern Apprenticeships.

Episode 3: The Higher Still reform (1994–)

In 1994 the government published *Higher Still* (Scottish Office, 1994a). This announced a new unified system to embrace all 16-plus provision below higher education level except for SVQs and the work-based sector. The new system will be based on 40- or 80-hour units, usually grouped into 160-hour courses, although stand-alone or 'additional' units are also available. Units and courses will cover the range of academic and vocational subjects, but will all be designed, assessed and certificated according to common principles. Where possible, core skills will be embedded in the new system. Units and courses will be available at five levels, and students will enter the system at the appropriate level given their previous attainment in the subject concerned. The top two levels correspond to existing Highers and CSYS courses, so high-flying students may continue to study a programme of Highers in their first post-compulsory year and pursue some of these at Advanced Higher (equivalent to CSYS) in the following year. A student may take courses at different levels at the same time.

Higher Still is a multipurpose reform which has nine main aims:

1. Higher standards of attainment
2. Recognised qualifications for all
3. An even gradient of progression
4. Expansion and rationalisation of existing provision
5. Breadth of attainment
6. Competence in core skills
7. Consolidation of earlier reforms
8. Making the system simpler and more efficient
9. Unification of curriculum and assessment arrangements

(Scottish Office, 1994a, pp.9–10)

To the extent that *Higher Still* has a single over-riding goal, this is expressed by the document's subtitle: *Opportunity for All*. *Higher Still* responds to the need for post-16 education to cater for the whole age group and it addresses the issues of differentiation and diversity that this raises. Instead of dividing students and allocating them to parallel tracks, it provides a single ladder for all students; it also caters for the diversity of students by allowing them to start climbing at different rungs on the ladder, to climb it at different speeds and to progress either vertically or horizontally. The system will be voluntary, in the sense that there will be no national prescription for the number, content or combination of courses taken. Students may, if they wish, take specified combinations of courses or units which will lead to Scottish Group Awards, available in a range of broad subject areas and at different levels.

The *Higher Still* approach is evolutionary. The new system will be built using elements of the existing system. Highers and CSYS courses will form the basis of units and courses at the top two *Higher Still* levels. NC modules will form the basis of new units and courses at all levels, particularly in vocational subjects. Scottish Group Awards will be based on GSVQs. But the reform is much more than a 'framework approach' (Hodgson and Spours, Chapter 1). The new courses and units are being redesigned with a new title and a new identity, and they will be subject to common principles for curriculum, assessment and certification. Curricula are being revised and updated and gaps in current provision are being filled, for example to provide more vocational subjects at Higher level. The two Scottish awarding bodies – SCOTVEC and the SEB – are merging in 1997 to form the Scottish Qualifications Authority, which will issue the new certificates.

Whatever its limitations, the Howie Report radicalized the debate; it based its proposals on a clear statement of the aims of education, and critics who rejected tracking had to provide a much clearer vision of the alternative. The *Higher Still* document itself did not maintain this radical visionary spirit; it presented the reform as a response to the perceived problems of the current system. Its style was low-key and it did not discuss its vision of the future except as this was implied by the nine aims. This style has been maintained in the debates which followed, and may have anticipated the public reaction to the proposals. When the policy was announced the reception was generally favourable, but the debate soon came to be dominated by practical issues such as the resources for development, the resources required to operate the new system, the timetable for reform, and the workload, stress and innovation fatigue of teachers and lecturers. The largest teachers' union, the Educational Institute of Scotland, took a distinctly cool attitude towards *Higher Still* – paradoxically, because its own response to the Howie Report had advocated a unified system very similar to the one pursued by *Higher Still*. The government has responded to these concerns by stressing the incremental nature of the reform, by emphasizing that it was responding to current practical problems, by delaying the start of the reform and by embarking on a major consultation process. In the process, however, it has down-played the visionary and future-oriented aspect of the reform. Discussions of the purposes of education or of the curriculum of the 21st century seem out of place in the *Higher Still* development, let alone discussions of the future economy or society to which education must contribute.

The Development Programme was established in 1994. Consultation rounds have been held in 1995 and 1996, based initially on draft frameworks for courses and units in each subject area, and latterly on more detailed course proposals (HSDU, 1995; 1996). Consultation documents have covered such issues as the curriculum, core skills, guidance, special needs and nomenclature. Many of the responses to the consultations so far have concerned the balance to be struck in reconciling the 'academic' and 'vocational' approaches. For example, there has been considerable discussion of the relative merits of the SEB and SCOTVEC approaches to assessment, especially the balance between external and internal assessment. There has been a similar debate over the balance between literature and linguistic competence in the English curriculum. However, most of the subject frameworks have been broadly endorsed in the consultations.

The consultations have also identified practical issues in developing a more differentiated set of opportunities for the whole age group. These include the problems of resourcing the wider set of opportunities, especially in small and isolated schools, the need for more collaboration across institutions, the likely increase in 'multi-level' classes and the implications for teaching and learning approaches, the need for the system to be simple and well understood by students and the wider public, and the need for clear pathways and guidance for student choice.

In 1994, the Scottish Office assumed responsibility for training policy and in 1995, education and training responsibilities were brought together in a newly-formed Education and Industry Department. A consultation paper, *Training for the Future*, started the process of developing a Scottish training strategy (Scottish Office, 1994b). In this and in subsequent documents, it became clear that training policy would build on *Higher Still* and that parity of esteem and 'the convergence of academic and vocational learning' would be core themes (DfEE/SO/WO, 1995, p.56). The government in Scotland can now adopt the 'whole-system' focus that had been lacking before (Fairley, 1996; Hodgson and Spours, Chapter 1).

Lessons for England and Wales

Any attempt to draw lessons for England and Wales must acknowledge the differences in the systems and in their contexts. The Scottish education system is smaller and more homogeneous. Its government is more centralized and its institutions less fragmented. Its courses and qualifications already have a degree of flexibility on which a unified system can build. It lacks an equivalent of the A-level lobby and the post-16 debate is less polarized – unification appeals to the Right as a way of raising the status of vocational learning, as well as to the Left. In contrast to England, the Howie debate revealed a widespread Scottish commitment to the principle of comprehensive secondary education, and to the idea that all school students should have access to 'mainstream' courses. By implication, however, this commitment excludes young people in colleges and training schemes, who, by leaving school, have put themselves outside the moral community invoked by the principle.

Despite these differences, there is much that England and Wales can learn from the Scottish experience and the experience of the *Action Plan* and the Howie debate are important sources of lessons, as well as the current *Higher Still* developments.

In their introductory chapter, Hodgson and Spours distinguish three main positions in the English debate: the 'trackers', the 'frameworkers' and the 'unifiers'. A first analysis suggests that the *Action Plan* introduced a 'framework', the

Howie debate toyed briefly with the idea of 'tracks', and *Higher Still* is introducing a 'unified system'.

The Action Plan: unifying vocational qualifications

The *Action Plan* was a 'vocational qualification framework', in Hodgson and Spours' terms, since it embraced all non-advanced vocational qualifications; it was also a 'credit framework', since it covered different institutions and credit was transferable. However, within its sphere it was closer to a unified system: it replaced existing qualifications and did not simply 'arch over' them to establish equivalences and credit ratings. The *Action Plan* experience has lessons for all these policy positions.

First, it demonstrated the potential of modularization, not only to enhance individual flexibility, but also to enhance the flexibility of the system as a whole and its capacity for incremental and manageable change. It revealed potential problems of modular approaches, for example concerning assessment and the fragmentation of the curriculum, but also allowed ways of overcoming these to be developed (Raffe, 1994). *Higher Still* addresses these problems with a multi-level curriculum structure, which groups 40-hour modules into 160-hour courses.

Second, a qualifications framework based on 'outcomes' is not a sufficient basis for a coherent system; inputs and institutions also matter. Despite the *Action Plan*, institutional barriers and rigidities persisted. The perceived value of the NC continued to depend on where and how it was obtained. Incentives to participate and progress depended more on the institutional context of provision (full-time course, training scheme or employment) than on the curricular pathways opened up by a credit framework. Part of the problem was the low status of the NC and its weak currency in higher education and the labour market. The *Action Plan* experience shows that the ability of a qualifications framework to promote system coherence is in direct proportion to the standing of the qualifications concerned.

Third, a qualifications framework (and, *a fortiori*, a unified system) will have particular difficulty in reconciling the demands and pressures of full-time and work-based provision. The *Action Plan* brought these two sectors together, but since 1989 they have diverged again, and they remain separate in the *Higher Still* reforms.

Action Plan and Highers: a kind of unified framework?

The *Action Plan* unified vocational provision, but it also contributed to a school curriculum in which students have increasingly combined academic and vocational study. As a result, the current school curriculum conforms to Hodgson and Spours' description of frameworks: 'Frameworks provide the means by which existing qualifications can continue but with greater flexibility (although no compulsion) to mix academic and vocational study'(Chapter 1, p.12).

Does Scotland thus represent the kind of system which Sir Ron Dearing (1996) proposes to introduce in England? If so, what conclusions should we draw from the fact that the Scots are dissatisfied with their system and in the process of reforming it?

To answer these questions we must recognize the different dimensions on which systems may vary. If systems vary on a continuum from tracking to unified systems (with frameworks somewhere in between), they may do so along several dimensions. Hodgson and Spours define tracks in terms of four dimensions of distinctiveness: purposes, content, assessment and structure. Academic and vocational courses in Scottish schools are distinctive in terms of assessment, content (especially pedagogy) and structure, and to a lesser extent in terms of purposes. In terms of distinctiveness, therefore, the current Scottish system is close to the 'tracking' end of the continuum. However, Scotland is close to the 'unified' end in respect of a further dimension: the flexibility of student 'pathways'. The Scottish system is therefore characterized by high distinctiveness but also by high flexibility, and the combination of these two has fuelled the pressure for change. This is because the problems of status and coherence that arise from the distinctiveness of academic and vocational courses are exacerbated when the same students are taking both. In England, the Dearing proposals will enhance both distinctiveness and flexibility; this will exacerbate the low status of the applied or vocational tracks and increase the pressure for unification (see Chapter 4).

The Howie debate: back to tracking?

The Howie proposals would have reduced flexibility; it is less certain that they would have increased track distinctiveness. The proposed lower track would have lacked purpose, ethos or any basis for esteem. The Committee insisted that it would not be a vocational track, and that it would differ from the higher track only in respect of the level of demand placed on students. In other words, it would have had low status by design.

An important lesson from the Howie debate is that the success of a 'multi-track system' depends on the strength of its lower track(s). This means that such a system must be designed from the bottom up, starting with the lower or vocational track(s) and working upwards. Howie's proposal, like the present system, was designed from the top down, with the academic track as the starting point.

Yet the Howie Committee showed how difficult it is to design a plausible vocational track. There are several reasons for this. First, there is a problem because of the weakness of the existing vocational and technical tradition, especially in full-time education. Second, the diversity of colleges' roles and the overlap with schools means that there is no clear institutional base for such a tradition to develop. 'Functional differentiation of institutions' is a further dimension of unification on which systems may vary. Third, there is a lack of labour-market demand for intermediate vocational qualifications and, related to this, a decay of occupational labour markets with weak links between vocational education and employment. Finally, the size and scale of higher education means that there are pressures for 'academic drift'. All these factors are common to the whole of Britain, even if the details vary north and south of the border.

A third and more speculative lesson from the Howie debate is that frameworks and other intermediate options between tracking and a unified system do not address the difficulty of building a strong vocational track, and are inherently unstable. I have suggested above that a Dearing-style framework, which combines track distinctiveness and flexibility, will be unstable. The more general problem is that an intermediate approach may get the worst of both worlds: it neither allows the vocational track(s) to develop their own identity and ethos as a basis of esteem, nor does it prevent academic drift and the flow of students into the academic track. The closer the tracks are brought together, the more likely that the lower track(s) will be judged by the values of the higher track, and found wanting. On this analysis, treating Dearing as a step towards a unified system is a matter of prediction, not prescription.

Higher Still: towards a unified system

Higher Still corresponds to the model of unified system described by Hodgson and Spours, with two main qualifications.

First, it excludes most work-based provision. This may change; Scotland is now capable of a 'whole-system' policy focus, and the next step may be to assimilate work-based provision – at least for young people – into the unified system. Alternatively, Scotland may pursue a model which sees the relation between school- and work-based provision primarily as one of progression. In this model, school- or college-based education would be followed by a period of work-based training for all people entering or re-entering the labour market, whatever their level of attainment.

Second, it is voluntaristic and has no compulsory 'core' or rules of combination. In Hodgson and Spours' analysis, one of the factors which distinguishes unified systems from unified frameworks is 'an in-built balance of general education and a variety of specialist units'. *Higher Still* only provides this to the extent that core skills and vocational relevance are embedded in all units and courses.

Higher Still has not yet been implemented, but we can already draw several lessons from the developments so far. First, it underlines the possibility – indeed, the necessity – of incremental, progressive change. The emerging Scottish approach to educational development, 'build[s] on our principles of partnership and consensus' and moves 'away from a model of fifteen years inertia followed by five years revolution, towards a situation where educational change is incremental, manageable and continuous' (Harrison, 1996, p.12). The Scottish experience confirms the value of planning each change as a step in a longer process, and of viewing it from the start as a learning experience – as did the authors of the *Action Plan*. It suggests that the next steps in England should give priority to enhancing the system's capacity for evolutionary change and it confirms the contribution which modularization may make to this. Above all, it demonstrates that incremental reform does not have to add new complexity, in the style favoured by NCVQ and Dearing, but may rationalize and simplify.

Second, it provides, if not a blueprint, numerous ideas for the design of a unified system. In particular, it shows how the need for differentiation may be addressed by offering a single progression ladder which all students may climb even if they start at different points, rather than by directing students to climb separate ladders. *Higher Still* will also clarify the practical issues that arise in this approach. For example, how easily can the same (eg, Higher level) courses cater both for high-fliers entering the system at this level and for students who entered at a lower level and may be proceeding at a slower pace?

Third, the experience of the *Action Plan* reminds us that the spirit of unification resists age boundaries, and that a unified system will cater for adults as well as young people. The current English debate still tends to be age-bound. The participation of adults may have implications for the balance between voluntarism and compulsory breadth. The experience of Scottish Group Awards may suggest how a voluntaristic unified system can provide a framework within which more prescriptive models may be designated for certain groups such as young people.

Finally, *Higher Still* provides lessons on the process of change. It reminds us that change is driven more by problems of the present rather than by visions of the future. It reminds us that principles which attract consensual support meet opposition or resistance when they become concrete proposals. The present English climate is not unlike the post-Howie phase in Scotland, when there was a consensus against tracking; but as soon as the *Higher Still* reforms were announced, the bread-and-butter issues of resources, timetable and workload dominated the subsequent debate. A change strategy for England must be incremental; it must share ownership of reform with those who must implement it; it must address immediate practical problems; but it must have a longer-term vision and keep this constantly in view.

References

Bennett, R, Wicks, P and McCoshan, A (1994) *Local Empowerment and Business Services: Britain's Experiment with Training and Enterprise Councils*, London: UCL Press.

Black, H, Hall, J and Martin, S (1991) *Modules: Teaching, Learning and Assessment: The Views of Students, Staff and Employers Involved in the National Certificate*, Edinburgh: Scottish Council for Research in Education.

Burnhill, P (1984) 'The Ragged Edge of Compulsory Schooling', in Raffe, D (ed.) *Fourteen to Eighteen*, Aberdeen: Aberdeen University Press.

Croxford, L, Howieson, C and Raffe, D (1991a) *Young People's Experience of National Certificate Modules*, Report to Scottish Office, Edinburgh: Centre for Educational Sociology, University of Edinburgh. Summary of same title published as *Interchange No 9*, Scottish Office (1992).

Croxford, L, Howieson, C and Raffe, D (1991b) 'National Certificate Modules in the S5 Curriculum', *Scottish Educational Review*, **23**, 2, 78–92.

Dearing, Sir Ron (1996) *Review of Qualifications for 16–19 Year Olds*, London: SCAA.

Department for Education and Employment, Scottish Office and Welsh Office (1995) *Lifetime Learning: A Consultation Document*, London: DfEE/SO/WO.

Department for Education and Employment and Cabinet Office (1996) *The Skills Audit*, London: HMSO.

Fairley, J (1996) 'Vocational Education and Training Reform in Scotland – Towards a Strategic Approach?', *Scottish Educational Review*, **28**, 1, 50–60.

Finegold, D, McFarland, L. and Richardson, W (eds) (1992, 1993) 'Something Borrowed, Something Blue?', *Oxford Studies in Comparative Education*, **2**, 2 and **3**, 1.

Gray, J, McPherson, A and Raffe, D (1983) *Reconstructions of Secondary Education*, London: Routledge and Kegan Paul.

Harrison, C (1996*) How Scottish will the Scottish Curriculum be in the 21st Century?* Dundee: Scottish Consultative Council on the Curriculum (mimeo).

Higher Still Development Unit (1995, 1996) *Consultative Documents*, Edinburgh: Scottish CCC.

Howieson, C (1992) *Modular Approaches to Initial Vocational Education and Training: The Scottish Experience*, Report for the PETRA Research Programme, Edinburgh: Centre for Educational Sociology, University of Edinburgh.

Howieson, C, Croxford, L and Raffe, D (1990) *After the Action: Young People's Reactions to the National Certificate*, Edinburgh: Centre for Educational Sociology, University of Edinburgh.

Keep, E (1991) 'The Grass Looked Greener', in Ryan, P (ed.) *International Comparisons of Vocational Education and Training for Intermediate Skills*, London: Falmer Press.

McPherson, A (1984a) 'Post-Compulsory Schooling: The Fifth Year', in Raffe, D (ed.) *Fourteen to Eighteen*, Aberdeen: Aberdeen University Press.

McPherson, A (1984b) 'Post-Compulsory Schooling: The Sixth Year', in Raffe, D (ed.) *Fourteen to Eighteen*, Aberdeen: Aberdeen University Press.

McPherson, A (1992) 'The Howie Committee on Post-Compulsory Schooling', in Paterson, L and McCrone, D (eds) *Scottish Government Yearbook 1992*, Edinburgh: Unit for the Study of Government in Scotland, University of Edinburgh.

McPherson, A and Raab, C (1988) *Governing Education: A Sociology of Policy in Scotland*, Edinburgh: Edinburgh University Press.

Murray, J (1996) 'General Scottish Vocational Qualifications (GSVQs) in Relation to the Six Themes of the Post-16 Strategies', in Lasonen, J (ed.) *Surveys of Strategies for Post-16 Education: Interim Report*, Finland: University of Jyväskylä.

National Commission on Education (1993) *Learning to Succeed*, Oxford: Heinemann.

Raffe, D (1985) 'The Extendable Ladder: Scotland's 16-Plus Action Plan', *Youth and Policy*, **12**, Spring, 27–33.

Raffe, D (1988a) 'The Story So Far: Research on Education, Training and the Labour Market from The Scottish Surveys', in Raffe, D (ed.) *Education and the Youth Labour Market*, London: Falmer Press.

Raffe, D (1988b) 'Going With the Grain: Youth Training in Transition', in Brown, S and Wake, R (eds) *Education in Transition: What Role for Research?* Edinburgh: Scottish Council for Research in Education.

Raffe, D (1991) 'Scotland v England: The Place of "Home Internationals" in Comparative Research', in Ryan, P (ed.) *International Comparisons of Vocational Education and Training for Intermediate Skills*, London: Falmer Press.

Raffe, D (1992) 'Beyond the "Mixed Model"', in Crouch, C and Heath, A (eds) *Social Research and Social Reform*, Oxford: Clarendon Press.

Raffe, D (1993) 'Multi-track and Unified Systems of Post-compulsory Education and "Upper Secondary Education in Scotland": An Analysis of Two Debates', *British Journal Of Educational Studies*, **41**, 3, 223–52.

Raffe, D (1994) 'Modular Strategies for Overcoming Academic/Vocational Divisions: Issues Arising from the Scottish Experience', *Journal of Education Policy*, **9**, 2, 141–54.

Raffe, D, Croxford, L and Howieson, C (1993) 'The Third Face of Modules: Gendered Patterns of Participation and Progression in Scottish Vocational Education', *British Journal of Education and Work*, **7**, 3, 87–104.

Richardson, W, Spours, K, Woolhouse, J and Young, M (1995) *Learning for the Future: Initial Report*, Post-16 Education Centre, Institute of Education, University of London and Centre for Education and Industry, University of Warwick.

Robertson, C (1990) *Trends in the Percentages of Scottish School Leavers Entering Higher Education 1962–1986*, Edinburgh: Centre for Educational Sociology, University of Edinburgh.

Rose, R (1993) *Lesson-Drawing in Public Policy*, Chatham, NJ: Chatham House.

Scottish Education Department (1979) *16–18s in Scotland: The First Two Years of Post-Compulsory Education*, Edinburgh: SED

Scottish Education Department (1983) *16–18s in Scotland: An Action Plan*, Edinburgh: SED.

Scottish Education Department (1991) *Access and Opportunity*, Cmnd 1530, Edinburgh: HMSO.

Scottish Education Department and Scottish Examination Board (1982) *Full-time Education after S4: A Statistical Study*, Dalkeith: SED/SEB.

Scottish Office (1994a) *Higher Still: Opportunity for All*, Edinburgh: HMSO.

Scottish Office (1994b) *Training for the Future*, Edinburgh: HMSO.

Scottish Office (1996) *Statistical Bulletin: Education Series: The National Certificate 1994–95*, Government Statistical Service.

Scottish Office Education Department (1992) *Upper Secondary Education in Scotland (Howie Report)*, Edinburgh: HMSO.

Weir, A and Kydd, J (1991) 'The National Certificate and Highers: A Case of Market Forces', *Scottish Educational Review*, **23**, 1, 13–22.

CHAPTER 13

Towards a Unified Qualifications System for Post-Compulsory Education: Barriers and Strategies

Ken Spours and Michael Young

Conceptual distinctions in analysing the reform process

The aim of this final chapter is to explore the process of change in reforming 14–19 qualifications and to suggest what might be involved in moving towards a unified qualifications system. It begins by making a number of conceptual distinctions which are intended to clarify the reform process. It then discusses barriers to change in the English system. This is followed by an exploration of reform strategies. Finally, the chapter restates a vision of a unified system.

In earlier chapters, we have conceptualized an approach to qualifications change in terms of a number of distinctions. First, there is the distinction between three types of qualifications systems: 'track-based', 'framework-based' or 'unified'. The Dearing proposals can be seen to lie somewhere between a track-based and a framework-based system (Spours and Young, 1996).

Second, these distinctions have been used to develop a model of qualifications change in terms of steps and stages. In Chapters 1 and 2 it has been recognized that the Dearing reform agenda, in some important respects, provides a basis for future change and that any further development towards a unified system is likely to involve a 'strengthening' of this approach.

Third, we have argued that qualifications systems are best seen as 'multi-dimensional'. The process of reform may change some dimensions and not others. Recent developments such as the DfEE merger and the Dearing proposals for the merger of SCAA and NCVQ take us towards a unified system insofar as the divided government and regulatory process are brought together. Other dimensions of the system, as a result of Dearing's emphasis on the curriculum distinctiveness of academic and vocational qualifications, remain more firmly located in the track-based approach.

Finally, it has been argued that the processes of change in moving to a unified qualifications system need to be seen not only in terms of curriculum and qualifications design, but also in terms of the effects of wider factors. These include fundamental influences, such as the level of resourcing, funding mechanisms, the local delivery of provision, the capability of institutions and the wider changes taking place in patterns of participation, in the labour market and in industrial and economic strategies.

Identifying different dimensions of qualifications and of the wider context can help with the process of conceptualizing qualifications change in a system which is complex, fragmented, politicized and without a strong tradition of consensus. These dimensions can also help us to understand the current conjuncture of the Dearing implementation programme and the degree to which there are agreements about the future direction of change. Some kind of consensus is now emerging, not only about the importance of system-wide aims, such as raising levels of achievement, but also about particular design features such as core skills, introducing new levels and the need to enhance and raise the status of vocational education. There is substantially less agreement, however, on whether it is desirable to introduce greater breadth, on the balance of assessment strategies and on the role of modularization. Before exploring reform strategies, it is important fully to appreciate the nature of the pressures for change and also the barriers to change in the English system of post-compulsory education.

Pressures for unification and barriers to change

Prior to 1990 there were many critiques of the inadequacy of the system of post-compulsory education and training in England. These came from researchers, notably Finegold and Soskice (1988), from government agencies (NEDO/MSC, 1984) and from business organizations (CBI, 1989). However, it was not until 1990 that there was an attempt to bring these critiques together and to develop a constructive strategy for change under the theme of unification (Finegold et al., 1990).

Since 1990 the idea of a unified system has been given additional support in a number of ways. First, a series of publications from professional organizations, not associated with the political Right or Left, appeared. All supported moves towards a unified system (APVIC, 1991; Ball, 1992; Royal Society, 1991). These rather diverse ideas were brought together again by the National Commission on Education in its report *Learning to Succeed* (NCE, 1993). Second, in the absence of any change in national policy there were a number of attempts to develop local unified strategies within the context of a divided system (Young et al., 1994). These developments, though lacking in national significance, were valuable in that they indicated the kinds of institutional inertia that might confront any unifying strategy from a new government. Third, by 1995 the problems of the qualifications system, arising from the 1991 White Paper, were becoming apparent and forced a series of reviews which include Dearing, Capey and Beaumont (see Chapter 1). The outcomes of these reviews, while cautious and limited, have resulted in some pressures for convergence between the three qualifications tracks, thus providing a basis for movement towards unification (see Chapters 2, 3 and 4). But, just as important, the renewed debate about the future direction of the system has resulted in a broadening of the basis of support for unification. The eventual move to a unified system is the aspiration not only of the majority of professional associations (Leney and Spours, 1996), but also of the Labour and Liberal Democrat Parties (Foster, 1995; Labour Party, 1996).

Despite the growing pressures for reform, there are also powerful forces resisting change. The possible election of a new government, while increasing the likelihood of a future unified system, will also reveal where the deep-seated resistances to change actually lie. The nature of conservatism in the English system has ironically been obscured by a Conservative government wedded to the A-level 'gold standard'. The election of a government without any 'ideological baggage' in relation to A-levels and with a modest reform agenda, outlined in *Aiming Higher* (Labour Party, 1996), will soon be confronted by a deeper conservatism. The effects of this will be much more powerful and diffuse than, for instance, the problems of change facing the Scottish system (see Chapter 12). Problems may be experienced not only in terms of qualifications design, but through the influence of the external context – vested interests, including the public schools and the older universities, the divisive effects of institutional competition and the results of cuts in funding. These factors could combine to affect the attitudes of educational professionals. Teacher organizations, which in the main currently support unification, might find themselves arguing for a slow pace of change as they have in Scotland.

Five major barriers can be identified which any attempt to develop a unification strategy will have to overcome. Furthermore, it will be apparent that these barriers will involve factors much wider than the curriculum and the qualifications system.

Uncertainty about the future shape of the education and training system

In the mid-1990s, the English education and training system appears to be caught between two possible futures. One argument is that a further growth of participation in the full-time route is the only future for the English system and that it should aim to become more like the 'schooling' systems associated with the Nordic countries, where participation rates at 19 are over 80 per cent (OECD, 1994). Those supporting the further expansion of full-time participation, despite problems of successful completion rates (Audit Commission/OFSTED, 1993), would point to the fact that this part of the system is more efficient than other routes at qualifying young people (Richardson *et al.*, 1995). A dominant full-time route beyond 16 would mean that a parallel work-based route for this age group would decline in significance, but would grow more important beyond 18 or 19.

The role of the work-based route in a high participation system would function, as in Scotland, as a continuation from more sustained full-time study, rather than as an alternative route at 16 for the 'school-weary'.

The alternative is to accept that the English system will never, at least in the foreseeable future, reach the kind of full-time post-16 participation levels of other European countries. It follows that any significant improvement in attainment and participation post-16 will depend on the reconstruction of the work-based route (see Chapter 5). However, this will mean employers developing support for training of a kind never previously seen in this country. Strengthening the work-based route is not just about qualifications or training; it will require a re-examination of the whole way that firms develop their human resource strategies. Given the difficulties that the work-based route is experiencing, even in Germany with its long tradition of employer commitment to training (Lasonen, 1996), such a radical change will not be easy for the English system.

The question then becomes whether a more systematic approach to mould the future shape of the system should focus on expanding full-time study, strengthening the work-based route or both. The reality is that both the full-time and the work-based routes are important and interdependent and that there is a common set of design problems to be confronted. Whatever the strategic options taken to alter the future shape of the English system, it will be important to confront the issue of voluntarism. Without a clear and planned strategy, it seems likely that we could face, once again, a period of drift, not unlike the mid-1980s when the Technical and Vocational Education Initiative (TVEI) and the Youth Training Scheme (YTS) set off in opposite directions.

Forms of qualification change: continuity or a break with the past?

The English system combines complexity of reform in the vocational track and long-standing conservatism in the academic track. So it follows that any future reform which attempts to build upon or to break with deeply ingrained habits and assumptions will be an important strategic issue. A brief contrast with Scotland is illuminative. Since the mid-1980s the reform of vocational qualifications in Scotland has been based on a broad acceptance of modular strategies and short courses, led from the centre by the Scottish Education Department. *Higher Still* (Scottish Office, 1994) is therefore seen as 'evolving' from previous episodes of reform and the process of incrementalism is accepted as a prerequisite of successful change (see Chapter 12). In England, the issue of continuity and a break with the past is more complicated. On the one hand, the movement towards a more unified system can be seen as a further development of a coherent National Qualifications Framework which has been an accepted policy aim since the mid-1980s. On the other hand, a concept of a unified system has to confront and break with deeply held cultural assumptions. In particular, there has been an acceptance of a divided curriculum for different levels of capability and the dominance of a specialized curriculum rather than one which provides for breadth of learning. A view about the best balance of 'continuity and break' with prevailing policy and attitudes will be crucial in determining how to handle the Dearing agenda.

The position taken by several contributors to this book is that the Dearing reform process provides a useful but limited platform for further changes. At the same time, it is shown to embody deeply conservative assumptions about learning and achievement. The current strategy of the government since the 1991 White Paper (DfE/ED/WO, 1991) and continued by Dearing, is to reach National Targets by making the qualification system more divisive and selective. This is based on the assumption that a divided system consisting of distinctive qualifications will allow different types of students with very different aptitudes to succeed. The implication of this analysis is that the movement towards a unified system in England will be less evolutionary than in Scotland and will involve more confrontation with the conservatism of the system.

A-levels undoubtedly still constitute the major barrier to any system-wide change. The view that A-levels represent the 'gold standard' makes a constructive educational debate about their future difficult (see Chapter 3). It has been argued in Chapter 3 that at a time when a change of government is possible in 1997, it is important to distinguish between the ideological and political barriers to A-level reform on the one hand and their educational function on the other. A Labour or Labour/Liberal Democrat government committed to a reform of A-levels would immediately face contradictory pressures from within the system about whether or not to extend the role of teacher-assessed coursework and whether to make the whole post-compulsory system in England and Wales modular. In contrast to Scotland, as Chapter 7 argues, there is no national modular tradition in England and modularization remains a contentious issue despite its popularity with schools and colleges. The strategic challenge of implementing a break with the past is that it would have to be undertaken in steps and stages and different strands of reform would have to be pursued simultaneously.

Both modularization and assessment remain difficult and contentious issues. They were not the focus of progressive policy proposals in the Dearing Report which, we have argued, adhered largely to the assumptions of the 1991 White Paper (see Chapter 2). But both these areas of qualifications policy have past precedents within the system, notably at the end of the 1980s (see Chapter 7).

The same cannot be said about the issue of breadth in the post-16 curriculum. The overwhelming assumption has been that subject specialization, associated with A-levels, is the basis for university study and that vocational specialization can motivate low achievers. Yet more effective continental systems provide a core of general education post-16 which not only promotes a greater breadth of knowledge and skill, but also provides a curriculum aimed at education in citizenship to promote greater social cohesion and inclusion (see Chapter 6). So far, breadth of learning in the English qualifications system has been largely confined to a debate about the role of core skills. Dearing's proposal for a Diploma, though at present voluntary, has begun to alter the nature of that discussion because of his recommendation of having core skills in both the academic and the vocational tracks. The problem of creating greater breadth in the post-16 curriculum will, however, not simply be confined to a debate about the curriculum. Even if the argument for more prescriptive breadth is won, the main sticking point will be resources. Recent expansion of post-compulsory participation in schools and colleges has been achieved on the back of reductions in course contact hours. As Chapter 6 argues, greater breadth of learning for all will require a substantial injection of resources and, possibly, longer periods of study. This would have to be properly planned and phased in over time.

Problems of continuity and break also exist in the vocational tracks, though for different reasons. In marked contrast to A-levels, which have managed to resist all but incremental change in 45 years, vocational qualifications have been constantly changing. After more than a decade of experimentation, the focal point of debate has become the future of the competence-based model (see Chapter 4). Despite many changes, GNVQs and NVQs appear incapable of attracting even the semblance of an educational consensus. This is because the competence-based model represents a radical break with previous vocational qualifications with its narrow definitions of competence, the bureaucratism of its assessment and the fact that outcomes are not complemented by inputs.

There is considerable support for a broadly-based outcomes approach when it is linked to support for modular syllabuses. If each module is defined in terms of a set of outcomes, students can see clearly what they are aiming to achieve (Young, 1994). However, if outcomes are linked to a narrow specification of competence, in the form to which NCVQ currently adheres, they lead inevitably to mediocrity and there are no incentives for encouraging excellence. The debate, which has hardly begun, will be about how to develop an outcomes-based model that encourages a broader and more common approach to both academic and vocational qualifications (see Chapter 8). This could lead eventually to replacing A-level subjects and GNVQ areas of study with a Diploma system based on national and regional modular banks.

The structure of national agencies for regulation and funding

Throughout the 1980s the administration of education and training was divided between the Department for Education and Science (DES) and the Employment Department (ED), a factor which contributed to the twists and turns of policy development. However, by the mid-1990s the situation is more fluid but presents stronger possibilities for unification. The DfEE merger has led to a single directorate for 14–19 qualifications and SCAA and NCVQ will merge to form the Qualifications and National Curriculum Authority (QNCA). Examining and validating bodies (EVBs) are also being encouraged to merge and this is taking place across the academic/vocational divide. Pressure for common standards and lower costs, as larger numbers of each student cohort attempt qualifications, is likely to accelerate this process. There appears to be an unmistakable trend towards a more unified organizational approach and a turning away from the principle of competition.

At the same time as this trend towards greater coordination, very different funding systems have been introduced: colleges are funded through the FEFC, grant-maintained schools through the Funding Agency for Schools, while maintained schools remain funded through LEAs. Funding mechanisms play an increasingly influential role in schools' and colleges' attitudes towards qualifications and achievement (Spours and Lucas, 1996). Divisions and complexity are growing features of school sixth forms and even more so of colleges, which are at the interface of full-time, work-based and adult programmes, all of which are subject to different funding and quality regimes (Lucas, 1997). Pressure is now building for some sort of convergence of funding regimes. This is another example of a more coordinated but not necessarily a more unified approach.

Comparisons with Scotland suggest that for a unified qualifications strategy to succeed there will have to be a single qualifications authority, a coordinated EVB system and funding approaches which encourage institutional collaboration rather than competition, and attainment rather than just recruitment. We are still a long way from this situation. In learning lessons from the Scottish experience we need to be aware that our population is ten times larger and that their more centralized system is probably not possible for England. We have inherited the typically English combination of fragmentation and ad hocery in the provision of post-compulsory education.

Two options are possible. However, both point in directions which go against the English tradition and are likely to be resisted. One possibility is a more centralized system, as in Scotland, France and the Nordic countries. However, such a system would challenge a tradition in which the responsibility for the 16–19 curriculum is still seen to lie with individual schools and colleges. Any attempt at greater centralization of policy, particularly if it were not properly planned or resourced, would encounter stiff institutional resistance. Another possibility is a more explicitly regionalized and cooperative system along the lines of the German *Lander*. This too would be a complete break with English traditions. What is needed is a model that draws more on the strengths of the English system, especially its capacity for devolving responsibility and institutional innovation, while minimizing the disadvantages of voluntarism.

Institutional voluntarism, competition and resource constraints

A fundamental barrier to a more unified system is the increasingly fragmented way in which post-compulsory education and training is delivered locally. Under pressure from LMS and FEFC funding methodology, the major issue shaping decisions made by schools and colleges is their own survival. Competition over students is endemic and collaboration, never part of the English tradition until it was explicitly funded by TVEI, has declined rapidly. Schools are often tempted to run vocational courses in which they may have little expertise, and to open sixth forms which are not economic. Current cuts in funding are forcing colleges to run down high-cost specialist courses and dramatically to reduce course hours.

Institutional competition not only endangers quality, it also undermines consensus. In a competitive climate teachers often go along with introducing new qualifications (eg, GNVQs) because they offer a lifeline, not because of their intrinsic educational worth. What perhaps is needed is a form of 'collaborative competition' – sometimes found in the private sector – in which colleges and schools in an area collaborate over some things (eg, staff development and innovation), agree to a division of labour on others (eg, specialist technical courses and less popular A-level subjects) and also compete in offering a choice of institutional learning environment and ethos.

Under resource constraints and with attacks on professional conditions, teachers can also be ambivalent about educational innovations that they would, in other circumstances, support in principle. Resistance to increases in assessed coursework, which might be promoted by a new government, is an example of a kind of conservatism that might need to be overcome. The problems of institutional division and the pragmatic conservatism of teachers point to the key role of institutions in any reform of the qualifications system (see Chapter 11). Overcoming institutional barriers to unification will require the creation of a positive and collaborative climate in which institutions and teachers are consulted, receive targeted funding and are adequately prepared for change through properly resourced staff development.

External contextual factors

The focus of the unification debate on overcoming academic/vocational divisions arises from the fact that it does not just point to an educational or a curriculum issue; it poses questions about the nature of English society and its occupational structure. Whereas academic/vocational divisions have their roots in the separation of mental from manual labour, the pressure to overcome these divisions arises from a different kind of occupational structure in which traditional 'working-class' jobs, which are either routine and make only minor intellectual demands or are based on craft skills, are disappearing. At the same time, there is evidence that many new jobs make considerable intellectual and practical demands on those who hold them (Reich, 1991). The old 'class society', at least from a functional point of view, was satisfied by an education system based on the division between academic and vocational learning. The emerging type of society, even from a functional viewpoint, depends on a very different type of education system in which general and vocational learning are combined in curricula and qualifications (Young, 1993). Unlike previous educational debates, which focused on access, organization, curriculum or learning/teaching styles, the current debate is not just about education but also about the interrelations between education and the society of which it is a part.

Opponents of a unified system argue that academic/vocational divisions respond to the diversity of learning needs of young people, many of whom, they assert, have neither the capability nor the inclination to continue their general education (Dearing, 1996). In contrast, the 'unifiers' argue that to limit a large proportion of young people to the current forms of vocational education from the age of 16 (or even 14) is to exclude them from access to the kinds of skills and knowledge they are going to need to be effective citizens and workers in the likely economy and society of the future (Finegold et al., 1990).

As far back as the early 1980s it was recognized that the success of qualifications reforms would be determined not only by their content, but also by the context in which they were being implemented (Raffe, 1984). Here, we shall discuss three such factors of particular importance: employer attitudes, the role of higher education and the economic situation of students.

Employers' views about qualifications are extremely diverse and contradictory. Some support selective A-levels as a screening device (eg, the Institute of Directors), whereas other employer organizations (eg, the CBI) want more core skills. Others support NVQs and, historically, there has been little support for broad vocational qualifications (Raffe, 1988). These divisions have been compounded by the voluntarism of training and apprenticeship schemes with no national training demand made on employers. This problem raises the issue of how a government can provide a strong framework steer to employer opinion and, at the same time, still be able to construct a consensus

Despite the fact that single-subject honours degrees are far less dominant in universities than in the past, they still influence the attitudes of admissions tutors and put pressures on colleges and schools to emphasize early academic specialization. In the context of resource constraints, a kind of anti-breadth collusion is produced, despite the widespread support in principle at least for a broader curriculum. Without some change in the structure of A-levels, some new type of incentive for higher education to recognize breadth and schools and colleges to promote breadth, it is difficult to see from where the pressure for a broader curriculum might come.

There is a growing perception amongst teachers that student poverty and the fact that more and more students are taking up part-time work, are beginning to affect participation and achievement (Spours, 1996). These trends have profound implications for qualifications reform. They make it more difficult to increase levels of full-time participation and, more crucially, to contemplate making greater curriculum demands of students. There are, therefore, strong arguments for the creation of a more flexible curriculum that allows different combinations of work and study. If it is also accepted that students should study more broadly, then they may have to study over a longer period. This points increasingly to a three-year, rather than a two-year, duration of study for most post-16 students in the future. However, this demand, without any additional funding, is likely to be resisted by teachers and students. On the other hand, it is untenable to think that current low successful completion rates can be improved on the existing basis of a combination of low course contact-hours and increasing levels of casualized part-time work.

In considering strategies to overcome the barriers that have been described, it is useful to contrast the position in England and Scotland (see Chapter 12). As can be seen from Table 13.1, there is a stronger consensus of support for an 'evolutionary' approach to a unified system in Scotland (Raffe *et al.*, 1996). The system already offers a significantly broader post-16 curriculum than in England and the unification of qualifications is at the centre of the *Higher Still* reforms. The English situation is more complex and inherits a more divided system and culture. While the Scottish experience highlights the importance of building on consensus and the scope for an evolutionary approach to reform, significant differences between the two countries and their recent educational histories point to the need for specifically English strategies for change.

Table 13.1 *England and Scotland compared*

	England	Scotland
1. Type of participation and shape of education and training system	Full-time participation 'peaking' and a lack of consensus about further expansion of the education-based model	More full-time staying-on and greater commitment to an education-based model (though not as strong as in France or Sweden)
2. Qualifications and curriculum	Lack of consensus about specialization and breadth of learning. Vocational qualifications still competence-based	Breadth through modular and short-course mixing. The system remains voluntary but strong cultural support for breadth. Uses a broader competence-based model
3. Regulation and funding	A tradition of divided ministries, different funding models and different modes of regulating qualifications	A tradition of leadership from the centre, more unified regulatory bodies and less impact of funding regimes
4. Institutions	Fragmented and competitive. Little collaborative division of labour	School-based model, colleges have a more vocational and adult role. A clearer division of labour between schools and colleges and more incentives for collaboration under greater central control
5. Labour market and educational culture	Weak endorsement of qualifications from labour market and strong voluntaristic tendencies	Weak endorsement of qualifications from labour market but a tangible presence of Scottish educational principles in the general culture

Strategies for moving to a unified system

The preceding analysis, which has highlighted both conceptual distinctions and barriers to change, suggests that strategies for moving to a unified system should have at their heart three fundamental considerations. First, there should be a strong vision accompanied by inclusive debates to deepen the consensus for change. Second, it is necessary to build on the idea of 'steps and stages' to change in order to preserve this consensus. Third, there is a need to consider different strands of reform, which are pursued simultaneously, so that qualifications change is reinforced by other measures.

Inclusive visions and inclusive debates

The disparate English system needs a strong and inclusive vision of change. The reform process cannot simply mirror the Scottish experience of evolution based on a consensus which has been built on responding to practical problems (see Chapter 12). However, such a vision should be one which can be seen to arise out of recent history, that connects to a diverse range of interests and concerns and that addresses long-standing weaknesses. What must be avoided at all costs is 'vision' being associated with the ideological pursuit of change, without due regard to practical consequences. This would simply reproduce some of the most serious mistakes of government policy since the 1991 White Paper.

Existing models of unification have undoubtedly grabbed the imagination of many in education (AfC *et al.*, 1994; Finegold *et al.*, 1990; NCE, 1993, 1995; Richardson *et al.*, 1995). Since 1990 several unification models, rather than one single model, have emerged, though none is fully inclusive. The work-based route is largely excluded from these models, which emphasize a baccalaureate-type Diploma or a unitized system based on full-time qualifications. Adult and lifelong learning still remain relatively on the margins of current designs, despite the recognition that unitization/modularization can connect the concerns of younger and older learners (see Chapters 7 and 8). Furthermore, these models remain generalized and do not yet sufficiently connect to the practical situations of schools and colleges. These inadequacies point to the value of starting from the Dearing proposals. Despite their limitations, they will at least provide some concrete experience of working with a framework approach.

It was the publication by the Institute of Public Policy Research of *A British Baccalaureate* in 1990 which established the idea of a unified system. A baccalaureate approach to unification has acted as one pole of the debate about the future of post-compulsory education and training. Since then, other perspectives have emerged to enrich the debate. It is now useful to recognize three positions in the qualifications debate which, we will see, are not mutually exclusive.

First, there are those whose primary concern has been to maintain the distinctiveness of different qualifications tracks. This position includes the present government, which emphasizes the distinctiveness of the academic track and the risks of dilution of achievement in A-levels. Researchers such as Prais, Steedman and Wolf, on the other hand, have stressed the importance of ensuring the distinctiveness of vocational qualifications. Their worries revolve particularly around the effects of competence-based methodologies, especially within GNVQs. Throughout this book, the government's view of distinctiveness has been strongly contested because of its pursuit of division. The researchers' concerns about distinctiveness, however, should be given altogether more serious attention.

It may be useful at this point to look briefly at the relationship between 'distinctiveness' and 'specialization'. Distinctiveness, in the Dearing Report, is defined in terms of differences of content, assessment and purposes of different qualifications associated with different types of learners. In this sense, it is synonymous with a track-based system. But it is possible to think of distinctiveness in another way: as a way of preparing for specialized functions in society for all learners, regardless of their level of achievement. It may be more productive to think less of 'distinctiveness' and more of 'specialization'. Specialization is applicable to both academic subjects (eg, preparing to be a physicist) or vocational areas of study (eg, preparing to be a skilled engineer). Specialization would be reflected, not through creating different types of curricula, but by clear progression routes and specialist groupings of modules/short-courses within a more common qualifications structure. This would seem to be the aim underlying the Swedish concept of 'lines of study' (Lasonen, 1996) or what we referred to elsewhere as the 'core/specialization model' (Spours and Young, 1995).

A second area of concern has been 'flexibility'. Unification proposals have emerged, based not on Baccalaureate-type proposals but on a framework of units, the principle of credit accumulation and an appreciation of the importance of access and flexible learning processes. The most important example of what can be called a 'Common Framework' was published in 1994 by the 'Group of Six' (AfC et al., 1994). The emphasis on flexibility in the Common Framework had a number of motives. At one level it was a politically pragmatic attempt to bring together those organizations which wanted to reform A-levels and those wishing to preserve them. At another level it reflected the experience of those whose work was principally with adults, for whom flexibility is vital. The Common Framework has made a very important contribution to the debate about unified systems. It has promoted the argument that any form of prescription has to be balanced by flexibility if it is to work in the English context and that change has to be as consensual and gradual as possible. This line of argument had a major effect in framing the proposals for a steps and stages approach to unification outlined in the Learning for the Future Project (Richardson et al., 1995).

The third group are those who see unification of the qualifications system as their ultimate aim. This group now includes the Labour and Liberal Democrat parties, most professional associations and many educational researchers. It is expressed most clearly in the IPPR proposal for a British baccalaureate and the NCE's Advanced Diploma. Arguments for this line of thinking are found throughout the book.

There are inevitably tensions between these three positions, but they can be reconciled within a strong and inclusive vision. Those in favour of a unified qualifications system can easily accept that commonality can be combined with distinctiveness of specialist pathways. The question is the degree of prescriptive breadth. If ideological and political considerations can be put aside, this is an issue of design and resourcing. At the same time, the question of prescription with flexibility and choice can be achieved through the unitization of courses. A more unitized/short-course design for all qualifications will help to arrive at a balance between core and optional areas of study.

A strong and inclusive vision of a future unified system should be able to articulate, and reassemble, the concerns of all of those whose arguments are educational rather than political or ideological. Any future system will need to include disciplinary study, multi-disciplinary inquiry, the application of knowledge and skill and common learning processes (core skills, action planning, recording of achievement and career education) within a single unitized/modular system. The key to the cementing of a consensus is not only the inclusiveness of the on-going debate, but the incrementalism of the reform process.

Incrementalism and steps and stages of reform

The concept of a steps and stages approach to reform has been outlined in recent analyses of possibilities for change in the English system (Richardson *et al.*, 1995; Spours and Young, 1996). The approach is based on seeing the 14–19 qualifications system as moving from a track-based system (Stage One), through a framework-based stage (Stage Two), and onto a unified system (Stage Three). As we have argued earlier, the Dearing proposals lie uneasily between Stages One and Two. They could, according to whoever wins the next election, be allowed to revert back to a track-based system, or they could be enhanced and developed into a stronger Framework Stage.

All contributors to this book, while not agreeing on everything, identify with a unifying approach. The issue is how this can be conducted in an incremental way, at the same time as confronting the underlying weaknesses in the English system. Earlier chapters referred to a strengthened Framework Stage of reform. The aims of this stage, which could last several years, would be to reduce the divisiveness of the tracks, to promote convergence of qualification design, to encourage student flexibility in combinations of learning and to introduce a 'limited broadening' of the curriculum. This Stage would not aim to move directly to a fully-fledged baccalaureate system, because this would require further debate, planning and resourcing. However, the Framework Stage establishes the basis of moving to the Third Stage – a fully unified system.

From Stage One to Stage Two: Strengthening the Framework

A stronger Framework Stage could emerge from the Dearing proposals. It would include proposals both to 'improve' existing qualifications, as well as to reinforce the framework proposals in the Dearing Report. The following design issues could be considered.

Short-courses, modularity and balanced assessment

The first development could be the creation of a three-unit AS and three-unit GNVQ, rather than the six-unit A-level, as the main building block of the system. This would provide a basis not only for greater mixing of study, but also for introducing limited broadening of the curriculum.

Modularization/unitization could be extended to all A-levels, GNVQs, traditional vocational qualifications and NVQs so that all qualifications have an identical internal structure. This could lay the basis for a common credit accumulation and transfer system. Such a move could also be accompanied by the introduction of a common and balanced assessment framework across both academic and vocational qualifications. Modularization/unitization and the introduction of balanced assessment might be the first steps in establishing a stronger Framework.

A flexible but mandatory Diploma

The Framework has to have a clear focus for relating different developments and this could be through the establishment of the Advanced Diploma as a mandatory requirement for entry to higher education. A flexible but mandatory Diploma is a realistic alternative to Dearing's proposal that the Diploma should be optional. For this to be a practical proposition at this stage would mean that the Dearing proposal for the Diploma would be used not to broaden study through domains, but principally to produce minimum standards and to promote cohesion and flexibility. Its main functions would be to ensure that there was a minimum of required study for all higher education entry (possibly the equivalent to two and a half or three A-levels), that academic and vocational routes led in all cases to a common title, that there was an academic/vocational equivalence based on structure and assessment, which was common to both types of study, and a common approach to core skills. It would mean that for the next four or five years the Diploma would contain existing qualifications which would be reformed into an aligned position with the addition of core skills or other forms of additional short-course qualifications or units.

Limited broadening of study

A mandatory but flexible Diploma could be used as a gradual means of making additional requirements over and above the internal specialist qualifications. In the first instance this would be core skill units but over time, as resourcing and teacher expertise permitted, other demands could be made. These might include accrediting work experience and introducing modern foreign language units for all students, though at different levels. The scope for developing a post-16 core curriculum would depend on considerations of student motivation, teacher expertise, institutional resourcing and striking the right balance and relationship between breadth and specialization. This limited broadening of study can be seen as a preliminary stage to a more structured domain approach in the future.

The introduction of more levels to promote access, achievement and progression

The Dearing proposals for an 'Entry Level' and the proposal for the 'Lateral AS' represent a hesitant and pragmatic recognition that the qualifications levels in England are too far apart and do not properly articulate with the National Curriculum. What is needed is a more thorough-going review of the qualifications levels and a commitment to replace the current three at 14–19 with four or more. The aim of a revamped levels system would be to provide a lattice-work for progression building on the National Curriculum. Levels would be much closer together than in the current system and, as such, could be motivating for students.

A revamped NRA as the reporting format of the Diploma system

Process-based learning has been one of the conspicuous strengths of the English system. Its weakness is that innovative learning has either been embedded in bureaucratic vocational qualifications or has remained extraneous to the more prestigious academic qualifications. The National Record of Achievement could become the new reporting format for the Diploma system, recording the type of qualifications in the Framework Stage, the range of units and their grades. There could also be school/college/employer reports as well as action planning documentation.

Inclusion of the work-based route

The failure to give serious consideration of the reform of the work-based route in 'unification blueprints' has been a notable weakness. A strengthened Framework Stage could build on the Dearing proposals for a ladder of progression in work-based learning, involving the proposed Traineeships leading to the Modern Apprenticeship (MA) programme. Qualifications reform is an important ingredient in building a credible and effective work-based route and could involve using a vocationalized variant of the Diploma to replace the current array of GNVQ and NVQ units used in MA programmes.

The Framework Stage: strands of the reform process

The analysis at the beginning of the chapter of different dimensions of the qualifications system and a recognition of the effects of the wider context for qualifications reform, lead to the conclusion that there have to be several strands to the reform process in the Framework Stage which work in a mutually reinforcing way.

Qualifications and curriculum

This itself has several internal dimensions (eg, content, structure, processes and assessment) which are aspects of the Dearing reform agenda. The preceding analysis would suggest that some of these dimensions are more immediately dynamic than others and that particular attention should be given to the roles of modularization/unitization and balanced assessment as a way of steering the Dearing proposals in the direction of a strengthened Framework Stage.

Regulation

In the wake of the DfEE merger, attention is turning to the coordination of different aspects of regulation. This can be seen to include the formation of the Qualifications National Curriculum Authority, the merging of examining and validating bodies and the possible convergence of funding mechanisms. There is a strong argument that a powerful centralized body for regulating qualifications should be complemented by a strong regional structure consisting of planning bodies, awarding bodies and funding bodies. The latter's role would be to respond to and to coordinate bottom-up initiatives and to encourage cohesion and collaboration across the whole post-16 sector. This 'regulatory strand' is also important because of its role in encouraging the new patterns of study required by the Framework Stage and its ability to support the type of local partnerships needed to bring about change.

Local delivery

This refers to the establishment of local delivery partnerships and the reduction of the negative effects of institutional competition. Any movement towards an 'expanded curriculum', a more effective delivery of vocational education and the full inclusion of the work-based route in the reform process will require a dramatic development in local patterns of institutional collaboration. It will mean institutions not deciding to 'go it alone' but working to their strengths and creating closer local links, not only between academic and vocational provision but also between full-time and work-based learning.

Institutional and professional capability

Institutional pragmatism and conservatism have been identified as a major potential barrier to reform. Particular care would need to be taken to ensure that schools and colleges, developing whole-institutional approaches to change, were adequately resourced and had planned human resource strategies directly linked to the demands of the Framework Stage, particularly with regard to modularization, assessment requirements and the evolution of the Diploma. This would point to the need for a unified development programme for institutions – perhaps a new TVEI-type initiative.

Student/trainee participation

The future shape of the education and training system will be determined by the patterns of student/trainee participation. A fundamental issue will be the role of funding. If more students are to be encouraged to engage in education and training beyond 16, how they can be financially supported is fast becoming a critical issue. This includes a consideration of the role of part-time work, as well as whether more young people can be financially encouraged to stay on full-time and for longer. The pattern of funding of institutions will provide important incentives for institutions to promote longer and more flexible periods of study rather than 'fast-tracking' students through the system.

External recognition

Qualifications reform cannot succeed unless the new qualifications are recognized by employers, higher education and parents. A precondition of recognition is not only improved quality, but the idea of the level playing field. This is behind the call for a 'single popular title' for all 14–19 qualifications, so that old qualifications cannot devalue anything that is new. Recognition will also require improved transparency of reporting, overall higher standards and sufficient flexibility to meet the requirements of different end-users. In practical terms, however, it may also require a mandatory approach developing the Framework Stage to ensure that the new framework certification is recognized for entry to university and is used as the qualifications base of Modern Apprenticeships.

Conclusion: a vision of a unified system

In terms of change processes, the main aim of a Framework Stage is to prepare the ground for moving to a fully unified system. What could emerge at this point is inevitably a matter of speculation, because we are moving into uncharted territory. However, some national systems, such as Scotland from 1998, Sweden and New Zealand, approximate towards a unified approach. It is important to observe at this point that these are relatively small systems compared to England. This underlines the need for caution in moving a complex and fragmented system in this direction.

A unified qualifications system can be distinguished from a Framework Stage in a number of ways. The most obvious difference would be that various qualifications contained within the Framework would be completely replaced by the single title – in this case the Diploma. A Diploma, offered at different levels from 14 onwards, would have some form of core curriculum and would have to be large enough to contain the scope for both breadth of study and for specialization. Compared to the current demands of Level 3 study through A-levels and GNVQs – often not more than 15 contact hours per week – the Diploma would represent an 'expanded curriculum'. If we are to move in this direction, and there are compelling arguments that we should, it has to be properly prepared for and resourced. The major function of the Framework Stage is to provide a gradual approach towards such an expanded curriculum.

Breadth of study could be a major objective of the third, ie, unified stage of qualifications development. Previous unification blueprints such as the British baccalaureate and the Diploma in the NCE Report, have argued for 'domains' as a means of encouraging broadening. Domains were also adopted by Dearing in his proposal for a voluntary Advanced Diploma. Domains offer the possibility of stipulating requirements for breadth while at the same time allowing students some choice. This kind of flexibility would also be assisted by modularization/unitization and short-course combinations of study.

Whereas domains are instruments of broadening, 'lines of study' as proposed in a unified system are the means of delivering specialization. Lines of study, which would consist of groupings of modules, are intended to replace the specialist function of different qualifications. The number of 'lines' made available will need to be discussed, though the experience of Sweden suggests that 15 or 16 may be appropriate.

A third feature of a unified system would be the emphasis on new types of inter-disciplinary study. A unified system is intended to be a curriculum for the 21st century (Young, 1993). In addition to the core and specialist elements in the Diploma, there could also be significant demands for project work, deliberately designed to cross-disciplinary and academic/vocational boundaries. Examples of this kind of work were beginning to emerge in TVEI projects at the end of the 1980s and are also found in modular higher education systems in other countries (Spours and Young, 1995).

Above all, a unified system will be intended to encourage personal achievement and progression. It means that arguments for greater curriculum demands will have to be balanced by those features which encourage flexible study. Balanced assessment, modularization and bringing levels closer together are key features of the Framework Stage, and will be important mechanisms for encouraging personal pacing of learning within the unified system.

To date, debates about a unified system have been largely confined to 14–19 qualifications and this book is no exception. This should be regarded not as narrowness and insularity, but as a recognition that the debates about unified systems are still at an early stage. If a unified curriculum is to be a curriculum for the 21st century, the boundaries of innovation will have to expand to embrace the concept and realities of lifelong learning. This book, however, has confined itself to the 14–19 qualifications system because its starting point has been the Dearing agenda which, combined with the possibilities of political change, marks a critical watershed. It is our belief that the Dearing agenda, though limited, is a basis for moving the complex and fragmented English system step by step towards greater cohesion. If we can move into what we have called the Framework Stage, which begins to break down the barriers of the system, new possibilities emerge. A staged approach to change is not about the pursuit of a mechanical blueprint, it is about the creation of a climate of innovation and debate which, at one and the same time, helps us to shape and to move towards a fully inclusive unified system.

References

Association for Colleges, The Girls' School Association, The Headmasters' Conference, The Secondary Heads Association, The Sixth Form Colleges' Association, The Society for Headmasters and Headmistresses in Independent Schools (1994) *Post-Compulsory Education and Training: A Joint Statement*, London: AfC.

Association of Principals of Sixth Form Colleges (1991) *A Framework for Growth: Improving the Post-16 Curriculum*, Wigan: APVIC.

Audit Commission/OFSTED (1993) *Unfinished Business: Full-time Education Courses for 16–19 Year Olds*, London: HMSO.

Ball, C (1992) *Profitable Learning: Summary Report, Findings and Action Plan*, London: RSA.

Confederation of British Industry (1989) *Towards a Skills Revolution*, London: CBI.

Dearing, Sir Ron (1996) *Review of Qualifications for 16–19 Year Olds*, London: SCAA.

Department for Education/Employment Department/Welsh Office (1991) *Education and Training for the 21st Century*, London: HMSO.

Finegold, D and Soskice, D (1988) 'The Failure of Training in Britain: Analysis and Prescription', *Oxford Review of Economic Policy*, 4, 3, Oxford: Oxford University Press.

Finegold, D, Keep, E, Miliband, D, Raffe, D, Spours, K and Young, M (1990) *A British Baccalaureate: Overcoming Divisions Between Education and Training*, London: Institute for Public Policy Research.

Foster, D (1995) 'Heat and Light', *Education*, 10 March.

Labour Party (1996) *Aiming Higher: Labour's Proposals for the Reform of the 14–19 Curriculum*, London: Labour Party.

Lasonen, J (1996) *Reforming Upper Secondary Education in Europe: Surveys of Strategies for Post-16 Education to Improve the Parity of Esteem for Initial Vocational Education in Eight European Educational Systems*, Finland: University of Jyväskylä Press.

Leney, T and Spours, K (1996) 'A Comparative Analysis of the Submissions and Responses of the Educational Professional Associations to the Dearing Review' draft discussion paper, Post-16 Education Centre, Institute of Education, University of London.

Lucas, N (ed.) (1997, forthcoming) *Recent Issues and Developments in the FE Incorporated Sector* Working Paper, London: Post-16 Education Centre, Institute of Education, University of London.

National Commission on Education (1993) *Learning to Succeed: A Radical Look at Education Today and a Strategy for the Future*, Report of the Paul Hamlyn Foundation National Commission on Education, Oxford: Heinemann.

National Commission on Education (1995) *Learning to Succeed: The Way Ahead*, Report of the Paul Hamlyn Foundation National Commission on Education, London: National Commission on Education.

NEDO/MSC (1984) *Competence and Competition: Training in the Federal Republic of Germany, the United States and Japan*, London: NEDO/MSC.

OECD (1994) *Education at a Glance: OECD Indicators*, Paris: OECD.

Raffe, D (1984) 'The Content and Context of Educational Reform', in *Fourteen to Eighteen*, Raffe, D (ed.), Aberdeen: Aberdeen University Press.

Raffe, D (1988) 'The Story So Far: Research on Education, Training and the Labour Market from The Scottish Surveys', in Raffe, D (ed.) *Education and the Youth Labour Market*, London: Falmer Press.

Raffe, D, Howieson. C, Spours, K and Young, M (1996) *Unifying Academic and Vocational Learning: English and Scottish Approaches*, paper presented to the British Association Annual Festival, University of Birmingham, 11 September.

Reich, R (1991) *The Work of Nations*, London: Simon and Schuster.

Richardson, W, Spours, K, Woolhouse, J and Young, M (1995) *Learning for the Future Interim Report*, Post-16 Education Centre, Institute of Education, University of London, Centre for Education and Industry, University of Warwick.

Royal Society (1991) *Beyond GCSE: A Report by a Working Group of the Royal Society's Education Committee*, London: The Royal Society.

Scottish Office (1994) *Higher Still: Opportunity for All*, Edinburgh: HMSO.

Spours, K (ed.) (1996) *Institutional Responses to Dearing and Aiming Higher,* Post-16 Education Centre Report for Essex LEA, Post-16 Education Centre, Institute of Education, University of London.

Spours, K and Lucas, N (1996) *The Formation of a National Sector of Incorporated Colleges: Beyond the FEFC Model,* Working Paper No 19, Post-16 Education Centre Institute of Education, University of London.

Spours, K and Young, M (1995) *Post-Compulsory Curriculum and Qualifications: Options for Change,* Learning for the Future Working Paper 6, Post-16 Institute of Education, University of London/Centre for Education and Industry, University of Warwick.

Spours, K and Young, M (1996) 'Dearing and Beyond: Steps and Stages to a Unified System', *British Journal of Education and Work,* December.

Young, M (1993) 'A Curriculum for the 21st Century? Towards a New Basis for Overcoming Academic/Vocational Divisions', *British Journal of Educational Studies,* **40**, 3.

Young, M (1994) 'Modularisation and the Outcomes Approach: Towards a Strategy for a Curriculum of the Future', in Burke, J (ed.), *Outcomes and the Curriculum,* London: Falmer Press.

Young, M, Hodgson, A and Morris, A (1994) *Unifying Strategies and Organisational Change in Post-16 Education,* Unified Curriculum at 16+ Working Paper 7, Post-16 Education Centre, Institute of Education, University of London.

Index